THE LIVING GITA

The Complete *Bhagavad Gita*

A Commentary for Modern Readers
By Sri Swami Satchidananda

Integral Yoga® Publications

Buckingham, Virginia, USA

Printed in the United States Of America
Library of Congress Cataloging-in-Publication Data

Satchidananda, Swami
The Living Gita: The Complete Bhagavad Gita
Includes index.
1. Bhagavad Gita translation, interpretation, etc.
1. Title
BLII38.66.S28 1988 294.5'924 84-27861
ISBN 978-0-932040-27-5

1st Printing - 1988
2nd printing (Henry Holt & Company), Inc. edition) - 1990
3rd printing - 1997
4th printing - 2000
5th printing - 2003
6th printing - 2005
7th printing - 2008
8th printing - 2013
9th printing - 2017
10th printing-2021

Integral Yoga® Publications
Satchidananda Ashram–Yogaville, Inc., Buckingham, Virginia 23921 U.S.A.
www.IntegralYoga.org

Books by Sri Swami Satchidananda

Beyond Words

Enlightening Tales

The Golden Present

The Healthy Vegetarian

Heaven on Earth

Integral Yoga Hatha

Kailash Journal

The Living Gita

To Know Your Self

Yoga Sutras of Patanjali

Bound To Be Free: The Liberating
Power of Prison Yoga

Integral Yoga® Pocket Collection featuring the Art of Peter Max

Meditation

The Key to Peace

Overcoming Obstacles

Adversity and Awakening

Satchidananda Sutras

Gems of Wisdom

Pathways to Peace

How to Find Happiness

The Be-Attitudes

Everything Will Come to You

Thou Art That

How to Know Your Self

Free Yourself

The Guru Within

Golden Moments

Books about Sri Swami Satchidananda:

Sri Swami Satchidananda: Apostle of Peace

Sri Swami Satchidananda: Portrait of a Modern Sage

Boundless Giving: The Life and Service of Sri Swami Satchidananda

The Master's Touch

Films about Sri Swami Satchidananda (DVDs):

Living Yoga: The Life and Teachings of Swami Satchidananda

Many Paths, One Truth: The Interfaith Message of Swami Satchidananda

The Essence of Yoga: The Path of Integral Yoga with Swami Satchidananda

In the Footsteps of a Master: The 1970 World Peace Tour

Journey with a Master

For complete listing of books, CDs and DVDs: www.iydbooks.com

Contents

— ॐ —

"Scriptures ought to be read again and again. If any of the lines here catch your eye and your heart, read them often. Learn them by heart and apply them in your life. You don't even need a whole sentence, not even half a sentence. Just a quarter of one line is enough to lift you like a rocket, not just to the moon or Mars, but to the heavenly sun itself."

Swami Satchidananda

—His Holiness Sri Swami Satchidananda

— ॐ —

Foreword

There have been many commentaries on the *Bhagavad Gita,* and there is room for many more. The *Gita* forms part of the epic poem of the *Mahabharata* and belongs to the culture of ancient India, but it has a message for all times and all places. Today, especially, the message of the *Gita* is coming with renewed meaning and value to Western Europe and America. Swami Satchidananda is one of the pioneers who have been able to interpret the *Gita* for the West with a power, which has changed people's lives. This commentary is therefore to be welcomed by all who treasure the wisdom of India and want to see it brought to bear on the problems of the West.

The *Bhagavad Gita* tells the story of how Arjuna, the great warrior, is seated in his chariot about to engage in battle, when he sees his own kinsmen and his revered teacher arrayed in battle against him, and he feels that he cannot fight. It is then that Krishna, the Cosmic Lord, comes to counsel him. The interrelation of this is that Arjuna represents the human soul seated in the chariot of the body and Krishna is the inner Spirit, the God within, who is there to counsel him. Today we see humanity divided against itself and threatened with nuclear war and mutual destruction. No political means are adequate to deal with this problem, and many are driven to despair. It is then that the message of the *Gita* comes to teach us that it is only when we rise above human schemes and calculations and awaken to the presence of the indwelling Spirit that we can hope to find an answer to our need.

Father Bede Griffiths, OSB Cam
Shantivanam
Tamil Nadu, India

Foreword

The Living Gita is the title of this book so beautifully written by Sri Swami Satchidananda. His life, with its ripeness in experience, gives a real commentary to the *Gita*. It is the calm and collected mind, far from the maddening materialism, that can enjoy the essence of the *Gita* to its fullest form. Sri Swamiji is one of the authorities or *Adhikaris* who can give us the commentary on the *Gita*. From Shankara, Ramanuja, Madhva, Ramakrishna Paramahamsa, Sri Swami Sivananda and Sri Aurobindo up to the modern scholars—like Tilak, Gandhi, Vinoba, Swami Chinmayananda, Swami Chidbhavananda and Dr. Radhakrishnan—all have enjoyed the nectar of the *Gita* which is known as *Dugdham Gitammtam Mahat!* The *Gita* has enchanted great Western scholars like Thoreau, who in ecstasy remarked: "In the morning I bathe my intellect in the stupendous and cosmogonal philosophy of the *Bhagavad Gita* in comparison with which our modern world and its literature seem puny and trivial."

Such a great work has been taken on by Swami Satchidananda. There is a reason behind it. Whether he is aware of the great quality he possesses or not, all his listeners and readers are very much aware of that quality; that is the simplicity and clarity of his expression. The *Bhagavad Gita*, through his pen, finds a lucid expression and meaning very essential for a modern reader. His words reach the very depth of the heart of the reader. What else should the expression need? Rhetoric, rhythm and rhyme are not that essential as the simplicity and sincerity of thought. Sri Swamiji is the foremost in that art. His listeners would certainly agree with this remark of mine. I am honored to write these words in this book of great significance.

I wish that all those who wish to know about the *Gita* will read and enjoy and be benefited by this book.

Dr. P. Jayaraman
Executive Director, Bharatiya Vidya Bhavan USA
New York

Editor's Preface

Many commentaries have been written on the ancient and always contemporary scripture, the *Bhagavad Gita*, or Song of God. However, the commentaries in this volume were not written originally, but were spoken by Sri Swami Satchidananda to his students. This has been the traditional method of imparting spiritual knowledge from Guru to disciple since time immemorial.

These commentaries began as a series of informal afternoon and evening talks by Sri Gurudev (as he is known to his students) during a ten-day Yoga retreat in Newport, Rhode Island. Subsequently, he elaborated on many of the *slokas*, or verses in the *Gita*, for his students at Satchidananda Ashram in Pomfret Center, Connecticut, and later at Satchidananda Ashram-Yogaville in Buckingham, Virginia.

The *Bhagavad Gita* is already the summary and essence of Eastern spiritual wisdom, drawing from the Hindu tradition in particular. I believe you will find Sri Gurudev's commentaries both wise and delightful. His teachings are always practical. He has a genius for clarifying the most obscure or arcane teachings with words and stories that make everything so clear you might not realize how very deep they are.

This presentation of the *Gita* is true to the spirit and, in most cases, to the letter of the original texts. It is not intended primarily for scholars, however. Rather, this is a practical manual on how to live in joy and freedom—wherever you are, and whatever you may be doing in life.

With Sri Gurudev's encouragement, I have reworded the *slokas* in contemporary English for modern seekers. I hope you find them easy to understand, unambiguous and instructive. I have tried to present the meanings accurately as I believe Lord Krishna intended and in accord with Swami Satchidananda's perceptive explanations. The overall intention throughout this undertaking is to make the *Gita* more comprehensible and, thereby, ever more illuminating.

Sometimes Sri Gurudev uses certain Sanskrit words in his teachings. These you will find transliterated in the text and the commentaries, together with their meanings in English—which may sometimes vary, depending on the context or the connotation intended. For example, karma in one *sloka* indicates an action; in another, a reaction to an action; and, in yet a third, the sum of a person's fate.

Dharma often means virtue or righteousness. On other occasions, it indicates essential religious teaching. And yet, it may be speaking of the appropriate duties of one's calling.

At the end of the text and commentary you will find a useful glossary of frequently used Sanskrit words and other yogic terms or concepts.

The *Bhagavad Gita*, after all, is a book of yogic wisdom. Yoga means yoking the finite, mental consciousness to Infinite Consciousness. This is accomplished through a variety of processes eloquently detailed in the *Gita*.

Even with Sri Gurudev's explanations and the accompanying notes, you may come upon a *sloka* that is still puzzling. In such cases, Gurudev's advice is to leave it and go on. Certain portions in every great scripture become clear only after further study and practice. As you grow spiritually, certain teachings in the *Gita*, which at one time may have been confounding, will open and spill their treasures before you. Sri Gurudev sometimes tells listeners that they can measure their growth by comparing their experiences with the authority of scripture.

This book would be unfinished without blessings from that unseen force that shapes our lives and lights our way. Sri Swami Satchidananda never asked anyone to do this book. We asked him to explain the *Gita* to us. And when a student asks sincerely, what else can a loving teacher do?

Here then is the cream of the cream, the purest elixir, the most precious gem of all—the way to be happy, victorious, prosperous and free. It's all in *The Living Gita*. I pray that this book will be a refuge of comfort and a fountain of enlightenment for many, many thirsty seekers over the years to come.

Acknowledgements

This *Living Gita* has been published through the dedicated and loving efforts of many students and friends.

I would like to make special mention of Reverend Vidya Vonne, who initiated this project a number of years ago at Satchidananda Ashram in Connecticut. She began the compilation and editing and inspired others to continue with *The Living Gita*.

Prahaladan Mandelkorn sacrificed his own personal time and put such concentration, skill and devotion into further compiling and editing these commentaries, often using modern language. His able and dedicated assistants were: Pushpa Smith, Uma Melinda Pedroso, Professor Walter Coppedge, John Buchanan, Sheila Fancher, Sarojini and Brian Sumner, Vasudeva Alan and Yasodha Karen Perry.

I would also like to express deep gratitude to Dr. P. Jayaraman and Dr. Lakshmi Barsel, who took time from their very busy schedules to review the Sanskrit transliterations in this volume and help with the glossary.

Artist Jim Ford generously donated his talents to the design and cover art for this book.

Special thanks to the devoted staff of Integral YogaPublications: Reverend Prakash Shakti Capen, Reverend Janaki Carrera, Swami Hamsananda Ma, Swami Sharadananda Ma, Reverend Kumari de Sachy, Bhaktan Bennetta, Leela Little, Vivekan Flint, Abhaya Thiele, Dharmavati Shapiro and Ratna Stone; and the Yogaville Art Department: Gretchen Uma Knight, Raghavan Rood and Prema Conan.

To all of them and to all the others who worked toward making this book a reality, my heartfelt appreciation.

—Sri Swami Satchidananda

Introduction by Sri Swami Satchidananda

The ancient Indian scriptures are known collectively as the *Vedas*. The *Bhagavad Gita* comes from the *Vedas*. But what are the *Vedas*?

The root *vid* means knowledge. According to the Hindus, the *Vedas* are holy scriptures. Any scripture that talks about the truth is a *Veda*.

Another name for the *Vedas* is *shruti*, which means "that which is heard." Sages "heard" these truths in their deep meditation. They didn't read them somewhere or hear them from some other human being. They were not written by somebody and they have no historical date. That's why the content of these *shrutis* is called the *Sanatana Dharma* or Eternal Truth.

Even today in India this philosophy is known simply as *Sanatana Dharma*, and not as Hinduism. The word "Hindu" is incorrect. That label appeared only when foreigners came to India, saw a beautiful culture around the Indu Valley and started calling the people of that area "Indu." Later it became "Hindus."

It was "heard," or you could say it has been revealed or realized. Such truth does not pertain just to India because truth has no limitation; it is cosmic. All those who go into a properly receptive state can get the same vision, or revelation. That's why you see the same truth if you go to the very core of any religion. It will be expressed in a little different way, according to the age, the people and the geographical area. But the truth behind it all is the same. Whether it's taught by Moses, Jesus, Buddha, Mohammed, Shankara or Krishna, they all had the same truth revealed to them.

Those revelations were passed on to their students. For this reason, the scriptures were called *shrutis*: the teachers said it and the students heard it. That is why the *shrutis* are called "*Elutha Marai*," unwritten scriptures, in Tamil. After some time, as normally happens, the mental capabilities slowly eroded. Brain power grew duller and the energy weakened. The students weren't able to retain it all by heart. They heard and could remember for some time, but slowly they began to forget. It was then they started noting it down.

That's how the *Vedas* came to be written. Until then, they were simply passed by word of mouth. That's why, even today, if you read the original *Vedas* you'll see they are like brief notes. Sometimes there are even incoherent parts. If you take notes while someone talks, only you can understand them. It was through their notes that the students passed on the teachings to their students—by expanding directly from the notes. And their students in turn took their own notes, and so on and on.

The *Vedas* cover the entire universe and all its activities. It does not talk only about something spiritual. There's the theoretical wisdom part, and also the day-to-day side. The *Vedas* explain the different levels of life in the world: *brahmacharya* (the student or celibate); *grihastha* (the householder); *vanaprastha* (the recluse) and how each should live. They say how a marriage should be conducted, how rituals are to be performed—everything in day-to-day life is given.

The wisdom portion is the plain truth, the theoretical part. That's also called *Vedanta, Anta* means end; *Vedanta* means the end or goal of the *Vedas*. This portion of the *Vedas* is also known as the *Upanishads*. The *Upanishads* say something directly about the final spiritual truth. But people found it difficult to grasp their meaning, so the great sage Vyasa (to whom the entire *Vedas* are ascribed), simplified it in his *Brahma Sutras*, teachings about the Absolute. Even the simplified *sutras*, or threads, were a little difficult for people; so again they got diluted.

It's something like giving medicine. If the patient finds it too difficult to swallow directly, coat it with sugar! Put the high philosophy into a nice story, the *Mahabharata*. The *Bhagavad Gita*, the Song of God, is a part of this story.

The *Gita* is the same *Vedic* truths presented as a story. Let us always remember that each religion has its *veda*. The *Koran* is also *veda*; the *Bible* is *veda*, the *Torah* is *veda*, the *Dhammapada* is *veda*. Each is a *veda* because each is a revelation of the same cosmic truth.

If we want to learn something from a great scripture, we should approach it reverentially. Thus, we place ourselves in a receptive state. Let us begin with a traditional prayer to the scripture.

Om,

O *Bhagavad Gita*, by which Arjuna was illumined by Lord Krishna himself and which was composed of eighteen chapters within the *Mahabharata* by the ancient sage Vyasa;

O Divine Mother, Destroyer of rebirth, who showers the nectar of oneness on us; O *Bhagavad Gita*, my affectionate Mother, on Thee I meditate.

All the *Upanishads* are the cows, the milker is the cowherd boy, Krishna; Arjuna is the calf; people of purified intellect are the drinkers; the milk is the supreme nectar of the *Gita*;

My salutations to the Lord who is the source of supreme bliss, whose grace makes the mute eloquent and the crippled cross mountains.

This means that, with the grace of God, nothing is impossible.

The Story Behind the *Bhagavad Gita*

My Master, Sri Swami Sivanandaji Maharaj, said this about the greatness of the *Gita*:

"The *Gita* expounds very lucidly the fundamentals of Yoga philosophy. It is a great source of wisdom. It is a great guide, a supreme teacher, an inexhaustible spiritual treasure. It is a fountain of bliss, an ocean of knowledge. It is full of divine splendor and grandeur."

Before we go into the text of the *Gita* itself, it's good to know the circumstances under which this sacred scripture was given. The *Gita* is a dialogue between Arjuna, a great warrior-king, and the supreme God, incarnated as Sri Krishna. To know who Arjuna and Krishna were, we need a little history of the *Mahabharata*, the great Hindu epic in which the *Gita* is found.

The story is this: There were two brothers—the blind Dhritarashtra and the fair-skinned Pandu—ruling a kingdom in ancient India, or Bharatavarsha as it was called in those days. King Dhritarashtra married Gandhari, and King Pandu married Kunti and Madri. Because Pandu was cursed, he couldn't have children. But by the grace of God he was given five sons through God's representatives. (This is explained through another wonderful story in the *Mahabharata.)* The blind Dhritarashtra had one hundred sons. Duryodhana was the name of his first son.

King Pandu didn't live long. His sons—called the Pandavas—were taken into Dhritarashtra's family and lived with their one hundred cousins, the Kauravas. Remember, we have five Pandavas and one hundred Kauravas. They grew up together; but because of the bravery and intelligence of the Pandavas, terrible jealousy arose in the Kauravas. Because of this constant dispute the Pandavas decided to live apart from the Kauravas, and the country was partitioned. The Pandavas ruled their section very well. Due to their wisdom and valor, their country grew so much and became so influential that the Pandavas were able to conduct a great ritual called the *Rajasuya Yajnam,* or Ruler of the Earth ceremony.

Great power was required to perform this ceremony, and only those who had no enemies could do it. It worked like this: the king of a country let loose a beautiful horse to roam wherever it wanted while the king and other friendly warriors followed it. If anybody stopped the horse from grazing or tried to control its movement, the king would fight with that person. This *yajna* was a way of proving that there was no one powerful enough to challenge that king. The Pandavas had that much status; there were no enemies strong enough to challenge them.

This great *Rajasuya Yajna* fueled the jealousy already in the hearts of the Kauravas. So Duryodhana, with the help of his cunning uncle Sakuni, plotted the destruction of the Pandavas. With the help of his uncle, Duryodhana invited the eldest Pandava brother, Yudhishthira, to a game of dice and defeated him through trickery and cheating. Yudhishthira lost all his wealth, possessions and kingdom. He lost everything—even Draupadi, his wife. It was a shameful moment for all the Pandavas. But they accepted the conditions of their defeat.

The Pandavas, including Draupadi, agreed to go into the forest and live there for twelve years, after which time they were to live incognito for another year, untraced by the Kauravas. If by any chance they were seen and recognized during the final year, they would have to return to the forest for another twelve years. Meanwhile, the Kauravas would rule all the land. If the Pandavas could fulfill the conditions, it was agreed that they would get back their share of the kingdom after those thirteen years.

Though they had a very hard time, the Pandavas did succeed in fulfilling all the conditions. With God's help, which came as the result of their faith and devotion, they completed all thirteen years. Then they returned and said, "We've fulfilled all the conditions. Please give us our kingdom back."

Duryodhana flatly refused. "No," he said, "I won't give you even as much land as can be covered by the point of a needle!" Those were his exact words. What a generous heart! "If you want anything," he added, "You'll have to fight for it."

Then the Pandavas' mother, Kunti, advised her sons, "Don't be fools, you should wage war against them. You have a just claim." And of course, Sri Krishna also inspired them in a way by saying, "You are virtuous people and the law of righteousness is on your side. You have a duty to do it. The Kauravas aren't fit to rule the country, You're the righteous ones. You must save all the people from these villains, even by fighting if necessary." That is the background situation that created the war.

Both sides wanted the help of Sri Krishna. So one day both Arjuna and Duryodhana decided, independently of course, to seek Krishna's help. Knowing they were coming, Krishna went into his bedroom and pretended to be sleeping. He did that purposely. (Krishna is usually very playful!) Before he reclined, he set a very comfortable chair just behind the head of his couch. Then he lay down and pretended to sleep.

Duryodhana arrived just before Arjuna. They met in the lobby adjoining Krishna's apartments and then entered. Duryodhana went straight to the chair behind Krishna's head and sat down waiting for Krishna to awaken. Arjuna walked in and, being a good devotee, went near Sri Krishna's feet and stood there waiting patiently.

That's an old Indian custom. No younger brother will sit before an older one, let alone before his father, mother, uncle or other older relatives. Even if he's only a year younger, he won't sit in front of his brother unless invited to do so. It's not out of fear; it's a way to show respect. Even today, this is still done in some places. You never lose anything by showing your respect. Now you will see what Arjuna gained through his respect.

He stood there patiently. After a few minutes, Krishna's "sleep" was over. What do you see first if you wake up and just open your eyes? The one standing by your feet.

"Hello, Arjuna," Sri Krishna said, "When did you come? Have you been standing there long? Why don't you sit?"

"No, I'm happy to stand, Sir."

Then Krishna turned and saw Duryodhana. "Hello, Duryodhana, you're also here. That's fine. When did you come?"

"I came here first to ask your help. You should give preference to the one who comes first."

Krishna looked at Arjuna, who nodded, as if to say he also had come for Sri Krishna's help.

Then Krishna spoke: "Duryodhana, I believe you when you say you came first, but I was sleeping when you both came. As I awoke my eyes fell first on Arjuna. You came first, but I saw him first. Therefore, I should help you both.

"To be neutral and impartial I'll give each something. I'll divide my energy into two portions. One of you can have my entire army. The other can have just me—unarmed, and I won't fight. Now you have the choice before you.

"As you know, the younger of two should be allowed to choose first. Now Arjuna, think well before you make your choice."

Duryodhana was thinking, "Oh God, don't let him ask for the army!"

"Without you, Sir," said Arjuna, "what can I do with your army? It's enough just to have you." And he fell at the feet of Sri Krishna.

"You get what you want," said Krishna.

"That's fine with me." Duryodhana was so relieved. "What am I going to do with you? I want your entire army, your power!"

"Okay, you get what you want and he gets what he wants. Good!"

After Duryodhana left, Krishna said to Arjuna, "You only got me. I won't use even a sword or a bow. I'll be simply empty-handed. What can I do?"

Arjuna laughed: "Do you think I don't know who you are, my Lord? Sir, I've been waiting for just such an opportunity as this. If I enter the field of battle with you as my charioteer, the world will see virtue established. Please drive my chariot. Take the reins."

That's how the supreme Sri Krishna became the charioteer of the warrior, Arjuna.

Even after this, Krishna went to see Duryodhana and said, "There is still time; can't we settle this peacefully?" But Duryodhana had plotted again.

Before Krishna came, Duryodhana had a beautiful throne built for him as if he were receiving Krishna with honors. But the throne was set on small reeds, with a huge pit below. Duryodhana was foolish enough to think he could destroy the Lord himself. Krishna came in—of course knowing everything—and sat down on the throne. When it broke, he remained seated in mid-air over the pit.

Then he said, "I'm sorry to see that nothing can help you now. You have decided to destroy yourselves." He returned to the Pandavas, and everything was prepared for the war.

Finally, both armies were arrayed opposite one another on a large field called Kurukshetra. At this point, Arjuna wanted to look more closely at the people he was about to fight. He already knew them. Still he said, "Let me just have a look. Krishna, please drive my chariot into the middle of the battlefield." It is here that the *Bhagavad Gita* begins.

But before we go into it, here's an important point about the *Gita*. The entire dialogue between Krishna and Arjuna, and the war itself can be seen as allegory. The historic Kurukshetra battlefield is symbolic of the human frame. Life centered in the body is a kind of warfare. The Pandavas and Kauravas are parallel to the good and bad human tendencies. The bad tendencies are the Kauravas—naturally in the majority. And why are they considered bad? Because they're born of a "blind" father, which is ignorance. You may remember that Dhritarashtra was blind, while his brother Pandu is said to be white-skinned. This isn't a reference to his race. The word *pandu* means white, which represents *sattva*, purity and tranquility. The five sons of Pandu are the products of tranquility and represent the virtuous human qualities.

There is a constant struggle between the good and bad, but both must get their energy from the supreme God or the *Atman*, the inner Consciousness. Without the *Atman* or Self, even the bad qualities couldn't do anything. Sri Krishna represents the *Atman*. The good qualities always seek the guidance of the inner Consciousness, the *Atman*, or Krishna; whereas other tendencies seek the help of the senses and physical forces—Krishna's army.

So this Kurukshetra battle didn't happen just once some thousands of years ago. It's constantly happening. It's within each of us. If the good tendencies will allow their conscience to guide them, they can have the grace and friendship of God, and they can win the battle of life.

On yet another level, the war chariot is the body; the five beautiful horses are the five senses; and the reins that control the horses are the *buddhi* or intellect. If that intellect, the discriminative faculty, is in the hands of the conscience, which is God in you, then your chariot runs well.

If the soul or desirous mind sits behind and simply follows what the conscience says, it will be always successful. That's the allegorical meaning behind the *Gita*.

Now, let's go into the *Bhagavad Gita* itself.

Chapter One

The Despondency of Arjuna

The first chapter is called "The Despondency of Arjuna." Some people say that this first chapter is unnecessary. But if we explore it in a little more detail, we'll see how Arjuna got into his present situation and why the entire *Bhagavad Gita* had to be given.

Actually, the entire *Gita* was seen in a vision by the pure-hearted Sanjaya. He had been gifted to see what was happening on the battlefield miles away, and even to know the thoughts of everyone there.

The *Bhagavad Gita* dialogue between Sri Krishna and Arjuna, and the ensuing battle, are all narrated to the blind king, Dhritarashtra, by the noble visionary, Sanjaya.

1. Dhritarashtra said: Tell me, Sanjaya, what did my sons and Pandu's sons do when they assembled on the holy field of Kurukshetra, eager to fight?

2. Sanjaya said: After observing the Pandava army arrayed for battle, King Duryodhana approached his teacher, Drona, and said:

3. Master, look at this great army of the sons of Pandu, marshalled by Drupada, your skilled disciple.

4. They have heroes, mighty archers, Yuyudhana and Virata, matching even the great Bhima and Arjuna—and Drupada who is the great chariot warrior.

5. There are Dhrishtaketu, Chekitana, the brave King of Kasi, Purujit, Kuntibhoja and Saibya, best of men.

6. They also have courageous Yudhamanyu, valiant Uttamaujas, the son of Subhadra and the sons of Draupadi—all great warriors.

7. Our leaders, too, are distinguished; let me name them for you who are highest of the twice-born.

8. There are you, Bhishma, Karna, Kripa, who is victorious in battle; Asvatthama, Vikarna and Jayadratha, son of Somadatta also.

9. And many more heroes and well-trained warriors fully armed and ready to give their lives for me.

10. Vast is our army under Bhishma; theirs is meager, in comparison, under Bhima's leadership.

11. Now, all of you take your positions throughout your divisions, and by all means protect Bhishma.

12. To embolden Duryodhana, Bhishma, the mighty great-grandfather and Kuru elder, roared like a lion and blew his conch powerfully.

How did the fighting actually begin? The mighty grandsire, Bhishma, the oldest in the family, was a very saintly person. But because he was head of the Kaurava family, he felt he had to fight on Duryodhana's side. He couldn't simply change his allegiance at the last minute. He accepted it as his *svadharma* or his predestined duty: "It's my duty to fight, even though I know I'm on the unrighteous side." And it was Bhishma who actually began the fighting. He gave a lion's roar and blew his conch shell. Then Sri Krishna, Arjuna and others blew their conches. This small point is to be noted: the battle was actually begun by the unrighteous Kauravas, not by the Pandavas.

13. Immediately, the Kurus sounded their conches, kettledrums, cow horns, tabors and trumpets, creating a tremendous noise.

14. Then Krishna and Arjuna stood in their magnificent chariot, which was yoked to white horses, and blew their divine conches.

15. The Panchajanya (conch taken from the demon Panchajanya) was blown by Krishna; the Devadatta (God-given conch) was blown by Arjuna, and the Paundra (conch) by Bhima of awesome feats.

16. King Yudhisthira, son of Kunti, blew the Anantavijaya (endless victory conch) Nakula and Sahadeva blew the Sughosha (great sounding conch) and Manipushpaka (jewel bracelet conch).

17. Immediately, the great archer and King of Kasi, the valiant charioteer Sikhandi; Dhrishtadyumna; Virata and the invincible Satyaki,

18. Together with Drupada, the sons of Draupadi and the mighty son of Subhadra blew their conches, my Lord,

19. Filling the earth and the heavens with such a roar that it tore at the hearts of the Kurus.

20. On observing Dhritarashtra's host arrayed for battle and ready to begin, Arjuna, flying the ensign of Hanuman, lifted his bow and said to Krishna:

21–22. Draw my chariot between the two armies so I can see whom to fight and with whom I must wage war.

23. I want to know who is gathered here intending to please the evil-minded Duryodhana in battle.

24–25. Sanjaya said: Thus requested by Arjuna, Krishna placed the best of chariots between the two armies. Then facing Bhishma, Drona and all the rulers of the earth, he said: Behold, Arjuna—all the Kurus gathered together—

26. Standing there, Arjuna saw in both armies: uncles, grandfathers, teachers, cousins, sons, grandsons, comrades, fathers-in-law and friends.

Arjuna no longer saw them as enemies. Until then he had regarded them as wicked, but the moment he stood between the armies he saw these familiar categories instead.

27. On seeing his friends and relatives positioned on both sides, Arjuna was overcome with pity and said despondently:

28–29. O, Krishna, my limbs fail me, my mouth is parched, my body is shaking and my hair stands on end seeing my relatives gathered here and anxious to fight.

It's good to know these symptoms which we too may face in similar situations, even when we try to fight our own undesirable habits.

It was not real compassion he felt, but a kind of attachment—like a judge who loses his neutrality when he sees a relative on trial. Arjuna forgot they were vicious people the minute he saw them as relatives.

> 30. Arjuna's bow, Gandiva, fell from his hand: My skin is burning, I can't keep standing and my mind seems to be reeling,

> 31. I see bad omens, Krishna. I cannot see any good resulting from the slaughter of my own people in battle.

See how the mind immediately finds excuses, and more excuses. Arjuna is an intelligent man, so he says:

> 32. Krishna, I do not desire victory, kingdom or even pleasures. What use is there for kingdom, pleasures or even life?

Is this true dispassion?

> 33. Those for whom we might desire kingdom, enjoyment and pleasures are here ready for battle, having renounced life and wealth.

Listen to the so-called beautiful advice he's giving Sri Krishna.

> 34. Before me are teachers, fathers, sons and even grandfathers, uncles, fathers-in-law, grandsons, brothers-in-law and other relatives.

> 35. Though they might kill me, Krishna, I do not want to kill them—even for the sake of dominion over the three worlds, much less, just for this earth.

Look at his approach. It's all based on his attachment.

> 36. What pleasure would be ours, Krishna, by killing the sons of Dhritarashtra? Only trouble will come to us for killing these murderers.

> 37. That's why we shouldn't kill the sons of Dhritarashtra, our own relatives. How could we ever be happy again, Krishna, after killing our own people?

> 38. Though their understanding is clouded by greed, and they feel no guilt about exterminating an entire family, or showing hostility toward friends . . .

Now Arjuna gives another excuse for not fighting. "They are all wretched people, murderers. What's the use of killing them and purposely committing sins ourselves?" Why does he call them wretched? Because it's true. If you go through the whole *Mahabharata*, you will see no criminal offense to which they were strangers. They were all confirmed scoundrels. They secretly set fire to the house where the Pandavas were expected to sleep during their exile. They tried poison. They openly attempted murder. They deceitfully tried to deprive the Pandavas of their kingdom, wealth and wife, Draupadi, who was married to all the Pandava brothers. Death is the reward that *dharma*, or destiny, will bring to such people, even if they happen to be Arjuna's relatives.

Overwhelmed with sentiment, Arjuna wants to save them, even though his duty as a *kshatriya* (member of the ruling, protecting caste) is to destroy evil. The duty of a king is to uphold righteousness. At the same time that he calls them murderers, still he wants to save them and speaks of committing sin. It's an argument based on sentiment.

39. Shouldn't we recoil from such sin, Krishna, seeing clearly the troubles that follow a family's destruction?

In *slokas* 38 and 39, Arjuna has been arguing: "By this war we are going to destroy the family unit." This is a reasonable excuse not to fight if it's an unjust war.

Sloka 39 clearly says, "Why don't we just avoid such momentous action which will cause so much sin. We know that this war will bring vast destruction and families will be dispersed. Many people will be lost in many families."

40. When a family is destroyed, its time-honored religious traditions also perish and impiety overtakes the survivors.

This *sloka* clearly says, "When there is a decline of the family, so not enough people are left to take care of the community and the country, then the sacrificial actions are lost."

41. As impiety spreads, the women become unchaste and the family is corrupted. This causes the intermingling of castes.

42. With the mingling of castes, both the family destroyed and the family destroyers must suffer in hell without the aid of their descendants' devotional offerings.

43. When castes are confused, religious traditions are ruined and with it the family's merits—all this caused by those who destroy a family.

And as you know, Arjuna continues, the men will be destroyed in this war. The survivors will be mostly women. And, he says, with more women and fewer men, the clean life will be disturbed.

Even the women may become unchaste and can be corrupted. That will bring confusion and a mixing of various bloods and mixing also of the castes.

This should not be taken literally. By castes, he means different calibers of people. There are different types of minds with different temperaments: the spiritual and most thoughtful thinking group; the warrior type; the business type; and the working type. Arjuna warns that these types of people will get all mixed up.

In those days, it was believed that people should marry in the same group to avoid cultural and intellectual differences. Normally, a warrior type of person wouldn't marry a working class person. Not that either one was inferior or superior, but the thinking mechanism was thought to be very different. Such a mixture, says Arjuna, will cause terrible confusion. And this purity of life is disturbed. These are some of the reasons why he didn't want to fight.

44. Krishna, we have heard that people must suffer for some time in hell when the religious practices of their families are destroyed.

45. Alas, we are bent on perpetrating the great sin of killing our relatives all out of greed for the pleasures of a kingdom.

Arjuna's reasons for not wanting to fight are good. But greater than any of these reasons, the necessity to go to war is there in this case because the wicked people have been unnecessarily disturbing the innocent people. So Sri Krishna will somehow educate him about the necessity of this war.

Because of this, some people say that the *Bhagavad Gita* propagates war. "Could this be scripture?" they ask. Yes, it is scripture—a teaching based on the truth. This shows that war is not always bad. Occasionally there is a just war, when innocent people are being victimized by the wicked and there is no way to stop it except by fighting.

Sometimes we lose sight of the truth when we get into emotional attachments to people. It is here that Sri Krishna tries to remove the sentimental feelings and bring Arjuna back to truth and his duty. But overwhelmed with sorrow, Arjuna sits despondently in the chariot and abandons his weapons.

46. It would be far better for me if the armed sons of Dhritarashtra would come upon me, unarmed and unresisting in battle and slay me.

47. Sanjaya said: Having said this, Arjuna threw down his bow and arrows and sat down in his chariot overcome with sorrow.

Thus ends the first discourse of the *Bhagavad Gita*, the science of Yoga, entitled: "The Despondency of Arjuna."

Chapter Two

The Yoga of Wisdom

In the first chapter we saw Arjuna, the warrior king who is supposed to protect the land from the unrighteous, come forward to do the job with the help of Sri Krishna. But when he saw his own kith and kin in opposition he was moved by sentimentality and momentarily forgot his duty. He underwent physical changes: shivering of the body, drying of the throat and nearly fainted from despondency. He decided not to fight. His bow, which had never failed, dropped from his hand. He lost courage and sat silent in his chariot.

To interpret the situation allegorically, we should each think that we are Arjuna. Very often we fail to perform our duties because we get involved in personal attachments, for example, thinking: "It's mine. It's dear to me. How can I do away with this?" Wherever there's this personal attachment, sentimentality arises and we fail to do our duties well.

This is Arjuna's situation. Now Krishna will try to remind Arjuna of his duty; that is the entire purpose of the *Gita*. It is not that Sri Krishna is interested in making Arjuna fight a war and destroy some wicked people. Had he really wanted to do only that, he could have done so with just a snap of his fingers. He doesn't need Arjuna or anybody else. Arjuna is only an excuse to show the entire world how people should perform their duties.

1. Sanjaya said: When Krishna saw Arjuna overcome with sentiment, despondent, eyes blurred with tears of despair,

2. The blessed Lord said: From whence arises this shameful and cowardly dejection, Arjuna, which at this dangerous moment bars the way to heaven?

He uses these words "Unmanly, heaven-barring and shameful dejection . . ." to kindle Arjuna's pride.

3. Yield not to weakness. It does not suit you. Shake off this petty faintheartedness. Stand up, Scorcher of foes, wake up!

Don't we often act like the despondent Arjuna? "Oh, I just don't know what to do. I can't do it. I can't!" I have heard this kind of mantra from many people. I say, "You *can* do it; you *have* the capacity."

"No, I can't," you still might say. If you keep on repeating "I can't; I can't," what is it but weak-mindedness? Instead just say, "I can!" and you *can*. Nothing is impossible.

But still Arjuna uses his own arguments—which seem to him very reasonable—to expound his view.

4. Arjuna said: O Krishna, how can I ever fight with the venerable Bhishma and Drona, who are worthy of my worship?

"My grandfather Bhishma and Drona, my own archery master, are there. Don't you see them? They are worthy of my worship. You know that." It's true. But what should come first, if the only choice is doing or sparing his own master? If he must choose between these, his duty comes first. Why? Because he is not really destroying the teacher. Sri Krishna explains that later. But until then, Arjuna goes on with his own intellectual arguments. Finally after all that, he reaches a point where he says,

5. It would be better for me to live as a beggar than to kill these great souls who have been my teachers. Even if I were to kill them, my enjoyment of wealth and desires in this world would be stained with their blood.

6. The sons of Dhritarashtra stand before us. I do not know which would be better—for us to kill them, or them to kill us. If we slay them, we won't even want to live.

7. I am weighed down with weak-mindedness; I am confused and cannot understand my duty. I beg of you to say for sure what is right for me to do. I am your disciple. Please teach me, for I have taken refuge in you.

It's a beautiful *sloka*: "I am your disciple. Instruct me." The *Bible* says, "Ask, it shall be given." Here Arjuna is asking. He realizes his situation. He's come to know that he knows nothing. That is the best understanding, because if you know that you don't know, you will *want* to know. If you don't know that, you won't even want to know. If somebody comes to tell you the truth, you will say, "I don't need it." That's why the proverb:

"If a person knows not that he knows not, ignore him. If he knows that he knows not, go teach him. If he knows that he knows, go learn from him."

So here is Arjuna ready to learn. The qualifications of a sincere student are clearly shown here. When you go to a teacher saying, "I know a little bit, can you add a little more?" Or, "I know, but can you verify it?" You are just going there to check your capabilities, not to learn anything new. If you want to learn, go empty and open. "I'm an empty cup; please pour in all you can." If you go with a cup already full, even if the teacher pours something good, where will it go? It's not that he or she is miserly; the teacher would like to pour, but it will overflow and go to waste. So empty your cup.

There's a good Zen story of a student who went to a *roshi*, a teacher, demanding to be taught the secret of enlightenment. Instead of saying something, the *roshi* began to pour the student a cup of tea. The cup became full; yet the master kept on pouring and the tea spilled over onto the floor.

"My cup is full, Master. Why do you keep on pouring more and more?" the student asked.

"Like this cup of tea, your mind is already filled with something. If I pour my knowledge into your cup, it will just go onto the floor because there's no room in your mind for it. You will interpret my instructions according to what you already think. Your mind will not be able to accept the truth I give you."

But Arjuna proves to be a good student and an honest person when he says:

8. I do not see any remedy for this deep grief that parches my senses—even if I were to achieve prosperous and unrivaled royalty here on earth and even over the heavens.

9. Sanjaya said: After speaking this way to Krishna, the Lord of the senses, Arjuna, who is the terror of his enemies, said: "I won't fight" and became silent.

After saying that, Arjuna was silent, waiting for Sri Krishna's instructions. Sri Krishna cast a beautiful smile at him and began to speak. In these next few verses he explains the immortality of the *Atman* or the Self.

10. Then, O great king, Krishna seemed to smile and spoke these words to the despondent warrior in between the two armies:

The *Bhagavad Gita* came into existence mainly because of the delusion and despondency of Arjuna. On the battlefield when Arjuna saw all his teachers, relatives, cousins and others, he felt sad. Momentarily, he forgot his duty as a warrior-protector and didn't want to fight; he wanted to back out. But at the same time, being the learned person that he was, he couldn't just say, "I'm despondent." He tried to hide that feeling by intellectualizing and saying, "Oh, what's the use of this fighting. After all, even if I win the kingdom, it's not going to last so long. Why don't we just allow these people to enjoy themselves. By killing all these people we, ourselves, may ultimately end up in hell." See, he made all kinds of excuses using various forms of logic. Sometimes we do that just to escape our duty.

Meanwhile, Krishna, the teacher, was just looking at him, nodding his head and smiling, "All right, come on, let me see how much you've learned. Go ahead—exhaust your vocabulary and all your arguments." Then finally, toward the end, Arjuna admitted, "Sorry, I'm simply blabbering. The fact is, I don't know what to do. Please sir, just tell me what to do. I'm ready to do it. I give up my ego and depend on your advice." Thus, he proved himself to be a good student. All his arguments were futile. He realized that all his learning wasn't helping him. And it is at this point that Sri Krishna started talking to him about the nature of the pure Self, the *Atman*, which is indestructible. At the same time, he tells Arjuna that, having come into this world, each one must perform his or her duty. "You have been born here as a *Kshatriya*," he says, "a king, a protector. You have to do your duty. You're not doing it for your sake, but for the sake of everybody, to protect the innocent from the wicked." And that's how he begins.

11. You are grieving for those who should not be grieved for, while uttering would-be words of wisdom. The wise grieve neither for the living nor the dead.

Here Sri Krishna gives the first step in Yoga, because all our understanding and practice should be based on knowledge of the immortality of the Self, which is what we aim to realize. These verses directly give the theoretical background of Yoga which is called *Samkhya*. That's why the entire second chapter is called *Samkhya Yoga*. Those who have read about different Hindu schools of thought may have heard of *samkhya* as something different, but what Sri Krishna calls *samkhya* is direct information about the Self.

First he explains the situation to Arjuna. "You haven't harmonized your thought, word and deed. You are thinking one way, but speaking another and acting in still a different way. You know the truth about these people. You have even called them wretched and wicked. They are not afraid to commit the worst crimes. Yet, you say some compassionate words and fail to perform your duty. So there's no harmony between your thoughts, words and actions. Such a person falls from Yoga." Thus he warns Arjuna about this falling.

12. There never was a time when I did not exist, nor you, nor any of these ruling princes. And neither will there ever come a time when we cease to be.

In terms of the *Atman*, the reality of the Self, we always *are*; we always exist. It's not that we were once non-existent, have now come and will stop existing later on.

13. That which is embodied experiences the body's childhood, youth and old age and also in time acquires another body. This does not disturb one whose mind is calm.

One with a calm mind isn't affected when the body undergoes changes. It was conceived, it grows up, dies, then decays and decomposes. There is impermanency in the body. How can that be the immortal Self? So Sri Krishna is explaining the nature of death.

And, here he gives the difference between the permanent and impermanent, the real and the unreal.

14. As the senses contact the objects of the senses, feelings of heat and cold, pain and pleasure occur, Arjuna. These sensations come and go; they're impermanent. Patiently endure them, great Prince.

15. In fact, that person who is not tossed about by sense experiences and always stays balanced in pain and pleasure is fit to experience immortality.

16. What is not, has never been; and what is, always is. This truth about the real and the unreal has been realized by the seers.

17. Know that all this vast universe is pervaded by that which is indestructible. No one can destroy what is everlasting and imperishable.

18. The indwelling One is eternal, indestructible and immeasurable. The bodies of the indwelling One are impermanent. Therefore, Arjuna,

19. Whoever thinks that *Atman*, or the Self, does the killing or can be killed misunderstands. That (Self) doesn't kill, nor is it ever killed.

Who is a seer? Who really knows the truth? The one who distinguishes between the unreal and the real. This is discriminative knowledge or *viveka*. With discrimination, the permanent—which is never-changing—is distinguished from the ever-changing. But the permanent and the impermanent are not completely different. When we say that something changes constantly, there must be something to change. Without that something, there cannot be any changes. Then what changes? The names and forms of the primordial essence, which is always there. The one is always there, but it appears to be many.

This basic oneness is what's real. For example, let's take water and say it is reality. Steam is one expression of it and ice is another. But in water, steam and ice, you see the same essence—nothing but H_2O, hydrogen and oxygen. Even though we see the changes and work with them, we can always remember that there's something permanent behind them all. That's clearly said here and is referred to as seeing the truth.

If ever we want to do something, we should keep an eye on the reality, and then do it. If we miss that reality, whatever we do on the superficial level will collapse one day. It's something like going to a lovely site to build a nice Yoga *ashram*, a training facility, there. You have decided on it. But somehow you come to know the plot isn't good for construction. The soil is loose and nothing can grow there. Or the soil is too full of clay and won't support a good sewage system. The location is rejected, however beautiful it is.

The following is a very well-known *sloka*:

> 20. It is not born and it does not die. Unborn, eternal and ancient, the Self is not killed when the body is killed.

He's actually preparing Arjuna. It's good to know this also, because many are so afraid of death. Why? We lose sight of our immortality. We lose sight of our being *Atman* and think constantly of becoming that. Sri Krishna simplifies death. It's surprising to see how easily Sri Krishna talks about it. That's why in the East particularly, people don't seem to worry much about death.

> 21. Whoever truly knows the Self—indestructible, eternal, birthless and changeless—in what way would such a person kill, Arjuna? Who would be killed?

> 22. Just like casting off worn-out clothing and putting on new ones, that which is embodied casts off worn-out bodies and enters others that are new.

If somebody takes off his worn-out shirt and says, "I'm going to get a new one," will you cry over it? Death is something like that. You have a new shirt and you show everyone proudly, "See how new it is? No wrinkles, so beautiful." But when you start using it, it gets dirty and wrinkled. You keep on washing and ironing it, but at a certain point that can't be done anymore. So you just discard it. The body is like that. And that's how we should think of death.

But the Self, isn't like that.

> 23. Weapons do not affect the Self; fire does not burn it, water does not wet it and wind does not dry it.

> 24. The Self cannot be pierced or cut; it cannot be burned, moistened or dried. It is endless, all-pervading, stable, immovable and everlasting.

> 25. It is said to be unmanifested, inconceivable and immutable. Knowing all this, there is no cause to grieve.

Why? Because the Self is not of nature's elements. All the elements are *products* of that same essence; thus, they can't affect it. They are the gross expressions of it.

After saying something about the immortal principle of *Atman*, Sri Krishna takes a different tack: "Now I've told you about your immortality, but you still may not want to believe this because it seems like mere theory. You may still have some doubts and insist, 'It is born and it will die.' All right. But even if that were so, why worry about it?"

> 26. Even if you imagined *Atman* (the Self) continually taking birth and dying—even then, mighty Arjuna—there is no reason to grieve.

It's natural that whatever comes, will go. The names and forms come and go; they constantly change. But the essence behind it all stays the same always.

> 27. Whatever is born will undoubtedly die; whatever is dead certainly will be born. You should not mourn what is inevitable.

> 28. Arjuna, beings originally are all unmanifested. At midstate they're manifested; and unmanifested again at the end. What is the point of lamenting?

> 29. One may perceive the Self as full of wonders; another speaks of It as marvelous; another hears It is wonderful, yet none completely understand It.

> 30. This Self, which exists in everyone, the Indweller, is invulnerable, Arjuna. Therefore, you do not have to grieve for anyone.

It's always changing. Just watch the changes and enjoy them. Now Sri Krishna takes still another viewpoint, a more worldly view.

> 31. Furthermore, looking at your own duty, you will see no reason to waver. For certainly there is nothing higher for a *Kshatriya* than a righteous war.

A *Kshatriya* is someone of the warrior or ruler caste and is supposed to protect the righteous from the wicked. A king is a *Kshatriya*, and the duty of a king is to maintain law and order. That's why he is a ruler. Krishna is reminding Arjuna of that: "Now that the war has come, you must uphold righteousness. By retreating from it, you allow unrighteousness to thrive. That's not fulfilling a *Kshatriya's* duty."

And if he doesn't do his duty, what will happen? Here Krishna gently pricks Arjuna's pride.

> 32. Happy indeed are the *Kshatriyas*, Arjuna, called to fight in such a battle that comes of itself— like an open gate to heaven.

> 33. But if you don't fight when it's your duty to do so, you lose your honor and incur sin.

You won't be doing the job for which you were created, which is your *svadharma*, your own duty.

Not only that, but . . .

> 34. People will continually recall your shame. And for one who has been honored, dishonor is worse than death.

"What will they think of you? All these days people were talking about your greatness. Don't you know that? Don't get into this shame."

> 35. The great charioteers will suppose you withdrew from battle out of fear. Those who thought so highly of you will take you lightly.

"You may have your own excuses. You may say you are compassionate and don't want to kill them. But do you think they'll believe that? No, they'll say you are a coward. You were highly esteemed by these people; hold onto their esteem."

> 36. And your enemies will deride your strengths and slander you. What could be more painful?

Sri Krishna makes three different points here. First, he tells Arjuna about the immortality of the *Atman*. Then, he says that even if it were possible for the soul to be born and to die, there's nothing to worry about anyway, because coming and going are inevitable. And third, speaking from a more worldly standpoint, he tells Arjuna to perform his duty by reminding him that if he ignores his duty he will incur sin and shame, which is worse than death.

> 37. If you are killed, you will gain heaven. If you are victorious, you will enjoy the earth. Therefore, rise up, Arjuna, resolved to fight!

"But when I say, 'arise and fight,' don't forget that you are acting on my behalf, not for your own sake. You have been created for this purpose in my cosmic plan and you are only fulfilling that purpose. Personally, you don't have anything to do with these things."

Here Sri Krishna begins speaking about the path of Karma Yoga.

> 38. Seeing the same in pleasure and pain, gain and loss, victory and defeat, in battle—just for the sake of the battle—then you will be sinless.

The cause is just. You are simply acting as an agent. So whatever the outcome may be, it's not going to affect you.

> 39. You have been given the ideal of Self-knowledge. Now hear the practical wisdom of Yoga by which, Arjuna, you can break through all the bonds of karma.

In this Samkhya Yoga chapter there are two sections—*Samkhya*, the theoretical part, and Yoga, the practical part. Merely knowing the theory is not enough. Put it into action. You may know the whole cookbook by heart, but you'll still be hungry if you don't cook the food and eat it. You should understand these two points—*Samkhya* and Yoga. Both are important. Why does Sri Krishna stress both? Because some people simply sit and inquire about the *Atman:* "Who am I? I am *Brahman*, the Absolute one. *Soham*—I am that." This is sheer Jnana Yoga, the path of discriminating wisdom. Others plunge into activity even without knowing the basic principles. There should be a beautiful harmony between theory and practice. Then life is more enjoyable and fruitful. That's the greatness of Raja Yoga, or to use our familiar term, Integral Yoga. You blend theory and practice. You apply the theory in your day-to-day activities.

Sometimes people say, "Probably it's too late for me now. I don't know how long I will live to practice these things. I don't have much time." Or, "I'm too old to do all this. I've wasted my life." But here Sri Krishna gives confidence to such people:

> 40. In these practices no effort made is lost, nor are there adverse effects. Even a little practice of this *dharma* protects one from great fear.

"Even a little practice of this *dharma* protects one from great fear." That's the great advantage of Yoga practice. With an understanding of theory and principle, even a little practice won't be wasted and will never cause adverse effects. Suppose you construct a house. You build the walls and then say, "I've spent all my money; I don't have enough to put on the roof." All the energy you used to build the walls is wasted. It's the same with all worldly things. If you begin, you have to go to the very end to get the benefit.

But in Yoga practice, it's different. Even if you practice Hatha Yoga postures and breathing for one day, at least you'll be relaxed on that day. It's like eating. Even if you eat on just one day, at least it will take care of that day. It won't go to waste. That's why Sri Krishna says that even a little bit is good. Try it. If you like it, take more. No bad aftereffects, like poisonous drugs that leave ill effects.

41. If your mind is unsteady and wandering, many-branched and endless are the thoughts and choices. When your mind is clear and one-pointed, there is only one decision.

Krishna addresses Arjuna about the difference between the people of firm and infirm mind. It's very simple. For the firm mind, there is only one decision, but for the infirm mind, "many-branched and endless are the decisions." He uses a beautiful Sanskrit word, *vyavasayam,* for a firm mind. *Vyavasayam* in Sanskrit means agriculture. To reap the harvest, cultivators needs firm minds with one conviction, that "by doing such and such, I will harvest this much." With such conviction they do everything toward fulfillment. Good cultivators never change midway. They don't prepare this soil, then sow the seeds somewhere else. Nor will they sow the seeds and then say, "I don't have time to take care of it." They continuously use their efforts until they reach their goals. That is what is meant by a firm mind.

So often we come across a fleeting type of mind. People with such minds don't stick to one thing. They choose one, then their minds soon become dissipated. Something that is worth obtaining won't come overnight. Rome wasn't built in a day. A seeker needs a firm conviction. "My goal is very high. It's the highest goal that, once achieved, will make me achieve everything else." As the *Bible* says, "Seek ye first the kingdom of God; all else will be added unto you." Having that big goal, we can't expect results overnight. A firm-minded seeker says, "I have to give all my effort, total one-pointedness, with unwavering mind." That seeker will certainly achieve what he or she wants.

But the others constantly change. If something brings a little irritation or is a little difficult, they say, "Let me leave it. I'll try something else; it may be easier and cheaper." They keep on switching. It's like digging many shallow wells and not finding water. Sri Krishna clearly gives the difference between these two kinds of people.

With a firm mind there is only one decision or one goal. Actually, there is no difference in goals between two firm-minded people—this is important to know. You are convinced of the highest goal. Another person is also convinced. Both are firm-minded. In that firmness the end is one and the same. The people who solve a mathematical problem will always find the same answer for that simple problem. There is only one right answer, but there can be many wrong answers. For the weak-minded there are many wrong answers. They try something and when it's no good they erase it, try again, erase it, try again. But to the firm mind there is only one conclusion, one answer, one goal that never changes.

A sincere seeker should have that total conviction about the goal. Then *sadhana*, spiritual practice, becomes easier. You are firmly convinced, and with that firm mind you begin. Then nothing will stop you.

Imagine a fisherman who really wants to catch a fish. He's in a small boat in the middle of the lake. It's raining, chilly and windy. He casts his line and keeps his eyes only on that. Nothing disturbs him. Just to catch a little fish, how much he forgoes. He could be sitting comfortably at home in an easy chair, but he wouldn't catch a fish that way. For a simple thing one needs so much concentration.

When you keep a keen eye on the goal you won't think of bodily difficulties. However much physical suffering is there, it doesn't matter. You won't even think of eating; you won't even sleep. People might say many things about you. Some might tease you. Some will say, "You're wasting your time." But you won't listen to those things. You won't be distracted—even by nice things. No one can move you from your purpose.

"Leave that, come on, there is something nice on television, a good movie."

But you say, "No, I'm catching a fish. I won't budge an inch until I do." Such a person is a true fisherman. For others, it's just a hobby. If they don't catch it, they think, "It's too much, forget it." You see the difference between the firm mind and the infirm mind.

42. In flowery discourses, the unwise focus on the letter of scripture and say there is nothing else.

43. With minds full of desires and heaven as their highest goal, they speak mostly of rites and rituals, which they believe will bring pleasure and power.

44. Those deeply attached to pleasures and power are not able to fix their minds one-pointed in meditation and enjoy *samadhi* (superconsciousness).

45. The *Vedas* discuss the three *gunas*. Arjuna, transcend the three *gunas* and you will be free of the pairs of opposites—ever-balanced, free of wanting to get or keep anything and centered in your true Self.

When Sri Krishna mentions the pairs of opposites, he means all dualities, such as pleasure and pain, profit and loss, praise and blame.

46. For those already enlightened, the scriptures are as useful as a water reservoir during a flood.

To an enlightened person all the scriptures are useless. When there's water everywhere, what's the use of a small well, or even a reservoir? A reservoir is needed when there's no water anywhere. Then at least you'll have some water to drink. But when there's water everywhere, who worries about a reservoir? It's the same way for an enlightened person; everything is there. They know what's what. There's no need for scriptures to tell them. Here's a simple analogy: You know you're living, don't you? Do you need scriptures to tell you: "Yes, you're living"? That's what enlightenment means. The one who knows what is to be known, doesn't need scriptures.

That's the essence of the 46th *sloka*. But that doesn't mean scriptures are unnecessary. They are something like a ladder. The one who has gone up doesn't need a ladder anymore. But what about the others still on the ground? They have to go up, too. So at least for their sake, keep the ladder.

47. As for you, do the work that comes to you—but don't look for the results. Don't be motivated by the fruits of your actions, nor become attached to inaction.

This is an oft-quoted *sloka*: "Your duty is to perform the act, but not for its fruit. Claiming the fruit of your actions is the forbidden fruit spoken of in the *Bible*. That was the first commandment given by God to the very first man, Adam. That commandment is given to "*Atman*" also. Adam and *Atman*—and even atom—are all more or less the same. Adam, *Atman* and atoms just function. Ask an atom, "Why are you constantly revolving?"

"It's none of my business to know that. I'm just doing what I'm supposed to be doing." It just acts; it never worries about the results. That's what Sri Krishna says here—"you are not to be affected by the act."

48. Equanimity of mind is Yoga. Do everything, Arjuna, centered in that equanimity. Renouncing all attachments, you'll enjoy an undisturbed mind in success or failure.

"Equanimity of mind is Yoga." Keep up that tranquility while allowing *prakriti,* or nature, to function through you. Sri Krishna goes on:

49. Work done for the sake of some results is much lower than that done in mental equilibrium, Arjuna. Wretched are those motivated by the fruits of their actions.

Sometimes the Sanskrit term is translated as "miser" instead of "result-seeker," because anyone who does something just to get something in return is not a giving person. If you are a giving person, you don't expect anything in return. If you expect even a little in return, how can you say you are giving? You give and you get. Then if you don't get, you won't give. Such a person is wretched, always thinks of getting. If you give, do it for the joy of giving. This is an important verse to remember: "Wretched are the result-seekers."

Imagine that you have arrived at a hotel. A porter immediately opens your car door, picks up the luggage and takes you to your room. Isn't that nice service? Picture his face—so much joy is there, particularly if you get out of a big car, dressed very well. You might have only a small suitcase which you could easily carry yourself. Just behind you, another car may pull in—a simple car. The people in this car may have three or four suitcases, but the porter won't go to them. He runs to "help" you instead. After you get to your room, if you simply say, "Thank you," look at his expression. He'll be completely dejected, even angry, because there are pits in his actions. That's why he waits for "tips." A tip is nothing but an inverted pit.

But what if, as you get out of the car, you see a good friend of yours going into the same hotel? He just picks up your suitcase. "Please, I'll take it for you." He brings it to your room and leaves. He won't even wait for your thanks, let alone a tip. Both men did the same job. Who really enjoyed what he was doing and kept a calm mind? The one who did it for the joy of doing. He's a *karma yogi*. The other one is a miser and is wretched. If he doesn't get the tip, or even if it's a little less than he expected, he's unhappy.

50. The one who has trained the mind to stay centered in equanimity, in this life, has cast aside both good and evil karma. Therefore, by all means practice Yoga; perfection in action is Yoga.

I often quote this *sloka* as a definition of Yoga. *"Yogah karmasu kaushalam,"* perfection in action is Yoga. An act becomes perfect when you do it with all joy and without expecting anything in return. All other acts, however wonderful they are, however beautiful they look, whatever religious label they get, are still imperfect acts because they will affect the mind. Then you are not free from the feeling of profit or loss.

You might ask: "Why can't I do something and get some merit? You say to let go of all the results. But what about good results? What's wrong with that?" Sri Krishna's reply is that whether they are good or bad, they are going to bind you, because the cause of birth and death is karma, actions and reactions, both bad and good. If you ask: "How about the good acts?" It's like a bird saying, "Take away this dirty, steel cage and give me a nice golden one." It looks prettier, but it's still a cage. You are born as a result of meritorious deeds also, the fruits of which you want to taste. It's better to renounce the fruits of all your actions.

But, of course, it's not that easy to renounce both good and bad to begin with. Therefore, we sometimes suggest, instead of bad acts, do good, at least for the sake of merit. But whatever it is, good or bad, it affects you in some way and brings birth and death. That's why at a certain point you are advised to renounce both.

When you do that, you just perform your own duty without any attachment. This keeps your mind clean. There's no reason to get disturbed, no disappointments, no grief, no fear, no competition.

Now we come to the most important and oft-quoted section of the second chapter, the *sthitapragnya lakshana,* the description of the enlightened person. Arjuna says, "You seem to be talking a lot about *samkhya* and Yoga—the theory and the practice. Are there people who have achieved this goal, who act with this realization underneath everything they do, whom you would call enlightened people? Are there people whose minds are always steady and tranquil, who perform perfect actions always? If so, let me hear about them."

51. Enjoying equanimity of mind, renouncing the fruits of their actions, free of the bondage of rebirth, the wise undoubtedly go to a stainless state.

52. When your understanding transcends delusion, then you are indifferent to things you hear about and things yet to be heard about.

When you've understood what is to be understood clearly, without any doubt, then you become indifferent to things you hear about or to those yet to be heard of. If such a person hears of something, he or she can say, "Well, I know that already." And if another says, "Oh, but there is something more to be heard," the first one can reply, "I don't have to hear anymore."

These are all the qualities of a person who has reached the height. In the *Upanishads* it's said, "For enlightened people there is nothing that is to be done or not to be done." Such people have risen above these duties. They have no personal responsibilities. There's nothing they have to do or should not do. This "do" and "don't do" no longer affect such people.

But until that time, certain things are to be followed—you have to do certain things and stop doing some other things. Mostly, these are the two guidelines, but there's another one also.

53. When your mind, which has been tossed about by conflicting opinions, becomes still and centered in equilibrium, then you experience Yoga.

It's a beautiful *sloka*. After being tossed back and forth by so many conflicting views, slowly you are pushed up and up. One day you rise to the heights. Then you're no longer tossed between these dualities or differing opinions—for and against, good and bad.

When your intelligence is shaken by the conflicting opinions of others don't get upset over it, because you know the truth. Just accept their opinions as mere words. You simply feel, "Yes, that's what they feel. Let them feel that way." It may appear to be conflicting, but you give the freedom to others to think the way they want and say what they want. The enlightened person is not affected by that.

Slokas 54 to 72 are very important, for they describe the one of steady wisdom. The summary of all these *slokas* can be said in one word: equanimity. The person of steady wisdom is the one who retains equanimity in all situations. Absolutely nothing shakes that person. Even though he or she may sometimes appear to be shaken, it's just an act to educate others. But such a person isn't really shaken.

Sthitapragnya, steady consciousness, is explained in *slokas* 54 to 72, how one is balanced between the dualities of pleasure and pain, profit and loss, praise and blame. Keeping your balance through all the ups and downs is Yoga. The sum of it all is: equanimity is Yoga. Arjuna asks the key question next.

54. O Lord, what is the sign of one of steady wisdom who is always in *samadhi* (superconsciousness)? How does this person talk, walk and sit?

Arjuna is saying: Please just let me know how someone like that will behave in day-to-day affairs.

Isn't it a wonderful question? We should thank Arjuna for having asked this question. Probably, Krishna wouldn't have said all this otherwise. That's why we say Arjuna is the calf. He goes forward and says, "I'm hungry." And the cowherd boy, Krishna, milks some truth from the *Vedas* for the sake of Arjuna. Some spills out, and we all enjoy it.

These *slokas* are really wonderful. This is the most important and oft-quoted portion of the second chapter—the description of the enlightened one.

The Blessed Lord says:

> **55. A person who has let go of all personal desires and is utterly content in the truth of *Atman*, the true Self, is one of steady wisdom.**

> **56. A person undisturbed by difficulties, who doesn't yearn to be happy, who has no favorites, no fear and no anger is a sage of steady wisdom.**

> **57. Whoever is free of all mental attachments, who is not excited when good things happen nor dejected when evil comes is poised in wisdom.**

> **58. When one can withdraw the senses from sense objects, like a tortoise draws within, one's wisdom is unwavering.**

A nice example is given here that will also illustrate *pratyahara* in Patanjali's *Yoga Sutras*. When your senses are completely under your control, you may see sense objects, but you are able to withdraw your senses from them. The senses should not draw you out against your will. That's *pratyahara*, withdrawal of the senses from the sense objects.

> **59. By abstaining from sense objects, they will drop away. Longing for them will also disappear upon realizing the highest truth.**

You may control the senses, but still impressions from past desires, the *vasanas*, are there. You may not be enjoying the objects of your desires, but that doesn't mean that you are completely free from them. You may have a little longing still. Sometimes when people fast, even though they are away from food, unfortunately they think more about food. So just staying away is not enough. The question really is: how do we get rid of this longing, these *vasanas?* The answer is, not by force, but by real understanding of the truth. Ask yourself, "Who is eating the food? Am I or is my body? It's the body that longs for the food. I'm not hungry. I'm not thirsty."

When you're rooted in this truth, then even the longing goes away. My Master used to sing: "I'm not the body, not the mind; immortal Self I am!"

When you're rooted in that, then you'll look at the body and say, "Hey, you're not really hungry. You've eaten enough. There's a lot of storage. Finish up all that and I'll give you some more later on." And you won't dwell on it. That's why they say: "When you realize the Supreme, even the longing goes away."

As long as you're still striving, be extremely careful not to be deceived by overconfidence, thinking, "I have achieved everything. Now I'm completely in control." You can be deceived at any time. Sri Krishna warns:

> **60. If the senses become excited, Arjuna, they will carry away even the mind of a wise person aiming for perfection.**

> **61. But the yogi learns to control the senses by meditating on me as the highest goal. As the senses come under control, the yogi's wisdom becomes steady.**

Now, he gives a chain reaction that shows how people ultimately destroy themselves. It is a beautiful part of the *Gita* to remember always.

> **62. From brooding on sense objects, attachment to them arises. Out of that attachment, personal desire is born. And from desire, anger appears.**

> **63. Anger confuses the thinking process, which, in turn, disturbs memory. When memory fails, reasoning is ruined. And when reason is gone, one is lost.**

Where does it all begin? Brooding on a sense object. When you start brooding, you end up perishing. Here's an example. You go to work every day by the same road. You see many people coming and going along your way, but you don't even notice them. All of a sudden one form gets registered in your mind. "Ah, who is this lovely woman?" Then you walk on. But something is fixed there. "Who could that be?" The next day you happen to see the same woman and your interest grows a little more. Within a couple of days you desire to find her address and telephone number. You're hoping for a date. Somehow, you come to know that someone else is already courting her. What happens then? Competition arises. When you see him getting in your way, you become angry. The anger ruins your discrimination. Because you're mad for her, an enmity develops and you want to destroy the other suitor. You get into a terrible fight. The law doesn't understand that it comes from a mental fixation, and you are both put in jail. Life gets ruined.

Everything begins with the mind. When the mind becomes attached to something, you don't usually question your mind. You don't analyze it. The mind wants it, so you just chase after it. That's what's meant here— not that you should totally avoid looking for good friendships. But let the desires be under *your* control. Don't just be carried away by the mind. That's the teaching. Personal desire creates anger. It's a temporary insanity. Basically, there's no difference between one and the other. If you are temporarily insane, they say you're mad.

> 64. But the yogi who has disciplined the mind and has control of the senses can move about amidst sense objects, free of attraction and aversion, settling more deeply in tranquility.

> 65. In that tranquility all sorrows fall away [because] the discerning intellect of a calm mind is soon secure in equilibrium.

> 66. There is neither wisdom nor meditation in an always-changing mind. Without a meditative, one-pointed mind, there is no peace. And without peace of mind, how can anyone be happy?

Without peace, how can you find happiness? These *slokas* speak of the *yukta*, the person of discrimination. In that discriminative knowledge, you get right understanding, which makes the mind profound. Without that profundity, there's no peace. And when there's no peace, there's no happiness. We are all looking for happiness; but, unfortunately, we're not looking where the *Gita* tells us to. We look outside ourselves for it. The very fact that we're looking outside disturbs the mind. But if we realize that happiness is reflected in the tranquil mind, then we won't disturb our minds—even to chase happiness. It's there in us always.

> 67. Like a ship tossed helplessly about by a gale, a mind subject to the roving senses loses all discrimination *(viveka)*.

> 68. When the senses are completely withdrawn from the sense objects, Arjuna, then the mind is poised perfectly.

69. What seems night to others is the state of awakening for one with a mind thus disciplined. And what appears day to others is as night to the sage who knows the Self.

Here is another beautiful verse that says in simple words: What is real to an enlightened person seems unreal to an ordinary person. And what seems real to an ordinary person is unreal to an enlightened person. Naturally, then, enlightened ones call the others insane, and we call him or her insane. When people want to lead the spiritual life of renunciation, you say, "I don't know why they are letting go of all of this. They could enjoy life so beautifully. They have wealth, youth and everything. I don't know why they are renouncing everything. Why can't they live like normal people? Are they crazy?" They ask the seeker: "Are you crazy? You're young; you're beautiful; you have everything. With all your beauty you could win a beauty contest! Why do you want to waste it?" As if youth and beauty can't be utilized for a higher purpose. And as if winning contests were the goal in life.

Now Krishna gives an example of the ocean:

70. Someone with personal desires will not experience true peace. But when all desires merge, like different rivers flowing into the vast, deep ocean, then peace is easily realized.

The ocean is contented. It never sends invitations to the rivers. It's just happy by itself. And that's the reason why all the rivers want to flow into it. They say, "You seem to be so happy while we're restless. By coming to join you, we'll be happy." So they all run into the ocean. The ocean doesn't want anything; it's not after the rivers. Therefore the rivers are after it. That's one important point. Another is that even after all the rivers have come into the ocean, the ocean retains the same contentment. It doesn't get excited: "Look how great I am! All the rivers are coming into me! The Missouri has come; the Mississippi is here; the Ganges also has come!" Excitement disturbs even the contented mind.

71. Peace is experienced by anyone who lives without longing for anything, free of all personal desires and with no individual sense of "me" and "mine."

72. This, Arjuna, is the absolute state. On experiencing it, there are no further questions. If established in this awareness at the time of bodily death, there is just the merging into the oneness of God.

This ends the second chapter. Isn't it sweet to study the *Gita*? But please remember that the entire *Gita* is right there in front of you. The best book to read is the book of life. With that book, you will be constantly learning everything. Written scriptures are only here to show that since they also say the same things, we can trust our experiences: "Yes, here in the *Bhagavad Gita*, Sri Krishna also said the same thing. Okay, then probably it must be right." We want an authority to confirm our experiences. Scriptural study is good for confirming our convictions.

Thus ends the second discourse of the *Bhagavad Gita*, the science of Yoga, entitled: "The Yoga of Wisdom."

Chapter Three

Karma Yoga: The Yoga of Action

Up to now we have seen something of the philosophy about the Self or *Atman* and touched on the practical side of Karma Yoga, which helps us go about realizing the *Atman*. We also covered the qualifications of a realized person whom the *Gita* calls one of steady wisdom. In this chapter, "The Yoga of Action," we'll learn the secret of action.

After hearing these first teachings by Sri Krishna, Arjuna still has a little doubt, and asks:

> 1. **Since you teach that the path of wisdom is better than the path of action, Krishna, why are you encouraging me to do this terrible act [of war]?**

Arjuna is asking, "Why don't you just allow me to sit and experience the truth right away? Your words seem perplexing."

> 2. **I am confused by what seems to be a contradiction. Please tell me a sure way to attain the highest.**

> 3. **The Blessed Lord said: Arjuna, in the beginning I gave the world a two-fold path: the way of discerning wisdom (Jnana Yoga) and the way of selfless action (Karma Yoga).**

For active people, there's the path of karma, action. And for people who can sit and analyze, depending entirely on their intelligence, the path of wisdom, *jnana* (also known as *samkhya)* is recommended. Some immediately will think, "Okay, I'm intelligent, that suits me very well." It's normal to think this way. Even if I suggest that you get involved in some work, you may wonder. "Does this mean he thinks I'm a little dull? Why can't he recommend the path of wisdom for me?" That's a natural reaction. So Sri Krishna explains:

> 4. **Ceasing to do things will not make you "actionless." Nor will you rise to perfection simply by renouncing actions.**

The karma, or desire to act, should fall away by itself, like a fully-ripened fruit dropping from the tree. If an unripe fruit, seeing the ripe fruit dropping from the tree, also wants to drop off, it will have to force itself. Renouncing action should come automatically instead of you forcing it by insisting: "I renounce." Instead of trying to push the desire out, you can develop a natural state of desirelessness in which you don't feel the need of anything. *Then* you've truly renounced. You can't force renunciation. But you can prepare your environment for this and let yourself mature.

5. No one is free of actions even for a moment, because everyone is moved to do things by the qualities of nature.

The qualities of nature, known as the three *gunas* (*sattva, rajas and tamas*) are the three qualities that function through *prakriti*, or nature. They are similar to positive, negative and neutral forces. We have the three *gunas* even in an atom: protons, electrons and neutrons. What are the differences between elements? The number of protons, the number of electrons, the number of neutrons. In the same way, if *sattva* is a bit predominant in someone, that person is said to be a spiritual seeker. Someone with a little more *rajas* (a few more electrons) just runs around. After all, what are the body and mind? Nothing but the same *prakriti*. Nature is composed of natural elements which themselves are the expression of the subtle essence which is pure consciousness. Everything that has manifested, you can call *prakriti*, Mother Nature. All expressions of that essence are called the Mother; the unexpressed one is the Father.

The Father, the essence of everything, cannot express himself. He must express, or manifest, through the Mother, or as the Mother. Therefore, know that anything and everything that is expressed is the Mother. In this sense, all we see is nothing but Mother. Don't think that only when you have a feminine body you are a mother. We are all part of nature. That's why we say Mother Nature.

As long as we are still identifying with our bodies and minds, we'll be tossed constantly by these three *gunas*. That tossing about can be called action. Even your hunger and thirst is action. To fulfill the hunger and thirst, there's more action. Everyone must pass through *prakriti*, but gradually when you're ripe enough in your wisdom, you just drop away from her; the *prakriti* won't affect you anymore. Though you've dropped away, you haven't disappeared. You're still in the same cosmos, but *prakriti*, won't affect you.

It's something like a patient who goes to the hospital to be cured. Until you're well, you have to be there. You can't just jump up and say, "I came for a week only; I'm going now." While you're there, you make use of the hospital and its facilities in order to be healed. On the other hand, after you're completely healed, you might still say: "This bed is so comfortable and the food is so good. There are sweet looking nurses all around. Why can't I stay a couple days more?" But now you'll be pushed out without your even trying to go.

Renunciation comes the same way, automatically. Even if you don't want it, it will come when you're ready. The Mother, *prakriti*, will nip you until you get out. The mother bird pecks at the young one: "Now you have grown wings. You can go around by yourself. Go!" That's what we see in Nature. That's Mother Nature's function. When you're ready, she won't bother to have you here, constantly feeding you. She has too much to do. There are so many children to take care of. But until that time, you should just wait. Be under her loving care. Learn all you have to learn.

6. Whoever stills the body as if seated in meditation, but mentally continues to think about sense objects, is deluded and a hypocrite.

Many times we think, "I'm fasting. I'm not going to eat anything today. But what about tomorrow morning? What shall I eat then?" Physically we may not be eating, but mentally we are. An action is evaluated by its motive, not by the action itself. Crimes committed without any planning are even pardoned sometimes. Even murder, if you prove that you have not concentrated on it ahead of time and that it just came up all of a sudden, unpremeditated, then you might be excused. But even if you don't actually commit the crime, if it's proved you were concentrating on it and planning it, then you'll get the punishment.

This shows that the mind is more important than the action. Often so-called renunciates will say, "I have nothing, no attachments. I don't desire to do anything." But in fact, they're doing many things mentally.

Maybe they go into a cave and sit there alone. But mentally they bring the entire world with them. That's not true renunciation. Meanwhile, a king ruling a country could still be a renunciate if he has no selfish desires.

King Janaka, for example, was ruler of a country, but many sages and saintly seekers went there to be initiated by him. Yajnavalkya was a well-known Guru, a great *jnani*, a renunciate. But he sent his own son, Suka, to King Janaka to be initiated into *sannyasa*, a life of renunciation. Look at that! A renunciate sage sending his son to get initiated by a king who is ruling a country. It shows that it's not your position in the world, but the attitude behind what you are doing that makes you a renunciate or a householder. It all depends on how much "house" you are holding in your heart.

So the mind and its attitudes should be seen behind this structure.

7. In order to excel, mentally control the senses, let go all attachments, and engage the body in Karma Yoga, selfless service.

That means the mind is totally in control, but he just allows his body to do certain acts for the sake of the actions themselves. Here a kind of discipline is necessary. For example, you might be preparing food, which we call *prasad*, to be offered at the altar. You sometimes make quite delicious dishes. From the very beginning, your feeling is that you are doing something for God, and it should be very fine and tasty. According to the Hindu way of thinking, you shouldn't even smell or taste it. If you've already tasted it by your senses—through your eyes, nose or tongue—it's already eaten. It becomes unfit to be offered. Complete control of the senses is necessary. Of course in preparing something for another, sometimes you taste it, but not for the sake of your own tongue. You want your guest to have a delicious dish. The action is not for your own sake.

If you do the act this way, you are cooking, and yet you are not cooking, because you aren't cooking for your personal enjoyment. This is a case where even though you act, *you personally* are not acting. It's called "inaction in action."

8. Do your duty; such action is better than doing nothing. If you attempt to renounce all actions, it would be impossible to maintain your body.

In this chapter, Sri Krishna also talks about a sacrificial ritual, a *yajna*, which often is thought to mean a fire ceremony: you sit, start a fire and offer everything to the fire. But that's not the true *yajna*; that's only the outward expression. Krishna explains what *yajna* really means:

9. The world is bondage when actions are done just for your own sake. Therefore, Arjuna, make every action a sacrifice, utterly free of personal attachment.

Anything you do for the benefit of others is true *yajna*. Not even a trace should be for your own personal benefit. If some benefit does also just happen to come to you, all right, let it come. Don't be repulsed by it. But don't do it for the sake of what will come to you.

10. After creating humankind together with *yajna* (sacrifice), the Creator said: Through sacrifice you will increase yourself and get everything that you want.

Prajapati is the word used here for the Creator. *Praja* means the created. *Pati* means lord. The Lord of the created is the Creator. *Praja* literally means citizen. You are the *praja* of the country. But here it doesn't mean only human beings. Everything that exists, visible and invisible, are all *prajas*. God is the One who *causes* the Creation.

When God created the beautiful Garden of Eden, God didn't say a word to all those plants, fruits, flowers, trees and animals. God could have said at least something to the dogs and cats, but just created them and allowed them to play around. God didn't even say anything to the snake or the scorpion. God could have said, "Don't sting anybody." But no, God didn't say anything. It was only when God created humans, that God said, "My children, don't eat the fruit." Why? It's because only at the human level have we been given the freedom to choose right or wrong. So naturally there should be guidance also.

According to this *sloka*, the guidance from God is: "Well, humanity, I have created you, and I am giving you the ability to sacrifice, to make an offering. By this you propagate yourself. Let this *yajna* or sacrifice be your milking cow. Of course, it doesn't mean just a regular cow. This cow represents: Everything that you want, you get.

Chapter Three

According to Hindu mythology, there is a cow known as Kamadhenu. *Kama* means desire. *Dhenu* means the giver. Whatever you want, you get. If you have Kamadhenu at your home, all your desires are fulfilled, you simply want it, you get it. Do we have such a Kamadhenu today? We do. It's not that there is only a mythological cow somewhere. No, everybody has been given a Kamadhenu, a boon-giving device. There is also a tree known as the boon-giving tree. I feel that this is the tree that became transformed into the Christmas tree, a tree with all the gifts underneath. It's a boon-giving tree: just go there, think what you want and you get it.

The great woman saint Avvayaar once said, "Even after having gone and sat under that boon-giving tree, if you ask for bitter fruit, that's your destiny." It's ready to give everything, but it won't give it to you unless you ask. And you should know what to ask for.

Once a fellow went into the jungle and became very tired. He found a beautiful tree and sat beneath it. But the ground was thorny. He couldn't lie down anywhere. "How nice it would be if I had a small cot!" The minute he thought of it, he found himself sitting on a cot. "Oh boy, I have a cot!" He lay down. "This is very comfortable, but I'm also hungry. I could use something to eat, maybe a banana." Immediately a bunch of bananas appeared. "What's this?" He couldn't believe his eyes. "It seems that whatever I want I can get here. Then how about some gourmet cooking?" Immediately, plates filled with delicacies, delicious dishes, pudding and desserts appeared. He ate sumptuously and then thought, "It would be nice if there were someone to massage my feet to put me to sleep." Even as he thought of it, there was already a beautiful angel-like person there massaging his feet. He became excited, "Oho! It looks like whatever I'm thinking, I'm getting. Now I have a comfortable bed, a good, sumptuous meal, and somebody to massage my feet. But what if, while I'm getting the massage, I fall asleep and suddenly a tiger comes from the jungle. What will happen?" Immediately he heard the roar, and a tiger appeared and devoured him.

What to do with such a person? He was under a boon-giving tree. Whatever he wanted, he got. Sometimes people are like that. They can get everything, but they don't know what to ask for.

That's why sacrifice was given by the Creator. "Don't look for anything just for yourself. Let your life be a sacrifice, *yajna*. If you use this guidance which I give you, certainly you'll prosper." In order to prosper, the most important thing, the one and only thing, is living a dedicated life. Let your entire life be a sacrifice. That means renounce all your personal interest and personal desires. Live for the sake of others. Sacrifice is the law of life.

This is said only to humankind because all other species are already doing it. Everything in this creation seems to exist to be used by others. Their very life is a sacrifice. They live not for themselves, but for others. They are all still under that direct guidance of nature's law. No other species in this creation has the freedom humankind has. In nature's college they are still under the control of the cosmic law. In a simple devotee's language, every minute God simply tells them what to do and they do it. They never misbehave.

Remember we all lived that life before. During our evolution we got all the lessons. When we were grass we learned something. When we became a little bush, we learned something else. When we became a worm, we learned something. We learned when we were cats, dogs, scorpions, foxes and cows. Sometimes traces from the past are revealed. We hear people say, "Don't trust him; he's a cunning fox." Why? Because that fox-like memory seems to be predominant even in this life. "Look at that woman; for every little thing she barks at others." That part was predominant. "My goodness, he stings you for everything." Or, "Don't stand there like a tree, man!"

We lived all those lives. We all have those *samskaras*, mental impressions, buried as part of our subconscious treasure. After having learned all that directly under the guidance of Sri Krishna, now at the human level he says, "Okay, I taught you everything. I held your hand, walked you everywhere and told you what to do. Now I want to test you. That means I give you the freedom. Let me see how you can use your education." That's what is happening at the level of humanity. "I have been bringing you up to live the life of sacrifice," says the Creator. "I'm simply reminding you that if you continue to live the same sacrificial life, you will prosper."

So, if any individual wants to prosper, to lead a comfortable and peaceful life, a life that's headed upward, he or she should keep in mind this question: "Am I leading a dedicated life? Is my life a sacrificial life?"

The entire world is a sacrificial altar. We should be constantly sacrificing ourselves. That's *yajna.*

11. Through sacrifice, you cherish the gods (*devas*) and they cherish you. Thus loving one another, you reap the very highest.

After giving the way of sacrifice, he says, "Come on, if you do this, the *devas,* the divine beings, will be happy with your sacrifice. So, offer everything to the divine beings, and in their turn, let them bless you. In this way you are helping each other.

Here the *devas* need not literally mean some beings "up there." All are divine. When you sacrifice your life and do things for others' sake, the others in return will do the same to you. Their good will is always present. As Thiruvalluvar says in the *Thirukkural:* if a person has decided to stay away from killing to eat, he will not kill, he will not eat meat. Neither does he kill nor does he eat what is killed by others. Such a person will be worshipped by all the creatures of the world. They will simply love him, praise and worship him. Even a wild dog will wag his tail at such a person, sensing he is non-violent: "You haven't caused violence to any animal." They know that.

Don't think that only we have modern, scientific communication. The plant and animal kingdoms have their own communication media. If you have saved the life of an animal somewhere, and if you come across another animal who may not be of the same species, it will express its gratitude, "Yes, you saved my brother. I know, I got the message." If you sacrifice for others, then all the souls will appreciate your sacrifice and bless you. Thus, ultimately you will reap the supreme blessing.

12. Cherished by your spirit of sacrifice, the gods give you everything you want. [But remember] whoever receives gifts from the gods without offering anything back is a thief.

There are five types of giving and taking. The *Gita* gives names to them. If you take one hundred percent and don't give anything in return, you can be called a thief. If you take one hundred percent and give fifty percent, you're a debtor. If you take one hundred percent and give one hundred percent, you're a good business person. (That's how business should be done: Give in return for what is received. If a business person gets $10, he or she should be sure to give $10 worth of goods or services. That's fair business.) Next, if you take fifty percent and give one hundred percent, you are called a righteous person. But if someone takes nothing and gives even ten percent, fifteen percent or one hundred percent—whatever possible—what do you call that person? A saint, a yogi.

We should always examine our transactions and discover in which category we put ourselves: one, thief; two, debtor; three, business person; four, righteous person; or five, a saint. And if you're already "one," try to be "two." If you're already "two," try to promote yourself to "three." Stop not until the fifth category is reached.

It's nice to keep this information handy. *Yajna* is so beautiful. So much could be said about it. The whole life is an offering.

> **13. Righteous people who eat what is left after *yajna* are freed from past sins. But those who prepare food only for themselves are creating more sin.**

What does it mean? You don't cook just for yourself, but to feed others. If there is anything left over, then you eat. Then you're free from sin. Not that you're doing any charity, but you're simply not committing a sin. I'll give you an example from the Hindu *dharma*, or virtuous teachings. Because I'm a little more familiar with the Hindu *dharma*, I often find examples there, but don't immediately bottle and label me. The same *dharma* prevails everywhere; without doubt it's Catholic *dharma*, Protestant *dharma*, Jewish *dharma* and Muslim *dharma*. The truth is the truth.

In the Hindu *dharma*, if a mother cooks some food, the father should come out of the house and look this way and that for at least fifteen minutes. If he sees somebody walking, he should ask, "Sir, ma'am, did you eat? Would you like to have some food?" If some passersby haven't eaten, then bring them in and give them food until they say, "Enough, enough." Then if there's anything left over, the family eats. If the guests eat everything, you shouldn't even cook again. It means God didn't want you to eat that day. Your own Self has already eaten in the form of those guests.

Chapter Three

There's a lovely story from another section of the *Mahabharata* epic. Once the Pandavas conducted a great sacrificial *yajna,* a royal ceremony. It was done with all pomp and show, and at great expense. Many people came and were enjoying it very much. As they all sat and appreciated the meal, they saw a strange looking mongoose running toward them. It started rolling in the remnants of the offered food and flowers there. Then the mongoose stood up, shook his head, looking completely disappointed.

The host stood and said, "What's this? You're not an ordinary mongoose. You seem a little peculiar. We see one half of your body is golden; the other half is ordinary mongoose color. How did this happen?"

"Oh, that's a long story. I don't know whether it's worth telling you." "Please tell us," they said. "We want to know."

"Well then, because you're asking, I'll tell you. I was just an ordinary mongoose before, without this golden color. One day as I was roaming around, I came across a small hut, and I just sat outside and watched what was happening there. A poor teacher, his wife, his son and daughter-in-law were living there. At the time there was a terrible famine. Food was scarce. They didn't have anything to eat. But fortunately one of his old students had brought some flour to be cooked into some *rotis* (a kind of Indian bread). The teacher's wife was preparing it. Everything was ready. As usual, the teacher, a pious man, came out looking this way and that to see if anybody was there, because the scriptures say to treat as God the one who comes in the form of the guest.

"The teacher saw somebody coming and said, 'Sir, would you like to have some food?'

"'Oh yes, I'm very hungry.'

"He was invited in. The wife had four *rotis,* one for each person. So the teacher gave his share to the guest. And the guest ate it.

"Then the wife came up. 'Sir, may I offer one more?'

'Oh, yes, yes. I don't know why I'm so terribly hungry.' So he ate that also.

"When the son and daughter-in-law saw this, they came with their shares, too. 'Sir, we would like to offer these also if you can eat them.'

"'I think I can.' And he did. Then he said, 'Thank you so much. God bless you all,' and he just walked out.

"In half an hour all the four collapsed and died because they were so weak from this terrible hunger. But I saw that they died in a state of joy.

"I was watching everything. I was also hungry, so I went in to see if anything had dropped to the ground as they made the *rotis*. I saw only a little flour and crumbs. It wasn't even fit to eat. So I just went there and rolled over in it. And when I got up, I saw half of my body had become golden. Then I understood: 'Oh, there's something mysterious, miraculous and divine in their actions. Yes, they truly dedicated their lives for the sake of another. They performed a truly beautiful *yajna*.'

"Somehow I got this crazy idea: 'How am I going to get the other half also golden?' So, ever since that day, I've been traveling and rolling about everywhere. Then I heard that Yudhishthira, the great Pandava, was preparing the royal *yajna*. So I thought, 'Surely this will be much greater than those four poor people.' I came running all the way here. But now, you see"—the mongoose indicated his body which was still only half golden—"not so good."

You should have seen Yudhishthira's face. So it's not the pomp and show, but the quality of your heart in the sacrifice that's important. In the Pandava's *yajna* there was also sacrifice, but probably it was mingled with a little pride: "We're doing it!" Those poor people had humility in their offering, and they really experienced God.

In this light we can judge our own actions. It might look charitable, but is it really? Does it have that touch of selflessness? If your actions are like that, you are already liberated. You may still be in the human form walking around like anybody else, but you are God on the face of the earth. That's the greatness of Karma Yoga.

14. From food, all beings arise. From rain, food originates. Rain is the result of selfless sacrifice (*yajna*). And sacrifice is the result of actions (karma).

This chapter says, "We are all born to act, which is karma. But if our karma, our actions, are selfless, sacrifice is born of that." That means your karma produces the greatness of sacrifice. And because of that sacrifice, the elements become happy and rain pours down. From *yajna,* rain comes. Now you know why there's drought in many places—there's not much sacrifice in people's lives. And from rain, what happens? Food comes. And from food, beings come. That's the essence of this *sloka.*

So your actions should be sacrificial. By your sacrificial actions, nature becomes beneficial to you. By that, you get abundance of supply. Food is not necessarily food that goes through the mouth. Here it means food that sustains you in every way. So for human sustenance, selfless actions that produce sacrifice are important.

15. Know that action (karma) comes from creative intelligence (Brahma) which is of the imperishable, the eternal. The all-pervading Brahma thus is forever centered in self-sacrifice.

16. Anyone here on earth, Arjuna, who does not align with the revolving wheel (sacrifice–action–God–sacrifice), but instead chooses to waste his or her life delighting only in the senses, lives in vain.

17. Whoever delights in the Self *(Atman),* finds satisfaction in the Self, and is centered in the Self—surely has no further duties.

18. Then at last there is nothing to get by doing something (action), nothing to lose by doing nothing (inaction) and no dependencies on anyone for anything.

19. Therefore, always do your duty without attachment. If you do things without desiring results for yourself, you will experience the highest state.

20. King Janaka and many others reached perfection through Karma Yoga, the path of selfless action. In order to guide others, you too should follow this path of action.

21. Whatever a great person does is followed by others who set their standard by his or her example.

22. Arjuna, there's nothing in the three worlds [earth, astral and celestial planes] that I ought to do, nor anything for me to achieve that I have not already achieved—yet I continue doing things.

What is it that the representative of God, an incarnation of God, would want to achieve? Nothing. No attainment is necessary. He has everything. He doesn't have to do anything to get anything. There's no need. God could just as well stay quiet, but says, "Having come into the world with a body and a name, I am continuously working."

So don't think that when you have obtained everything you'll just stop doing things. The mere fact that you are still a member of humanity means there is something for you to do. Sri Krishna explains, "Even though I don't need to obtain anything, if I do nothing, you know what will happen? All my students will follow my example. They'll say, 'Look, he's not doing anything. Why should I do things?' At least for their sake then, I must be doing something." It's almost like seeing both the students and the professor also going to college. There's no need for the professor to go to the college to learn. But if he or she doesn't go, the students won't go. This is a nice thought to remember.

> 23. If I ever stop doing my continuous work, Arjuna, everyone would follow my example in every way.

> 24. If I stop doing, the worlds would perish; I would confuse all species and cause the destruction of all creatures.

> 25. The unenlightened do things with attachment (wanting some results for themselves). An enlightened person does things with the same zeal, Arjuna, but without attachment, and thus guides others on the path of selfless action (Karma Yoga).

Just as an ordinary person performs actions with selfishness, the enlightened one also does things, but without selfishness. The only difference: the ordinary person does things for his or her own benefit; the enlightened one does things for others' benefit. The performance of actions for others is in no way inferior. In fact, Sri Krishna says, the selfless person should even act a little more carefully and more efficiently than a selfish person. A yogi is acting for everybody's sake, and should do a little better job. Sometimes the attitude is, "Since I'm not gaining much from this action—it's mainly for others—it doesn't matter how I do it. I'll just let it happen." Probably Sri Krishna knows this attitude is part of human nature. So he says, "Don't think that because you are acting selflessly you can get away with something haphazard. In fact, you should do a better job."

Who is a yogi? The one who performs actions skillfully and efficiently. Why? Your interest is to serve others. Since so many are going to be benefited by your action; you should do a better job. If an ordinary person doesn't do a good job, then only he or she loses. But if you don't do a good job, imagine how many people will lose.

26. A wise person will not disturb the mind of an unwise person who is still attached to the fruits of his or her actions. But by continuously performing perfect (selfless) actions the wise person influences others in all they do.

At one point Sri Krishna says, "Even though at a certain point the need to perform actions naturally drops away, a realized person should not stop doing things." He gives himself as the example. "See, I am Krishna, an incarnation. There is nothing for me to gain in this world. There is nothing I should gain by doing anything; but I work. Why? If I don't, others will say, 'He's not doing anything, so why should I? Not working must be the sign of realization.'"

Suppose a small child asks his uncle, "Who is that man with something hanging around his neck?"

"He's a doctor. That's a stethoscope around his neck."

"Uncle, I want to be a doctor, too. Buy me a stethoscope."

It's easy to copy. That's why teachers do things that actually there's no need for them to do. Their actions aren't for their own sake, but to set examples for their students. If they stop doing these things, the students will immediately follow their example. That's what Krishna is saying here.

And he's also basically answering the question: How should we work if we are not doing it for personal gain, but just for the sake of others? Should they be grateful for what we're doing? Can we do the work any way we want?

Krishna says no, that's not Karma Yoga then. Even an ordinary, greedy person will do things well for his or her own benefit. We should do things just as well, if not better. Don't think that because it's a dedicated or karma

Yoga action, it doesn't matter how it's done. In fact, Karma Yoga actions should be done perfectly, even neater and tidier because they're offerings.

Suppose that every day you simply make a little pudding and bread for yourself to eat. When you expect a hundred guests and you're offering them something, would you still do the same thing? No, you'd do something special. It's not for yourself. That's the beauty of it. Whatever you do for your sake can be ordinary, but when you do it for the benefit of others, you're doing it for God. That should be a better job, not just equal to what you'd be doing in your own home.

See how much is to be considered just in this path of action.

27. The qualities of nature [calmness, restlessness, inertia] do all that is done. But because the mind is clouded by ego, a person thinks: I am the doer.

28. Arjuna, one may intuit the relationship between nature's qualities (*gunas*) and action (*karma*). Whoever does so knows that nature, as the senses, merely abides with nature, as the sense objects. That person identifies with neither, and thus does not become entangled.

29. Those still deluded by nature's qualities become attached to nature's functions. But one of perfect understanding should not disturb the mind of someone who does not know better.

30. Dedicate all your actions to me. [Then] your mind will rest in the Self (*Atman*), free of the wishing and selfishness fever and you can engage in battle.

31. Whoever lives by these teachings with faith and without complaining will transcend karma.

32. Those who don't live by these teachings, however, but look instead to criticize them, misunderstand everything. They have no discrimination *(viveka)* and are ruined.

33. Even a wise person follows his or her own nature, as all beings follow their own natures. Why try to force anything to be otherwise?

34. It is natural for the senses to be attracted or repulsed by various sense objects. But don't for a moment come under their domination, or surely they will be your enemies.

35. It is better to do your own *dharma* (calling) even imperfectly, than someone else's *dharma* perfectly. Even better to die in your *dharma* than in another's, which brings great fear.

Is this a little confusing? What is your *dharma* and what is somebody else's *dharma?* What you're truly called to do is your *dharma*. It fits your aptitude, your capabilities and your natural inclination. Constitutionally, your *dharma*—physical and mental—is to walk. Look at a snake. If you try to crawl like that, it's not your *dharma*. It might look cute, but remember you're created to walk. Don't try to imitate a crawling species.

This is just a rough example. But often we come across this situation, for example, in the name of equality. "I must do everything he does. Only then am I equal to him. If he jumps, I should jump. If he flies, I should fly. If he drives a tractor, I should drive a tractor. Only then am I equal." That attitude is terribly wrong. Remember, even science has shown that there is no duplication in creation. No two snowflakes are exactly the same. As such, you are also unique, you have been created unique with certain abilities that no other person can do. That's your *svadharma,* your individual duty.

Find out what your *svadharma* is. Ask yourself, "How do I feel when doing certain things? Does something come easily? Is it natural for me or am I trying to imitate somebody?" First, take stock of your natural inclination and your capability which is your taste, temperament and capacity. With some things it's so natural, you're like a fish in the water. You just know: "Ahh, that's what I'm meant to do." In Sanskrit, it is called your *svadharma*.

But remember, that *svadharma* is different from karma, which is just an action based on a selfish interest. *Svadharma* is something righteous. It's something completely natural to you that you could do to benefit others. That's *svadharma*. You can't say: "My *svadharma* is to steal. I feel naturally inclined to take something from somebody's pocket. It's to my taste." No. The word "*dharma*" always implies the benefit of others. There's no personal desire behind it. Think what your *svadharma* is and try to do it. If you're an expert cook, that's your *svadharma*. It just came to you naturally. Good! Cook for everybody. But if you're naturally inclined to work somewhere in the field, then that's your *svadharma* at this time.

Your *svadharma* may change over the years. As you grow, your thinking becomes different. The *svadharma* of a baby is to crawl; an adult, to walk. It can change, but it just flows. It's not that you consciously decide, saying, "That's no good. I'd like to do this instead." It flows. Even without your knowledge or planning, new things come.

I can give you an example from my own life. From the very beginning, I never planned anything. Even from the time of birth and childhood, I was taken to school, from there to high school, from there into the business field. All this happened so naturally. It wasn't that I said, "This is no good, and this is nice." I got some special education in a technical field. But later I was naturally drawn to take care of a temple. Look at that! From technical education to temple management! But it happened so naturally, so I just went along. I moved from one place to another place to another until I went to Rishikesh. Even from there naturally I was pushed to Ceylon (Sri Lanka), and from there to the Far East countries—all by nature and without my planning. And from there, naturally into Europe. And later into New York. Probably that's why they call me a "naturalized" citizen.

See, it develops. Remember that you have been brought into this world not for your job. You have nothing to do here. You have nothing to gain, nothing to lose. You didn't come planned. "Did you consciously plan to be born in California in the womb of so-and-so?" No. You were just pushed along. You are brought along stage by stage. You don't have any responsibility of your own. Remember that. You didn't come according to your own plan. You are not going to leave according to your own plan. You have been brought here, and you will be kept here as long as that One up there needs you. Whoever it is. The minute He or She thinks your job is over, all the Divine One has to do is just turn off the switch. No air will enter your lungs. Finished.

The doctors say: heart failure. The yogis say: stopped breathing. The breath refused to go in. That's it; finished. Somebody was pumping the air in and out and stopped pumping. So, you don't get the air anymore.

It's okay; just flow. Feel the unseen hand directing you every minute, taking you along from one thing to another. Know that it's always unplanned by you and for the good of everybody. That's *svadharma*.

But very often people think some other person's work would be better. That's the tendency of the mind. The other's grass is always greener. Turn the tide of that mentality. Know that you are wanted. You have been sent here and given special skills. You might think: "I don't seem to have any special skill." But you eat and you sleep, don't you? Even these are special skills. Don't belittle yourself. Don't degrade yourself, thinking, "I'm no good. I'm wasting my time. I'm a burden to people." People go crazy thinking like that.

You aren't a burden to anybody. If that Supreme Intelligence thinks that you are a burden to somebody, it won't be wasting the breath on you. The next minute it will be turned off, finished. God is no fool to keep you as a burden here and still keep you and put breath into you.

36. [Then] Arjuna asked Sri Krishna: What force is it that drags us into sin, even against our will—as if by some compulsion?

You want to know the origin of sin?

Arjuna asks: What drags people into committing sin? Though they don't want to do such things, still unwillingly they are dragged into it. Is there some force behind it? he asks. Often we come across this in our lives. We don't want to do certain things. We even know it's terribly wrong. But still some force seems to be pushing us: "Go ahead and get it. It's all right." No wonder Arjuna asks Krishna, "What is this?"

37. The blessed Lord said: Know that the enemy here on earth is [personal] desire and anger, which arise from the all-consuming *rajasic guna* (restless quality of nature).

The blessed Lord says, "It's nothing but personal desire. Your wanting it." Your desire overpowers your intelligent discrimination. It's a fight between your lower selfish desire and clear thinking. Such desire is caused by *rajas*. It's all-consuming and it's the cause of sin. "Remember, this is your deadliest enemy," says Krishna. Selfish desire and the wrath that comes out of that—when you don't get it, you get angry. Both the desire and the wrath are caused by *rajas*.

38-39. Like fire covered by smoke, like a mirror covered by dust, like the unborn fetus completely surrounded by a membrane—just so is the wisdom in humankind covered over by the insatiable fire of desire, the constant enemy of the wise.

40. The senses, mind and intellect are the seat of desire. It is this desire that veils wisdom and deludes people.

41. Therefore, Arjuna, first take control of your desire—the sinful destroyer of wisdom and Self-realization.

In other words, learn to control the mind through *pratyahara*, withdrawal of the senses from the sense objects. By controlling the senses, indirectly you're controlling the mind. The senses by themselves are senseless. It's not the eye, the ear or the tongue that sins. The tongue doesn't overeat. The hand doesn't pick someone's pocket. It's the mind using all these senses.

To stop the car you apply the brakes while sitting at the wheel. The wheels are more or less like the senses. The engine is like the mind. The engine makes the wheels move. Disconnect the engine from the running shaft. Though you disconnect the engine by declutching, for a time momentum will continue to move the car. Even though you put the clutch into neutral, the car isn't going to stop immediately if you're going at a good speed. So, apply the brakes also.

That's why there are two pedals next to each other. Try to detach your mind from the senses. But if they are already away from the objects of the senses, then also make a determined decision. For instance, if you are trying to control the tongue, say: "I won't eat anything between meals, no matter what." You're also putting on the brakes. If you refuse to go, what can your tongue do? That's the way. Put blocks on the senses. And through the senses, you control the mind.

42. The senses are stronger than the body. The mind is stronger than the senses; the discriminating intellect (*buddhi*) is stronger than the mind; and *Atman* is above the intellect.

43. Now that you know that *Atman* is beyond even the discriminating intellect (*buddhi*), you can control the (lower) self with *Atman* (the higher Self), and, although it is difficult, utterly destroy your deadly enemy, [personal] desire.

Thus ends the third discourse of the *Bhagavad Gita*, the science of Yoga, entitled: "Karma Yoga: The Yoga of Action."

The Wisdom Yoga of Action and Renunciation

1. The blessed Lord said: I taught this indestructible Yoga science to Vivasvat (the Sun God), who taught it to Manu (the father of humanity). Manu in turn taught it to the great sage Ikshvaku.

2. The Yoga science was thus regularly passed from teacher to disciple over the ages; even the saintly kings knew it. But over a long time, Arjuna, the succession was broken and the teachings were lost.

3. Now I am giving you this supreme secret of Yoga because you are my devotee and friend.

4. Arjuna asked: You were born long after Vivasvat. How is it possible that you taught this in the beginning?

5. Sri Krishna said: You and I have taken many births, Arjuna. I know them all but you do not.

6. The truth is that I am eternal; I am not born, I never die and I am the Lord of everything. Still, by controlling the elements of nature (my *prakriti*), I appear to take births by my power of illusion (*maya*).

In this chapter, Sri Krishna gives the reason for his incarnation:

7. When righteousness is lost and wickedness prevails, I appear on earth in bodily form.

Sometimes I'm asked about the coming of the Messiah. The Messiah is the one who brings a message from God. Whenever people forget the true message of God, there is *adharma* or unrighteousness. Then God comes to remind, transform and redirect people back to the proper path. If need be, God even destroys their physical bodies, then allows them to go through another birth to learn better. It's a form of purgation.

Why should God come into existence in the physical world? The seventh *sloka* gives a promise: Whenever there is decay in *dharma* (virtue) and rise of *adharma*, I come embodied, to be in the midst of people, to move as one with them, to help the needy people and to help the people who really want to escape from this dilemma.

It's a promise given to us by God. The *Bible* says God sent Jesus as the son of God. Why couldn't God come then? Nobody would recognize God because God doesn't even have a name. We say God or He. But who says God is He or She or It?

God knows: "If I go as God, either people won't recognize me or they will be afraid of me, because they don't know who I am. I can't just go as me because I am neither human, animal nor plant. I'm formless and nameless. How will they recognize me? So I'll just go to them in ways they can recognize me."

That's why among human beings, God comes as a human being. When God decides to be in the midst of buffalo, certainly God doesn't come as a human, but comes as a buffalo. Among pigs, God comes as a mother pig. There are stories of that. We recognize God only when God comes as us.

God comes through a form that we understand and with whom we can communicate. When God came to England, God spoke English. When God came to North India, God spoke Sanskrit and Hindi. When God came to Tamil Nadu, God spoke Tamil. That's the promise here: "I come to people in their own way so they can understand me and communicate with me. I come to help them get out of this turmoil, take them from the unholy to the holy land, from *adharma* to *dharma*, from the unreal to the real."

What is Israel? In essence, it means that which is real. When the children of Israel wanted to escape the unholy land and go to the promised land, God didn't just come and pull them out. First they had to feel deeply:

"Oh, we don't want to be in this wicked place. We want a place where we can practice virtue and truth."

The minute you feel that you want help and guidance, someone to save you, *then* the savior comes. And nothing can stop God from saving you; neither land nor sea. Even the sea will part. All scriptures also have their esoteric meanings, over and above the story itself. When God wants to help you, nothing can stop God. That's the promise that God gives in this oft-quoted *sloka*. The only thing is, you have to follow God.

Who thinks about God when everything is comfortable and going fine? You have to be really hungry for God to appear like this for you. You have to ask with all your heart. *Then* it shall be given. Why only then? It's not because God is a miser. God waits to see that you're very hungry. Then God can really feed you. That's the secret. If you aren't hungry, even if I give you delicious food, you won't enjoy it. You might even throw it back in my face. So, God waits to appear until you're fit for that, and you have the need.

Of course, God is here always. It's not that God is coming and going, sometimes here, sometimes away. In one sense it's all right to talk this way. But where is God actually? Everywhere. Where can God go or come from? But unless you need to feel that Presence, you won't be looking for it. It's not that God doesn't want to come. But only when you thirst for God, will you relish God's coming. Then you'll know the value of it.

When God comes to communicate with you, God just plays with you, talks with you and sometimes even does mischief with you. God doesn't want you always thinking God is so lofty, because then you put a gap there and lose the benefit. To communicate, God sometimes comes as your playmate and friend.

8. Age after age I take birth to protect the good, destroy the wicked and establish virtue.

"I come age after age," Krishna says. "This is not the only time. I have come many times because the world goes through the same cycles constantly."

It's a continuous process. Very often *adharma* accumulates, and I have to come and clean it away. Then everything goes on smoothly for a while. Then slowly *adharma* accumulates again.

It's like cleaning our houses. Just because we clean the house once, it doesn't mean we won't need to do it again. Some do it once a week, others twice a month. It all depends on how many kids run around or how gently we use the house. This world is God's house, and we are all children running around doing so many things. That's why God has to keep coming and cleaning up.

9. When people die who truly know me, instead of taking another birth, they come directly to me.

10. Many enter my being directly because they're free from passion, fear and anger; because they take refuge in me; and because their hearts have become purified through austerities that led to wisdom.

In the next *sloka*, Sri Krishna speaks of the different human approaches and the aim of each approach.

11. However people sincerely call on me, I come to them and fulfill their hearts' desires. They use many paths to reach me.

It might sound philosophical, but we can make it a little clearer by saying that God, the Supreme One, the Incarnation, is not a person. Then what is God? Simplest to understand is that God is the peace in us. We are born with joy. We are peace and joy personified. We are purity personified.

Unfortunately we seem to be ignoring that. We're ignorant of our own true nature. So we run after things to make us happy and to find peace. Behind all our efforts, our basic motive is to find happiness and thus to find peace. All our actions are for that good. They need not be religious. We're all working toward that happiness. Even all these wars, fights and competition are ways people look for happiness. Even when people steal things, they think they're going to be happy by stealing. So the ultimate motive behind all our actions is to find that joy and peace.

That's what Krishna means when he says, "Whatever people do, ultimately their interest is in me." When he says "me," it means that peace: "I am that joy. I am eternal. Unfortunately many don't realize that I, as peace, am already there in them."

Sometimes you put on your earrings and then forget them. Then you spend hours pulling out all the drawers until somebody comes, pinches your ears and says, "Here they are."

It's the same way spiritually. Peace, or your true Self, is something subjective. You look about for it outside of you as some object, something different from you. That's why you miss it. If occasionally you seem to be enjoying some happiness or peace, that's nothing but a reflection of your own peace within.

It's something like this: you go around your house looking at all the walls. Suddenly you come across your face, and say; "Ah, I found it after looking for it all this time." What happened? You're in front of a mirror. Then you pass by and don't see it anymore. "My God, what happened? I just had it, and I've lost it!" Then you look all around. And if you happen to come before another mirror: "Ah, here, I got it back." It's not that the mirror brings your face. You always had your face. You are seeing now with your own face; the face is the subject that wants to see things. The subject can never see itself as an object. But at certain times and places, your own self, your true face, reflects on a refined surface.

If you feel you're happy because you got something, it's not really the object that brought you the happiness. If it were, then the more of it you get, the happier you should be. But that doesn't seem to be so. Sometimes if you get a little more, you become unhappy.

If we imagine a glass of milk will make us happy, we drink it and think, "I got the milk. Now I'm really happy. But I want to become still happier. So I'll drink a few more glasses." What happens? We get sick. If the milk could bring happiness, the more we drink, the happier we should be. We seem to forget where true happiness is to be found.

This is why Sri Krishna says, "Whatever your effort is, it's always to seek me, to enjoy me, to feel my Presence." That's why there are various religions. Each has a different approach with a different label. We might go into different prayer halls. One person kneels and prays. Another falls and prays, and a third stands and prays. Maybe you've come across people who roll and pray. What does it matter whether we stand, kneel, fall or roll—we pray. We have that in common. Too often we miss what we have in common. That's why we disagree. In fact, all religions have the same goal. In a way, everybody has his or her own religion. Because our minds vary, each mind has its religion. Your approach is your religion.

Chapter Four

12. In order to succeed, people worship the gods *(devas)*. Success soon comes by actions in the world.

When he says, "gods," he's referring to the minor deities. There's the supreme God, and then there are the minor deities. If you approach at that level, you probably get a result more quickly, but you get only that. If you want more, go to the highest. Actually, they're not different. There is one and the same energy coming through different channels. Sometimes the minor one is easier to handle. But for a big purpose, it may not be enough. It's better to aim high.

Electricity provides a good example. Electricity comes in thousands of volts. We can't approach it directly. It has to be transformed by step-down transformers. When it comes to our home, it comes as 110 volts. Then even if we get a shock, it won't hurt us so badly. Suppose we say, "I'm rich and my house must have bigger voltage. I only want the big current." Then we'll have bigger shocks also. With 110 we can do certain things, but if we want to do more, we need more voltage. If we want to cook with a microwave, probably we'll need 220. The greater the purpose, the higher the voltage.

God's power is also like that. It takes time to reach the highest One. You have to learn how to handle it, how to protect yourself before you go to a high voltage transformer. It's like getting friendly with a person of high position; it takes a long time. You can easily be friendly with a junior officer. But sometimes, it's worth the waiting and working for the acquaintance of a senior officer.

God's energy also works on different levels. Ordinary people are satisfied with something small. But gradually through that, they'll go to the highest one. There is no need to condemn or discourage them. If an opportunity comes, just tell them, "This is not all there is. A little further on you will see much more. Keep on going."

13. By variously distributing nature's qualities *(gunas)* and activities (karma) throughout humanity, I thus created the four castes (mental tendencies). Though I am the author of it all, know that I am not the doer and I never change.

Many have heard of the Hindu caste system. There's much controversy about it. But the *original* purpose and meaning was beautiful. The castes were grouped according to the capacities and inborn temperaments of the people. The Sanskrit term for caste is *varna*, which means color. It refers to the color of the mind. And again, the color is according to the three *gunas: sattva, rajas* and *tamas. Sattva* is white, *rajas* is red and *tamas is* black.

It's not the color of the skin or of anything you can see. It's just symbolic of the mental color. A dull mind is always clouded. That is why if you see all clouds in meditation, you know your mind is *tamasic.* When it's *rajasic,* you will see bright colors. If it's *sattvic,* you will see golden colors. So from the colors you can guess the calibre of your mind at this time.

Ideally caste is defined according to the color of the mind. People can't easily change from one to another unless they really work on their minds.

14. **I am unaffected by all actions, nor do I desire any results. Whoever experiences this quality in me is also free.**

15. **Even the ancients who realized this freedom from all duties, nonetheless continued to work in the world. Like those sages, you too should continue to act.**

16. **Even the sages are sometimes confused about action and inaction. However, I'll tell you now what action is and you'll be freed from evil.**

With this assurance he goes to the next *sloka.*

17. **Distinguish between right action, wrong action and inaction. The way of karma is nearly impossible to understand.**

It's important to discriminate between appropriate action, forbidden action and inaction. Note the three: right action, wrong action and inaction, or the actionless state. Scholars argue about the meaning of this *sloka.* But the majority think Krishna speaks of what is to be done, what is not to be done and what is not doing anything. This is explained in the next *sloka.*

18. **The person is wise who sees the inaction in actions, and the action in inaction. He or she is a yogi and can accomplish everything.**

Chapter Four

Sloka 4.18 says the one who sees inaction in action and action in inaction is a wise person, a yogi. Having reached this point, you have accomplished everything. You do, and at the same time, do not. You do not, yet still you do. You sleep and sleep not. You eat, yet eat not. So on and on, two different things that look like opposites. But the wise person knows the difference. You see inaction amid all the actions. That means you know there are two different things in the same experience, two sides of the same coin. One acts, the other observes. The observer is the witness. As a witness you don't act. As an actor, you don't witness. If you are a wise person you take both positions simultaneously. You know who is doing and who is observing. And because you know how to be the witness, then even though your body and mind may be doing things, you know it is not you who is acting.

But in the previous *sloka*, Krishna finishes by saying, "The way of karma is impossible to understand—from the viewpoint of the onlooker who sees somebody doing something." The onlooker cannot tell whether the person is acting or not acting. Only the one doing the action will know. This is very deep. To understand karma one has to rise up to a certain level where it is possible to discriminate between correct action, wrong action and inaction.

A simple example is that of the lotus flower which blossoms when the sun comes up. When the sun goes down, it closes. Is it the sun that causes the blossom to open in the morning and close in the evening? Ask the sun, "Why are you doing that?" The sun says, "I don't know anything. All I know is I'm here. I don't even come and go. It's you who says the sun rises and sets. I'm never up. I never set. I don't get upset. From your standpoint you think I'm coming and going."

Similarly, a yogi appears to be doing things: coming and going, accomplishing this and that. Sometimes he may even say he's doing things. But in fact it's Nature, making things happen. The yogi is a constant witness to it all. That way he or she understands the secret of karma. The yogi perceives action from the state of inaction, at the same time enjoying inaction in the midst of action. This may sound a little philosophical. It's nice to hear, but hearing is not enough. When you reach the stage where you experience this, then you'll say: "Yes, now I know what he means."

Prakriti, the manifested universe, is controlled by the three *gunas.* Our minds and bodies are part of that *prakriti* which is constantly moved by these three *gunas: sattva, rajas* and *tamas* (balance, restlessness and inertia). But who are you really? You are the Self; you are the Knower. You are not affected by *prakriti.* You are completely different.

That's why you say, "*my* mind" or "*my* body." When you say, "my mind has been disturbed," you're really right. It's not you, but your mind that's disturbed. But if you immediately add, "and I'm really unhappy about it," that's not right. That's not the real you. But you insist, "I'm unhappy because my mind is disturbed." If you were unhappy, you wouldn't even notice that your mind was unhappy. An unhappy or sick person can't recognize another unhappy or sick person. Only the sane person can discern if another is insane.

If your very knowing itself were unhappy, you wouldn't be able to recognize the unhappiness of the mind. This means your knowing is always sane. For you are the Knower, the awareness, you are aware of everything that's happening in your body and mind. This awareness never ceases to be. That is the constant, eternal, permanent you—the Self. But unfortunately, you usually identify *yourself* with the mind or the body and talk in those terms: "I was happy, I am unhappy," and so on.

The true you, which is the Self or *Atman,* doesn't do anything. The "*prakriti* you" (nature operating through the mind and the body) does it. Here is the action and the inaction at the same time. Even though I (as mind-body) did this action, I (as Self-*Atman*) didn't do it. See? I *did* it, and certainly I didn't. That means two "I's" are there. The true "I" (the Self) knew that my little "I" (body-mind) did this action. Even though you see me (body-mind) acting, I (the Self) am not acting. Just my mind and body are doing. See—inaction in action.

Do you understand this? If you can keep this in mind, it's surely very helpful. Even when you feel depressed, you can just pull back quickly and ask, "Who is depressed? Certainly it's not me. I know someone is depressed. Who? My mind. Why? Well, I told it not to do all that mischief. What can I do for it now?" See how quickly you can separate away from identifying with your mind. It's very handy. You'll never get lost. You can rescue yourself from drowning in wrong identification. The very moment you separate from it, the agony is gone. It's like turning off the main switch. You become the person witnessing.

Even with pain. You burn your finger, feel the pain, then quickly take it from the fire. Then inquire: "Pain? Where does it come from: Who is complaining of pain? Who got burnt? Who knows that?" As you start analyzing the pain, the pain disappears. But when you identify with the body and mind, which experience the pain, you are in agony. The minute you separate from it and start analyzing, it no longer affects you. If you get this point, it's very useful in day-to-day life. There's no need to get lost in all the ups and downs.

19. Whatever you do without personal desire for the results is called wise by the sages. Your actions are pure and you know the truth.

A wise person is the one who seems to be doing things without any desire to do them and without any desire for the result. He or she seems to be doing things, but the actions of the wise person are all completely fired by the absolute truth, by real knowing.

After you gently roast seeds, they still might appear to be like they were before—ready to germinate. They keep their shape, their name and appearance. But they don't germinate. They've lost the germ of their desire. Because there's no desire, the seed doesn't grow.

From all appearances you might appear to be acting and doing everything. People naturally might think: "See, you are doing the same things we do. Sometimes you seem to be quite eager to get things done. If it doesn't happen, you seems to be scolding us." But remember an earlier *sloka* (3.25): An enlightened person does things with the same zeal [as an unenlightened person], Arjuna, but without attachment, and thus guides others on the path of selfless action.

Moreover, the enlightened people don't act because they personally want to do these things. Nature's force functions through them in a special way; they are catalysts. Some chemicals are used as catalytic agents. They don't have any special purpose for themselves. They're used for getting something done. Once that is achieved, they go away. That's a catalytic agent. During welding the rod is coated with flux as a catalytic agent. Its purpose is just to make the metal flow freely. The flux is not there for the sake of the flux, but just to fulfill a purpose and go away. Sometimes you see people in that role. That is what's meant here.

20. Because you have let go [of] attachment to the fruits of your actions, you are ever content and have no dependencies. Though you appear to be doing things (karma), actually you're not the doer.

21. Because you don't want anything for yourself; and because you have control of your mind and ego; and because you do not consider possessions as your own, you are completely pure despite the actions of your body and mind [which move according to the forces of nature].

22. Because you are content with what comes of its own accord; and because you envy no one; and because you have gone beyond the pairs of opposites and maintain your equanimity in success and failure, even though it appears that you are doing things, you are not bound by your actions.

23. When you let go of all attachments and experience liberation, your mind becomes absorbed in the truth. Then everything you do becomes a sacrifice (*yajna*), and all your karma melts away.

24. The offering itself is *Brahman*. The oblation is *Brahman* which is offered by *Brahman* into the fire of *Brahman*; the one who sees nothing but *Brahman* in all that he or she does, certainly realizes *Brahman*.

A very important *sloka*, but there's not much to say because it's all *Brahman* ultimately. When performing a devotional offering or worship, the various parts are mentioned: the fire, that which is offered, the water or oblation, the fuel or clarified butter and the one who is offering it. Everything, every part and the entire sacrifice is ultimately *Brahman*. That's what it means. At one level you see everything as one, no dividing one part from another. Then there's not somebody offering something into some fire and somebody getting the benefit. All are the same. Differentiation is gone. Then you realize the oblation is *Brahman*; the clarified butter is

Brahman; the person is *Brahman* offering into the fire of *Brahman.* So, unto *Brahman* everything goes.

Actually taking a meal is a *puja,* a devotional offering. If we rise to that level, we understand the meaning, and experience it when we eat: "The food is *Brahman;* the hand that takes the food is *Brahman;* the mouth that chews is *Brahman;* the alimentary canal is *Brahman;* the person who eats is *Brahman;* the process of eating also is *Brahman.* Everything is *Brahman.*"

One day we should all experience this truth. Until then, if we think this when we eat, it's useful.

> 25. Some yogis make sacrifices to the *devas* (gods, angels), while others offer their very selves as a sacrifice to *Brahman* (the Absolute God).
>
> 26. As an offering, some restrain their senses (such as hearing, seeing, tasting), while others sacrifice sense objects (such as sounds, etc.) that otherwise would be enjoyed by the senses.
>
> 27. Motivated by wisdom, still others offer their senses and vital energy (*prana*) as a sacrifice in the form of self-restraint.
>
> 28. Some offer their wealth as a sacrifice, or their suffering, or the fruits of their Yoga practices. Others, who tend toward austerity and extreme vows, offer the fruits and the knowledge of sacred study as their sacrifice.
>
> 29. Among those primarily interested in control of the life force by restraining the flow of the breathing (*pranayama*), some offer the out breath as a sacrifice to the in breath, and the in breath to the out breath.
>
> 30. Others, who restrict their diets, offer the additional vitality of such austerity as their sacrifice. All these yogis are purified by *yajna* which utterly destroys their sins.

The incoming air, the outgoing air, the retention: it's all *Brahman.* Your breathing itself becomes a sacrifice. It's happening anyway; just become conscious of it, that's all. Actually the breath is sacrificing itself for our life support. It goes in and gets burned. If it didn't sacrifice itself, we wouldn't be alive today. The incoming and outgoing breath are examples of sacrifice.

31. This world and the world to come are for those who sacrifice. Those who partake of what remains of sacrifice go to *Brahman* (God).

32. In many ways do people sacrifice of themselves and reach God. Each sacrifice is according to their karma. Understand this well and you will be free.

33. Giving knowledge is even better than giving wealth, Arjuna, because all other sacrificial actions lead to the attainment of knowledge.

Now Krishna talks about giving wisdom to others. The charity of knowledge is called *jnana yajna.* You can give many material things to people, but these won't last long. But if you can give wisdom, it will save their souls, because it takes them out of this cycle of births and deaths. If you give them food, they're all right for a few hours; but then they'll have to go to somebody else for more food. If you give them some academic education, maybe they can earn some money. They can do a job and earn some dollars; that's all. But if you give wisdom, it will save their souls. It will free them from misery in life. So *jnana yajna,* the gift of wisdom, is the best gift.

34. If you seek enlightenment from those who have realized the truth, prostrate before them, question them and serve them. Only then are you open to receive their teachings of sacred knowledge.

This *sloka* shows the qualities of a student. Sri Krishna says: Become enlightened by surrendering. By prostrating you annihilate your ego. Also, by questioning and service, only then will the wise instruct you in that knowledge. They won't until then. That means you prove yourself to be a qualified seeker by humbling yourself and by asking. To get such knowledge you can't just simply say, "Could you give me that?" In this case, literally cry and beg for it. That's what prostrating means.

But just because you asked doesn't mean you accept it blindly. If it doesn't suit your intelligence, ask, "Why is it so? Why this way and not that way?" A seeker has every right to question, but with humility. Receiving this knowledge is impossible without the humility. You are the receiver;

the teacher is the transmitter. Humility allows you to receive. But after you receive, if you have doubts, or if you don't understand something, you have every right to question. A good seeker *should* question.

It is also the duty of the teacher to convince the student. If the student isn't convinced, he or she won't be a good student. If the teacher can't convince the student, maybe this particular teacher isn't the right one for that person. But to be convinced, the student must listen. If you have your previously fixed opinions and then say, "Come on, convince me," it's not possible. You have to be open-minded. You have to receive first.

People sometimes ask questions, and as you answer, they'll be planning to ask another question. They won't even hear the answer. Moreover, they want the answer to be in such a way that they can agree with it. Such people are not really asking questions to learn. They're just testing the teacher.

Prostrating doesn't always mean you fall at someone's feet. It's mostly an attitude of humility. You feel that you don't know that much, and you trust that the teacher knows a little more than you. You place yourself below the teacher and you receive. Receiving knowledge is possible only if you can humble yourself. To understand, you have to stand under.

That's what Arjuna does. "I don't seem to know anything," he says. "I've lost my intelligence. I've lost my mind. I don't know what to do. Please direct me." Then Sri Krishna starts talking to him. It's easy to pour something into a mind that has been emptied and says: "I'm empty, please pour."

Even scientifically this is so: one beaker is empty or has just a little water in it. Another beaker is full of water. If the empty beaker wants more water from the full beaker, a tube is connected—a kind of siphon. If the tube is filled with air, the water won't flow. The tube should be a vacuum. Then the water is sucked in. The empty beaker can receive the water only as long as it's below. If the receiver says, "I should be equal to you," then the flow stops. When it says, "Actually, I'm a little better than you," then it loses whatever it had. It's a simple siphon system. Now you see how scientific religious teachings are.

The flow of electricity is another example. Did you know that this human body itself is a magnet? Every magnet has two poles: north and south.

Normally on a map, up is north and down is south. If you are a magnet standing upright, your head is your north pole and the feet are your south pole. If you have only a little magnetism and there is a powerful magnet somewhere close by, where would you go to get some magnetism? Which part of you should rub which part of the big magnet? Your head, the north pole, should rub the feet, the south pole, of that big magnet. That way you can draw the magnetism.

This is another reason for prostrating: put your head on the teacher's feet. Don't think it's such a joy for teachers to see many people falling at their feet; they get drained. It's not that easy to be a Guru. Very soon they will be totally drained unless they know how to bring in more energy. That means they should put their heads somewhere under the greatest feet. If they say, "I know everything; now I can give to you," they are no longer holy people; soon they'll be hollow people.

The more teachers give, the more they should know how to receive from higher still. Probably because students can't see those greater feet, they see the Gurus as the big magnets. But the Gurus know of another bigger magnet which they keep hanging on to while students hang onto them. That way they aren't drained. And whatever comes to the Guru is passed on to the students.

Of course just prostrating and questioning is not enough. Service is also necessary. Serve your teachers. That means obey them and do what they say. Service is very important. Some students say, "I came only to learn. Why should I work for you? I can work anywhere." But by service you show your obedience and the readiness of your mind to receive. Through service the teacher imparts the teaching.

Mere words are not enough. Physics and chemistry cannot be taught just from the books. The student has to go into the lab and work. In the case of spiritual knowledge, the lab is the entire world—wherever you are. The teacher will say, "Go and wash that toilet." It's Karma Yoga. In the olden days when disciples went to Gurus, they seldom saw the Guru for years. They only saw a few of the senior students. Whether king or peasant, they were simply asked to do some work. "Okay, you've come. Cut the lawn;

gather some grass for the cow; bring some wood for the kitchen." And that's what they'd do.

There was a case in the *Vedas* where a student approached a teacher who said, "Here is a cow. Go and let her graze. Stay there until the cow multiplies into one hundred. When there are one hundred cows, come to me again." See how long it took. A normal course of study under a teacher was twelve years. You might say, "That was way back in the bullock-cart age; now we're in the jet age. Can't we learn in twelve minutes?" I'm sorry, no. Truth is the same always. Actually, you can learn it in twelve minutes if you have the right attitude. But it still takes a long time to rub, scrub and clean the ego to get the proper receptivity of mind. It's covered with so much mud. To empty the mind and clean it takes a long time.

35. When you realize this truth, Arjuna, you will never be confused again, and you will clearly see that all things in creation are part of you and part of me.

36. Even if you had been the worst sinner, on the raft of this realization, you will certainly pass over the ocean of sin and evil.

37. Just like a roaring fire reduces its fuel to ashes, the fire of your realization of the truth reduces all your karma to ashes.

38. Undoubtedly there is nothing in the world that so purifies you as the awakening of true knowing. Whoever rises up through Yoga, in time realizes this truth in his or her own heart.

Another important qualification for the student is *shraddha*—wholehearted sincerity, complete and total interest in what you're doing, true zeal.

39. Anyone who has sincere belief and devotion, and takes control of his or her senses, will rise to this wisdom, which in turn leads to the realization of profound peace.

40. Because of ignorance, some people have no sincere belief and are constantly skeptical; they are ruined. A mind like that is unhappy in the present and the future.

What a great truth he gives here! When even an atom of doubt gets into your mind, your first and foremost duty is to remove it. Doubt enters like a drop of poison falling into a pot of nectar. That poisonous doubt can arise anywhere—between friends, in the family, in your business partnership, between you and your teacher or in your own practice. The first duty is to remove the doubts.

41. If you dedicate all your actions so your work becomes Karma Yoga, all remaining doubts will be destroyed in the fire of your awakening. At this point all bondage falls away and you remain poised in the true Self.

If all that you do is Karma Yoga, selfless action, dedicated to God or humanity—and there's no doubt in your mind—automatically true knowledge dawns and nothing in this world binds you. Such a person is liberated.

42. With the keen blade of knowledge, sever any doubts due to ignorance that you may still hold about *Atman*, the true Self, which abides in your own heart and thus—well-established in Yoga—stand up, Arjuna!

Thus ends the fourth discourse of the *Bhagavad Gita*, the science of Yoga, entitled: "The Wisdom Yoga of Action and Renunciation."

The Yoga of Renunciation

1. Arjuna asked: You seem to be advising both renunciation of action and the performance of action. Is one better than the other?

2. Sri Krishna said: Both paths lead to freedom. Of the two, Karma Yoga, selfless action, is better.

3. True *sannyasis* (renunciates) neither hate nor desire [anything just for themselves]. Freedom from such dualities of mind brings liberation, Arjuna.

4. Unlike the wise, those with childish attitudes try to distinguish between the paths of wisdom (Jnana Yoga) and selfless actions (Karma Yoga). Whoever becomes well-established on either path receives the fruits of both.

5. Both *jnana yogis* and *karma yogis* experience the same heightened states of consciousness. They see clearly who see Jnana Yoga and Karma Yoga as one and the same.

6. The state of true renunciation (*sannyasa*) is hard to reach, Arjuna, without Karma Yoga, the performance of selfless actions which purify the mind. Anyone who meditates regularly with a mind made pure by Karma Yoga soon realizes God.

7. As your mind becomes pure through Karma Yoga and well-disciplined through meditation, the senses quiet down and you see that your own self is none other than *Atman*. At that point you are no longer subject to karma.

In this chapter, Sri Krishna describes a renunciate.

8-9. By identifying with the true Self, you will be a sage seeing clearly that it is not you but the senses that move among the sense objects. Even while seeing, hearing, touching, smelling, eating, walking, sleeping, breathing, speaking, letting go, holding on and opening and closing the eyes—you think: I am not the doer.

This means that whatever happens through the body or even the mind, it's just the senses functioning through the sense organs. You know all those actions are happening, but you're not affected by them. You realize that you are just the Knower. You're like a person sitting in the movie theater of your body and mind, watching the whole show. And not just things outside you. As the Knower, even your own body and mind are somewhere outside. It's as if you're surrounded by a sort of cinerama with not just one screen, but screens all around, and you're constantly watching. If everything goes smoothly, if there are only nice heros and heroines, then you'll be looking for a villain to come. Why? For tempo changes and some suspense. Only then is the movie really well written.

In the same way, to make our lives more adventurous, we have various scenes. We've been given a constantly moving show. It's best just to watch all that's happening. Unfortunately, even in a normal movie theater, people don't just watch. Very often we hear people weeping and blowing their noses because it's a sad scene. If we go to a soccer game, we might even get kicked by people sitting nearby, who forgot they were only witnessing the game. Instead, they began to take part and started kicking everybody around them.

That's exactly what's happening in our lives. We forget that we're just seeing a show. We forget that we're just witnessing. We start acting and joining in. It's better to always say, "I'm the witness." Then we won't get caught. That's the sign of a sage or total renunciate. If you are a total renunciate, there may be many things happening to you, and it may appear that you're thinking, doing and talking. But to you, it isn't so. Just as others see you doing things, you also see yourself doing. They're observing, and so are you.

10. Whoever lets go [of] attachment to the fruits of their actions, and instead dedicates their actions to God, is not touched by sin, like the lotus leaf is not touched by water.

11. Yogis abandon attachment to results. To purify themselves further, they still continue to work with the body, mind, intellect and senses.

12. By steadily letting go of the fruits of their actions, yogis attain peace. But unyogic people, motivated by personal desires, are bound by their attachment to the fruits.

13. By mentally renouncing the fruits of their actions, yogis' minds becomes disciplined. Thus, they know themselves to be the *Atman*, happily abiding in the city of nine gates (the body). They know that they are not the doers who act or cause to act.

14. God (the Indweller) does not directly create forces that move in the world or anything that happens here. Nor is God in any way affected by them. Nature (*prakriti*) does all this.

15. God, who is omnipresent, does not measure anyone's virtues or vices. Because inner wisdom is veiled in ignorance, people therefore are misled and err.

16. When you know who you are, you are enlightened. In that Self-realization, the darkness of ignorance disappears in the light of true knowledge that shines like the sun, revealing the Supreme.

17. Those who continuously think about That (Self), merge with it and settle into it. Whoever holds this as their goal will no longer be subject to rebirth [because] Self-realization dispels any remaining flaws.

18. Those who have realized the Self see that same Self equally in a humble scholar, a cow, a dog or a dog-eater.

Such a person has that equal vision. Having equal vision means you don't see anybody as low or high. To you both thief and police officer are equal. You don't see the superficial. The Self of the thief is the same as that of the police officer. Something is playing the part of the thief, and that same something is playing the part of the police officer. Because the sage is rooted in the Self, he or she sees them both as Self. So, for the sage, they're equal.

This explains the biblical commandment, "Love your neighbor as your Self." It doesn't say, "Love only your good neighbor as your Self," or "Love your neighbor who has the same label. If he's Catholic, love him. If she's Protestant, throw stones at her." No. It simply says, "your

Chapter Five

neighbor." And who is your neighbor? The one sitting next to you now, or in the next room, the next house, or the next town. Everyone close to you is your neighbor.

But how to love your neighbors as your own Self? You have to see your Self in them. Otherwise, you can't love them as your own Self. How can you see your Self in another if you don't know your Self? Suppose I say, "Here's a banana. Please see the banana that you had yesterday in this banana." To do that you should have had a banana yesterday in order to know what a banana is. Only then will you recognize one and the other as the same. If I don't know what a banana is, I can't say this one is the same as the other, and that I love this as I loved the other banana.

The clue here is to know your Self and then see your Self in your neighbors. Then love them as your Self. That's why someone who has realized the Self will always have equal vision based on that Self or that spirit. A God-realized person will see nothing but God everywhere, even though that God may be clothed in different forms and using different names. That's why Sri Krishna says that whether it's a dog or an outcast or a great spiritual person, it's all the same to a person of wisdom.

How can we truly come together? Only with this spiritual knowledge— not by mental, physical or financial knowledge. We can never find the oneness in any of these areas, nor in the name of country, race, creed, community, money or education. The only way to see everybody equally is in that divine vision. Then we see the same truth colored different ways.

When children go to a candy store, there are so many chocolates packaged in so many ways: different designs and different labels. But, ultimately, they're all chocolates. If you ask for a pound of assorted chocolates, the shop owner will just take a little from here, there and everywhere and weigh out one pound. You are being charged for a pound of chocolate. The shopkeeper doesn't worry about the color or shape, the name or label of the candies. You could say the shopkeeper's vision is in the chocolate. But the children will say, "I love the square chocolate," or "The oval one is very good." "The green is beautiful." Each will buy something different. "Mine is so good." "No, mine is best." They even fight among themselves. Nevertheless, they're all licking the same chocolate. So the shopkeeper has the chocolate vision, and the children have the vision of the form and name and the different labels.

Someone who goes to the very root of it all doesn't worry about any of these differences. Whatever label you have, it doesn't matter. It's all the same to the sage. That's what we call a person of equal vision.

I'm stressing the point here because we often talk about unity, oneness and harmony. But true harmony can be experienced only by realizing the spirit and seeing that spirit in everybody. In all other areas we see only differences. Such harmony won't last long. When people dress the same way or speak the same language, they're in a sort of harmony. But if somebody speaks a different language, they see him or her as different. It's not universal harmony then. There's only one universal truth. That's the great advantage of realizing one's own true Self.

19. When you see the stainless unity of God (*Brahman*) everywhere, you become established in *Brahman* and rise above the constant changes of this world.

20. When you become established in the Absolute, your understanding is without doubt; there are no delusions. Those who have realized *Brahman* are not excited by pleasures nor do they suffer from pain.

21. If you let go [of] attachment to external things, you will delight in the bliss of *Atman* (the true Self). Persistent meditation on *Brahman* (the Infinite) brings a state of uninterrupted joy.

In the next *sloka* Sri Krishna talks about the wombs of pain.

22. Pleasures that come from sense contacts, Arjuna, actually are the womb of pain. A wise person does not delight in pleasure that comes and goes.

Buddha is the one who has *buddhi*, or discerning intellect, one who is wise. A wise person will never expect joy from the outside world or by contact with outside objects. The truth is, joy can never come from outside. *That's the truth.* Happiness can never come from outside. Even if it seems to be coming from outside, it's only a reflection of your own inner happiness.

When we depend on the pleasures that seem to come from outside, each has its pain behind it. Such pleasure begins with pain and later ends with pain. Even as you begin seeking the pleasure, you are in a sort of pain, thirsting for it. Soon after you get it, you feel the pain or anxiety to protect it for fear of losing it. Then who's wise? The one who will never, ever look for happiness from outside things. This doesn't mean running away from pleasures. Instead simply understand, "I can't be happy by having this, by acquiring that, or by achieving something." The world has yet to see anyone who could say, "I'm happy because I got everything I wanted." Never! One want begets ten wants. True, you may want things just for the fun of wanting, but not for the happiness.

And if you don't get what you want—that should be fun, too. "Hey, I wanted it, I didn't get it! This is great fun." Enjoy the wanting; enjoy not getting and enjoy losing it also: "Hey, I got it. See, look at that, I lost it now. Isn't it wonderful?" Don't lose your happiness while wanting, getting or losing something. It's like playing chess or cards. Don't lose your joy if you lose the game. It's all just fun.

With this understanding, life becomes fun. Whoever has this understanding is wise. Otherwise, we're making a big mistake trying to get happiness from outside. This is what Sri Krishna is trying to drive home.

The same was said by Sri Patanjali in his *Yoga Sutras:* "For a *viveki*, a person of discrimination, everything is painful." He means that outside pleasures ultimately are followed by pain. In and of themselves, things aren't painful. Only when our approach is wrong do they become painful and tell us, "Hi, don't look at me for your happiness. Just have me for the fun of it, like a game. But don't ever expect to be happy by using your own ego or your intelligence." If you think: "I'm very intelligent; I can be happy always," you may be disappointed. Sometimes your own intelligence brings both pleasure and pain.

Nor does your body always bring you joy. The body also in a way is outside you. The real you is just simply you—an isolated "I." All that you have or possess is part of the outside world, part of nature. Even by always controlling the mind and using your intelligence you can't be truly happy. That's the meaning of this teaching. Instead, act not for the happiness, but as the appropriate duty of the moment: "Well, I'm here. This is what I should be doing, and I'm doing it." Opportunities present themselves, and we respond to them. And if there's nothing to do, we're just as happy.

Dig a hole and put a seed inside. Then close it. Before you put the seed inside the hole, it was in a gunny bag. The seed wasn't unhappy. It was just a seed. Then you put it in the hole. It's just there. It's not extra happy. Instead of being in a gunny bag, it's in a hole. Does the seed demand: "Come on, pour water on me. I want to grow?" No. When you pour water, it grows. Is it happy? "Ah, you poured water, now I'm growing." No, it says: "You poured water, now it's my duty to grow. If you stop pouring water, I'll be there. I'm just doing my duty according to the conditions present." A wise person functions that way—never, ever losing happiness for any reason. He or she knows that looking for happiness from the outside brings pain. The cause of pain and the womb of that pain is ignorance.

23. While still in a human body, if you can stand fast amid the forces of desire and anger, then surely you are a yogi destined for happiness.

24. The yogi who discovers happiness and joy within is also illumined solely from within. That yogi becomes one with God and marvels in the ecstasy of God.

25. Those who have realized their unity with *Brahman* (the Absolute) are the *rishis* (sages) from whom sin and doubt have dropped away. They have transcended the dualities of nature and delight in the welfare of all beings.

26. Lust and anger naturally drop away from those who successfully renounce attachment to the fruits of their actions (*sannyasis*). With their minds now calm and controlled, they easily realize their true Self and enjoy the bliss of oneness with God.

27-28. By withdrawing attention from external things, mentally focusing back between the eyebrows and equalizing the in and out breaths (*pranayama*), thus you control the mind, the senses and the discerning intellect (*buddhi*). [Then] by aiming for nothing else but absolute and unconditional freedom (*moksha*), personal desires, fear and anger naturally drop away, and you undoubtedly experience final liberation (*moksha*).

How easy it is to say: shut out all external things, focus between the eyebrows, balance the in and out breaths, control the senses, mind and intellect, only pursue liberation, cast away desires, fear and anger. And then you are a liberated sage.

The first thing to do is withdraw the mind from external things. That doesn't mean closing your eyes, nose, ears and everything. It means don't get distracted by these things. Develop dispassion, which is detachment from the objects of the senses.

Then he speaks of meditation: "Focus between the eyebrows." It need not be "between" the eyebrows. It could even be the crown *chakra* near the top of the head. It doesn't always mean with the eyes open, which might cause some problems to the optic nerves. He means the mental gaze.

Equalizing the breath means very gentle breathing. If your concentration is well focused, the breath becomes balanced automatically. You don't even have to do anything consciously. You might have noticed this even when you're working, if you are totally concentrating on something, such as a math problem or just deeply thinking or while writing an article, wondering what to write next. At that moment, if you notice your breath, you'll see that it has almost stopped. That's equalizing the breath.

When the mind is still, the breath is still.

It can go the other way also. If you can't still the mind and through the mind, stop the breath, then try to stop the mind by quieting the breathing. That's why we do a little *pranayama* before meditation, because breath and mind go together. The sage Thiruvalluvar says: "Wherever the mind goes, the breath runs." When the mind is agitated, the breath becomes agitated. When the mind is calm, the breath is calm. When coming out of deeply concentrated thinking, you take a big sigh, because your breath had completely stopped. It's natural retention. It's not that you took a breath consciously and held it. It just stopped by itself.

All these steps in meditation are connected with each other. If you do one, the others come automatically. So whichever is easy for you, begin that way. Either detach from external things if that's easy, or fix your mind on a *chakra* if that's easy; or equalize your incoming and outgoing breath; or control the senses, control the mind, control the intellect; or cast away your desires, fear and anger—whichever is easy. They are all different links to make the chain. By pulling on one link you get the whole chain.

Try it and become a liberated sage.

29. **Whoever knows me as the Lord of self-sacrifice and asceticism, as the master of the universe and as the friend of all, reaches the state of supreme peace.**

Thus ends the fifth discourse of the *Bhagavad Gita*, the science of Yoga, entitled: "The Yoga of Renunciation."

The Yoga of Meditation

1. The blessed Lord said: If you do your duties without desiring the fruits for yourself, you are a true renunciate (*sannyasi*) and a true yogi, unlike those who live without sacrifice and devotion.

2. Renunciation is the essence of Yoga, Arjuna; you don't become a true yogi until you renounce personal desire.

3. Karma Yoga, selfless service, is the way of the wise in order to attain the state of Yoga. Serenity is the nature of those who have reached that state.

4. You experience the true yogic state when you let go [of] attachment to sense objects and the desire for the fruits of your efforts.

5. You can rise up through the efforts of your own mind; or in the same manner, draw yourself down, for you are your own friend or enemy.

What does it mean? Who are you and who is this friend? There must be two of you there. Your higher Self is making a friend of your lower self. In other words, when your own mind behaves as your good friend you get all the benefits and you see friends everywhere. But if your mind behaves as your enemy, you hardly find a friend anywhere. With that inimical vision you see everybody as your enemy. And when you perceive everybody as your enemy, you actually create enemies. There's a saying: "If you're a thief, you don't trust anybody." It all depends on the "glasses" that you wear. You see everybody through your own mind's eye. The following *sloka* is more or less the same idea:

6. As you gain control of your mind, with the help of your higher Self, then your mind and ego become your allies. But the uncontrolled mind behaves as an enemy.

This means that if you are a friend of your own higher Self, and if you have no enemy within you, then you see friends everywhere. This is so because the world is nothing but your own projection. If your own mind is inimical, it will see everybody as an enemy. If you don't know how to conquer your own lower self, then it acts as your enemy. It doesn't behave for your benefit or to your advantage. Instead, it always tries to fulfill its own desires whether you get the benefit or not.

Once Sri Ramakrishna Paramahamsa told this fine story: A few people were walking along the road early in the morning, and they saw a man lying on the side of the road. The first one said, "He must have spent the whole night gambling and couldn't reach home, so he fell asleep here. Gamblers are like that. They don't reach home safely." Then he walked away.

The next one spoke, "Poor man, he must be very ill. We shouldn't disturb a sick man. Let him rest there." Then he walked away.

The third one came and said to the man on the roadside, "You're a bum. You don't know how to drink. Don't you know one or two is enough? Probably they gave you free drinks, and now you're down." He treated him as a drunkard.

The first fellow thought the man had been gambling and was sleeping. The second thought he was sick, and the third thought he was drunk. Then the fourth man spoke: "A saint doesn't care where he is. Probably he's in higher consciousness, *samadhi*. A saint can be anywhere. He may be near the ditch, near the river, in a temple, sitting and meditating or even lying down meditating. This man is probably above physical consciousness. Let's not disturb him." He then bowed and walked away.

We don't know who was right. All four may have been wrong. They all saw the same person differently because they projected themselves. A drinker thinks the other is drunk. A saint sees a saint. The world as you perceive it is nothing but your own projection. If there is hell in your mind, you won't see heaven anywhere. If there is heaven in your mind, you can't see hell anywhere. That's why it's said, "Correct your vision, and you will see the truth." Self-reformation will bring the right view. If your mind itself isn't corrected but is poisoned and acts like an enemy, then the whole world is an enemy. That's why Sri Krishna says you are your own friend; you are your own enemy. The teaching given here is: Take care of your own mind first.

7. With a self-disciplined mind, you experience a state of constant serenity, correctly identifying with your highest Self (*Atman*) who remains unaffected in heat or cold, pleasure or pain, praise or blame.

8. A true and steady yogi is utterly content with the wisdom of real knowing, is not disturbed by anything, has controlled and calmed his or her senses and looks with equal vision on a dirt clod, a stone or a nugget of gold.

9. A person stands supreme who has equal regard for friends, companions, enemies, neutral arbiters, hateful people, relatives, saints and sinners.

Friends are friends; enemies are enemies. How is it possible to see sinner and saint the same? You must go beyond saintliness and sin, beyond friend and enemy. Something is common in them all. Everybody has a clean Self, the image of God. Each also is an expression of the same God. You can perceive that divine element pervading everywhere, functioning through every mind and body. When you do that, you'll always recognize the Self that is common to everything and everybody. That means you go beyond the so-called sinner and saint.

After all, what makes someone a sinner? It's not the higher Self that sins. It's the ego or the mind. *Manas, buddhi, ahamkara:* mind, intelligence and ego. They're one and the same, but at different levels. It's the mind that sins. If that same mind develops a beautiful character, you call the person a saint. But the real Self is never affected. The Self is always pure.

An example is a clear bulb or a colored bulb. If the bulb is colored, it gives colored light. But you wouldn't say the electricity inside is also colored. The energy that runs through all the bulbs is the same; external variations are caused by the bodies through which the energy passes. If it's a colored bulb, it sheds colored light.

The same Self functioning through a clean mind shows a saint. If the mind has all lower tendencies, you call the person a sinner. The one who stands supreme is the one who looks beyond the mind-body element and sees the genuine or real spirit behind it all, even in the so-called sinner. The supreme person still loves that other one as the pure spirit, though in a way such a person is spoiling his or her own vehicle.

Chapter Six

Some people keep their cars clean. Some people never clean them at all. Feel sorry for them. They were given beautiful instruments but didn't take care of them. Feel for them, help them, but do not dislike them, because they are still the same as you. If your vision always sees the spiritual side of the person, you'll be unaffected by all these external things. That's called Yoga *drishti,* yogic vision. You just transcend all these superficial things. Look not at the vehicle, look not at the *prakriti,* but look at *Purusha* behind *prakriti*—the essence behind the changing forms in nature.

10. Yoga practitioners should continue to concentrate their minds until they master their minds and bodies, and thus experience a state of solitude wherever they may be; then desires and possessiveness drop away.

This *sloka* suggests that a yogi should always be in solitude, and it is easily misinterpreted. In the mind is God. In the hand is the job. God and job should go together. But if you insist, "I want to be a yogi, I must always be in solitude," then you won't even come to the kitchen for something to eat; you won't leave your solitude.

If you're interested in coming to the dining room, then you should also be interested in going to the workshop. The idea here is to perform one's duty with the hand. Yet in the midst of performing the duty, keep the mind in solitude. Head in solitude, hands in multitude.

The *sloka* says always try to concentrate your mind, feeling yourself in solitude. That means you don't associate yourself with everything. It doesn't mean you don't move along with everything, because the rest of the *sloka* says you achieve solitude only after subduing the mind and body. Doing so, you rise above all desires and possessions that you accumulated fulfilling previous desires. You may still be in the midst of many people and many things, but in fact you're in solitude, you're not affected by it, like a boat on the water or like a lotus in the mud. It's in the mud, but it's unaffected. When you go to the lake, you see lotus leaves floating in the water. But the moment you take the leaf out of the water, you won't find even a trace of moisture there.

Swim like a duck in the water. But the minute you come out, shake everything off. All the water drops away, you come out free. That's real *dhyana,* true meditation.

Now Sri Krishna gives some meditation information. It's general, useful information that will be very helpful. First, what sort of setting should one have?

> 11. To practice meditation, fix up a clean meditation place with your seat neither too high nor too low. Insulate the seat with a grass mat, then a deer skin, and over those, a clean cloth.

But don't kill a deer just for the sake of meditation. The idea here is simply to have some good insulation between the body and the ground. During meditation you are trying to develop a new form of energy, which shouldn't be drawn down by the pull of the earth. It's like an electrician who stands on a piece of wood before touching an electric line. These recommendations are given to help you insulate yourself when you sit for regular meditation. Bring a clean towel if you like, it's easy to do. If you want, you can even use a Yoga mat. Lay it first over the carpet, then put a clean towel on top. (The towel should be used only for your meditation. After you finish the meditation, don't even stand on it. Immediately roll it up and keep it in a clean place.)

The purpose is to let the meditation seat become charged with the meditative vibrations. Have you noticed that the minute you go to bed, you feel sleepy? In the same way, the minute you sit on the meditation seat, you'll feel like meditating.

Even the way you dress can help your meditation. Have clean, comfortable meditation clothes nearby. Before you sit to meditate, bathe or take a quick shower, put on your meditation clothes, then sit at your seat. All these things help a lot. As your practice continues, you'll be charging those things with meditative vibrations. That's the idea behind these suggestions.

Some might even wonder, "Why all these things? Why not a more comfortable seat with a back?" If you used such a seat, soon after sitting there, you would slowly begin to lean back until very soon you'd fall asleep. Something too soft is not good because it won't give you steadiness. Don't sit on soft cushions. Something similar to the *kusha* grass mat is better.

> 12. Then sit and calm the mind and senses by concentrating on one thing; thus you practice Yoga (meditation) for self-purification.

The first practice is to purify. That's also why we do *pranayama*, the breathing practices that cleanse the body, alert the mind and drive away dullness. The main purpose of meditation is this purification. "You get rid of all the wild thoughts by filling the mind with one chosen, beautiful thought. That's why it's called self-purification.

Now he speaks of the physical position.

13. Keep the body, head and neck erect without looking about; gaze instead toward the tip of your nose.

The neck, head and body should be in a straight line. That means the spine is in one line. A crooked spine may hinder the process when the consciousness rises up. It should flow easily through the spine along the *ida, pingala* and *sushumna*. These are important *nadis* passing through all the *chakras*.

There's another advantage in keeping the spine straight. The entire weight of the body falls right on the base. Thus you find your center of gravity. Then your seated position becomes quite steady. If you sit leaning forward, more of your weight is on the legs. If you lean backward, you feel your legs coming up. That's why when you sit, ask, "Where is my weight falling?" Your weight should fall right in the center. The feeling itself will tell you whether you are sitting straight or not. Once you find that center of gravity, then the whole body very easily becomes still.

It's the same with trees. Wherever the branches go, the trees maintain their center of gravity. They stand on that one trunk. If trees can find their center of gravity, so can we.

To meditate effectively, you must prepare first. It's not that the minute you sit, you just close your eyes and start repeating your mantra. Preparation for meditation is even more important than meditation itself. Sit comfortably. Find your center of gravity. Then make a firm assertion. Tell your body, "I've been obeying you all these days. Now the moment has come, and you must listen to me at least for half an hour until the end of my meditation. I'm not going to budge an inch, even if you complain. I know you're not going to break. Know for certain that I am your master. You're going to listen to me. If you obey me for the entire half hour or even one hour, maybe I'll give you some free time. You can run and jump for a while. But first, obey me and then I'll give you your freedom." Yes, it's a transaction.

This is all necessary for good meditation. If you prepare well, nothing is difficult. The proper preparation itself makes it very easy.

When Sri Krishna says to prepare by gazing at the tip of the nose, he doesn't mean for you to take this literally. It might create tension in the optic nerves. Let the eyes be half closed, with your *mental* concentration at first at the tip of your nose. To others, it appears that you are looking at the tip of your nose. But your concentration should be above and between the eyebrows or in the very center of the head. The best location is the center of the head.

Touch your two ears. Mentally draw a line between them. Now touch the center of your forehead and the back of your head. Mentally draw another line. Where the two lines cross is the place. It is more or less the location of the king and queen glands: the pituitary and pineal. They are very psychic glands. This is actually the location of the seat of consciousness, the brow *chakra,* not on the forehead between the eyebrows—although sometimes people think that's the place. No, let your awareness be right in the middle of the head. Now, let the eyes be half-closed; keep the awareness there in the center.

If you close your eyes completely there's the danger of falling asleep. If the eyes are wide open, everything is visible to distract you. As your mind turns inward, automatically the eyes turn up halfway. If you watch a cow chewing its cud, you will see the eyes are half-closed. For meditation— neither asleep nor awake, but halfway between. Keep the head, neck and body erect, mentally gaze at the tip of the nose; don't look around.

14. Sit thus in Yoga meditation, serene and fearless. Firm in the vow of *brahmacharya* and with the mind calm, think of me and only me.

If we could all do that, there would be no need to meditate. "Erase all fear from the heart," means don't even be afraid of God. Just be serene. Think that you are the child of God. And you will experience fearlessness.

When Sri Krishna says, "Think only of me," he means the oneness. Please know for certain that it's not his form or his name he's talking about. When he says "me," he means that cosmic essence, that spirit.

It's exactly the same when Christ said, "Only through me can you reach the Father." He didn't mean his body. That body didn't attain anything. It was just a composition of elements. He meant the spirit. Put your mind completely on that Self. Think of it, and you will be "serene and fearless."

Brahmacharya literally means constantly thinking of the Absolute, which is easy if you control all the senses. This is why controlling the senses came to be called *brahmacharya*. Actually, the true meaning of *brahmacharya* is to put your attention entirely on *Brahman,* the Absolute one. That's not possible if you allow the senses to go astray.

Another important understanding of *brahmacharya* is strict celibacy. For married people, moderation is advised. That means preserve as much *prana* or vital energy as possible.

Sri Krishna says:

> **15. By steadily and continuously practicing Yoga in this way, the yogi wins over his or her mind and realizes the peace that is my nature. This in turn naturally leads to *nirvana*.**

Nirvana is a term very often used by the Buddha. *Nirvana* is "mind nakedness"—absolute serenity and peace. Your mind isn't clothed; your Self isn't covered or colored with anything. It's completely free. A totally liberated person is naked. The Self is naked, uncovered. That's the meaning of *nirvana.* In order to experience this, says Sri Krishna, "Just think of me and only me." That means think of the Absolute. Try to eliminate all other thoughts.

It's a beautiful teaching, but how can you even think of the Absolute? It's very hard. But at least you can feel that the Absolute is something vast. Actually, that's the idea behind the personification of Vishnu, a name that means the Absolute, unlimited, omnipresent, omniscient, omnipotent. Omni-this, omni-that. Repeat "*Om*"—think of omni. Nothing can limit you. Don't just think of little or fractional things. Patanjali says in his *Yoga Sutras,* "If you keep thinking of the infinite you feel bigger. You feel yourself expanding." Why? What you think, you become. You feel unlimited. Don't think "I'm just this body. I belong only to this, or that."

Don't always keep the mind in petty, limited things. All of them are simply aids that just come and go.

Saint Ramalingam once said, "If a seeker constantly thinks of food, all the merit attained by his or her practices will melt away like a bundle of salt thrown in the river." How much time we spend thinking what to eat in the morning, what to eat at noon, what to eat in the afternoon: menus, diets, balanced diets, macrobiotic diets, organic diets. Too much time spent thinking of food, making food, eating food. Another saint, Thayumanavar, said, "I just want to be in solitude, Lord. I know I have a body. Occasionally, it might need some food. So when I feel hungry I should be able to just grab anything that's available—a ripe fruit, a dry leaf or a root." That means take anything simple just to satisfy the hunger. Gandhiji would say, "Eat to live, but please do not live to eat." How often people live to eat. They forget the goal and let petty things take priority and fill up their lives.

A true yogi shouldn't get tangled in these things. Yes, you need a little food, a little clothing, a shelter. If you're really sleepy, you can sleep anywhere. You don't even need a cozy bed. If you don't feel sleepy, then sit and meditate. So don't waste your time with all these daily petty things. Keep them very simple, then you'll have more time to spend in spiritual pursuits, which is what Sri Krishna is saying: "Think on me, intent on me alone."

That means that everything you do is all for good; it's all for God. Do everything as an offering. Let this constantly be in your mind—when you sit and type, when you're outside digging, cooking or eating, everything. Then it becomes a continuous meditation. In your regular, seated meditation practice, be thinking, "How can I make my entire life a meditation?" To make the whole day a meditation, you plan here. Like winding a clock early in the morning so it goes the whole day, sit and meditate early so you'll unwind in meditation the whole day.

Ultimately put more time in meditation. If you use up your only time for meditation doing Yoga postures and breathing practices, the next day cut those short; increase the meditation. You can even do those separately in the afternoon or evening. In the mornings, if your practice time is limited, you can spend all the time for meditation, but do a little *pranayama* (breathing practice) first. *Pranayama* also is part of meditation.

It's not the length, but the quality of the meditation that's important. Some try to meditate for an hour and can't. But if you prepare properly, even ten minutes will be a very good meditation. A person should know how deep he or she is going in meditation. If it's not so deep, then better do more preparation. That's why you shouldn't think, "Meditation is the most important thing, so I don't need to do any of the other practices." If you sit half-sleeping or thinking of many things, you might say you meditated for one hour, but you didn't. See, the quality is more important. And that's the very reason why we suggest a little of all the different Yoga practices. Slowly, we prepare the body with *asanas*, Yoga poses and prepare the mind with *pranayama*. This leads to deep meditation.

16. It is impossible to practice Yoga effectively if you eat or sleep either too much or too little.

17. But if you are moderate in eating, playing, sleeping, staying awake and avoiding extremes in everything you do, you will see that these Yoga practices eliminate all your pain and suffering.

In simpler language, Yoga is the middle path—moderation in everything. You have everything on this middle path, including peace of mind and tranquility. By eating too much, you just satisfy the body and senses. This means you identify yourself with your body and the senses, and you just want to satisfy them. By not eating, you don't satisfy the body, but you may satisfy your ego: "Look at me! I've fasted for the past ten days." This is just another form of ego satisfaction. Instead, a yogi should have a purpose in eating, a purpose in sleeping and a purpose in doing everything. These two are just examples. You don't need to satisfy the body, the senses or your own ego. Do it just for the joy of doing it, and then you maintain your Yoga.

You're not achieving Yoga. You are a yogi already. But you disturb the Yoga by over- or under-eating. It's the golden mean: moderate in eating and recreation, temperate in actions, sleep and wakefulness. Then Yoga becomes the destroyer of pain. To destroy the pain means to uncover your

Yoga, which means ease. When you lose your *Yoga,* you fall into *roga,* which means disease.

This is not to say it's best to take a little bit of anything and everything. That's not moderation. You don't take a little poison "in moderation." There are many foul things lying on the road. Would you eat them "in moderation?"

18. When you have your mind well-trained so it rests solely in *Atman,* without wanting anything, then you are established in Yoga (union with God).

19. The well-trained mind of a yogi, concentrating on the Self, is as steady as a flame in a windless place.

20. Disciplined by Yoga practices, the mind becomes calm and tranquil. Then the individual self (*jiva*) beholds the true Self and is completely satisfied.

21. Once your intelligence actually experiences this greatest joy— which surpasses all pleasures of the senses—you become consciously established in absolute reality, and never slip from that again.

22. Once you are established in this (reality), there's absolutely nothing else to achieve, nor will anything ever shake you again— not even the worst possible affliction.

23. Yoga is a means to disconnect your identification with that which experiences pain. Therefore, be determined to steadily practice Yoga with a one-pointed mind.

24. Completely let go of all personal desires and expectations. Then with your own mind, you can withdraw the senses from all sides.

25. Little by little your mind becomes one-pointed and still, and you can focus on the Self without thinking of anything else.

26. However your mind may wander away, continue to draw it back again to rest in the true Self.

27. Yogis who learn to calm their minds and quell their passions unquestionably experience the greatest joy, become one with *Brahman* (Infinite Consciousness) and are free of sin.

28. All sins fall away from yogis who continually direct their minds this way; they naturally ascend to experience the infinite bliss of *Brahman*.

29. As your mind becomes harmonized through Yoga practices, you begin to see the *Atman* in all beings and all beings in your Self; you see the same Self everywhere and in everything.

Sri Krishna speaks of the "mind harmonized through Yoga." Without equanimity of mind, one can never see oneself in all beings and all beings in oneself. That means you rise above superficial differences to the very essence of which everything is made. You rise above the changes of name and form. Nature is filled with name and form, but behind these is one essence.

Even the scientists agree. They say all that you see isn't real in the ultimate sense. It's real in a relative sense. But relative reality has limitations, and it changes constantly. That's part of nature. Anything that constantly changes cannot be absolutely real. Sometimes you say one thing, sometimes you say the opposite. Are you truthful or are you a liar? In the same way, when things constantly change, they can't be real. Once I was called a little baby. After a few years I was called a boy. Then I was called an adult. Now they might call me an old man. What is true then? Which is real? The name keeps changing.

That's the very nature of nature. Outside the mouth it was an apple. Inside the mouth it becomes pulp. When it goes into the stomach, it becomes carbohydrates, sugar and roughage. Then, when part of it comes out, again it's totally different. So nature constantly changes. The changing aspect isn't the real essence. But the essence that gives room for all the changes is what's real. That is the absolute reality.

There are two realities in life. Always remember both. Forgetting either one brings problems. If you only think, "Yes, we're all spirit," then you cease to function in a normal way and aren't fit for worldly life. At the same time, if you live only on the superficial level, then you constantly see the differences, and that creates many problems: "Who is she? Who is he? I'm different. You're different." Tension comes, then rivalry and hatred. Likes and dislikes arise. But the real yogic way of living is to keep both these realities in mind—the absolute reality and the superficial or manifested reality.

30. **Those who see me wherever they look and recognize everything as my manifestation, never again feel separate from me, nor I from them.**

It's the same teaching put in a different way. When you learn to see the essential unity, you're in full communion with the Ultimate, and you are never apart from that.

31. **Whoever becomes established in the all-pervading oneness [of Brahman] and worships me abiding in all beings—however he or she may be living, that yogi lives in me.**

32. **The yogi who perceives the essential oneness everywhere naturally feels the pleasure or pain of others as his or her own.**

Having achieved that state of perception, you feel others' pain as your own pain, others' pleasure as your own pleasure. You put yourself in the others' place. It's like saying, "Do unto others as you would want done to yourself." "Who sees the essential oneness everywhere" means you see the same spirit everywhere, functioning through various bodies and minds that, ultimately, aren't different from your body and mind. All the bodies and minds are made of the same *prakriti,* the same elements of nature with which your own body and mind are made. Naturally, when you have that consciousness you feel the suffering or pleasures of others as your own.

33. **Then Arjuna spoke: Krishna, you say that equanimity of mind is Yoga. But I do not see how that is possible, because the mind by nature is constantly changing.**

34. **Not only is it restless, Krishna, the mind is often turbulent and powerfully obstinate. Trying to control the mind is like trying to control the wind.**

35. **Then Sri Krishna said: O mighty Arjuna, undoubtedly the mind is restless and very difficult to control. But with steady practice (*abhyasa*) and non-attachment (*vairagya*), it can be controlled.**

36. Success in Yoga (Self-realization) is extremely difficult if you cannot control your mind. But if you persist [and] control your mind, and earnestly strive for realization using the right methods, you will certainly be successful.

Arjuna says to Sri Krishna, "The mind is continuously turbulent. Don't you think it's difficult to control?"

"No doubt it's very difficult to control," Krishna agrees, which probably gives Arjuna a little consolation. Then he continues, "But if you have both *abhyasa* and *vairagya,* you can do it." Yes, it's very hard to control the mind. But just remember, by continuous practice and enough non-attachment, certainly it can be controlled.

It's difficult but it *is* possible; that's the beauty of it! What's the use of doing anything that's too easy? Anybody can do it. The glory comes only when you do something others can't easily do. And it is possible to achieve anything if you practice continuously, not just one day a week or five minutes in the mornings and evenings while the rest of the time you do anything you want. Always keep your high aim to control the restless mind. If you meditate for ten minutes a day and then just leave the mind uncontrolled to go where it wants the rest of the day, it's like holding the rudder for only ten minutes, then leaving the boat uncontrolled, letting the wind toss the boat any way it wants. That way you'll never reach the other shore.

That's why constant vigilance is necessary. Somebody must always hold the wheel and watch the compass. Are you going in the right direction? If, by chance, you make a mistake or are caught by a wind, then you correct your course. Immediately, the navigator works out the course correction. Without that course correction, you can never reach the destination.

Be constantly at it. That's why it's called practice. But mere practice alone is not enough without proper *vairagya.* Here's a story to illustrate this point.

Once upon a time there were two boatmen. They knew how to row, but they didn't own a boat. They had been drinking and decided to "borrow" a boat and go to a neighboring town on the Ganges River. At about midnight they came to the shore and saw a new boat there. The moment they saw the boat, they were happy.

"We have a boat. Come on, get in." They found the oars and started rowing. All night they were just singing a song as they rowed. Slowly dawn came.

As you may know, people normally come to take a bath in the Ganges in the early morning. The boatmen saw a couple of people coming whose faces were familiar. "That's strange," they thought. "How did they get here so easily? We've been rowing half the night."

Soon there was a little more light, and they saw familiar buildings.

"Hey," they called to the bathers, "we are still in the same place. What happened?"

The bathers replied, "What did you expect? Whose boat is this?"

"We just wanted to go to the neighboring town and come back soon. We have been rowing the whole night. Why are we still here?"

"You fools," they said. "You forgot to undo the knot. All the while you were tied to the shore."

They had been practicing, no doubt—rowing steadily. Even if you do months and months of practice, repeating the mantra, all the breathing practices, going to all the Gurus and every other technique, still you'll be tied down if you don't release your anchor lines of personal attachment.

Mere spiritual practice alone is not enough. Know that positively, you must have non-attachment. I won't say the yogic practices alone are no good. It's better than doing nothing. At least you're doing something positive, instead of something detrimental.

If they hadn't been rowing the whole night, those boatmen might have been in a gambling den. No doubt, there is an advantage to such practices. But we can't attain the goal that way. We can't reach the shore unless the bondage is removed.

Unfortunately, in our boats we have more than just one anchor line. There are thousands of anchor lines everywhere. Everything we call "mine" is holding us. That's why I say if you want to know how far away you are from your goal—call it God or peace—I can give you a good method. Get some paper and write down everything you call "mine:" my house, my body, my brain, my intelligence, my child, my wife, my money, my race, my country, my this, my that. List everything. Don't omit even one. If the list goes very long, you are that far away from your goal. As you reduce the list, you're coming closer. If there is nothing at all you think of as "mine," then you're already there. That's all. It's very simple. Then you don't need to practice anything. This could be your only Yoga practice.

When you achieve dispassion, you are not attached to things. You can keep them around, but you won't call them "mine." Now, for example, I may be using this chair. It's very comfortable. I can even say it's *my* seat as long as I'm sitting in it. But when I leave, I can't take it with me and go. It's just given for my use. Similarly, everything, even your body, is given for your use.

This detachment must be properly understood, you can't become irresponsible and just leave everything and run away. That's not detachment. Wherever you go, you'll still be attached to something. If you've run away from your mansion, within a few weeks you'll be attached to your hut. It makes no difference if it's a mansion or a hut. It doesn't matter whether it's your fine suit and coat or all the patches on your worn-out jeans. How many people become attached even to these jeans with hundreds of patches? Clothes are just something to cover the body, that's all. But they should be neat and clean and comfortable.

So many problems arise from personal attachments. Unless there's non-attachment, practices won't bring many results. Side by side there should be *abhyasa* and *vairagya,* practice and non-attachment, two wings of the same bird, in order to fly.

Nothing is impossible to achieve. You see it in these modern times also. We sent a man to walk on the moon. A few decades before, probably nobody would have thought this possible. Nowadays, you can film a little baby in the womb moving around, playing, rolling and show it on a screen. Whoever thought it possible fifty years ago? It's the result of continuous effort. Keep working, keep working; nothing is impossible to achieve. If your want is really that strong and great, you get it. Yes, people can get whatever they want if they think deeply and strongly. That's *abhyasa.* That's meditation, too. Everything is possible.

37. Arjuna asked: Krishna, what happens to those who have sincere belief, but cannot yet control the mind, or those who fall away from these practices before achieving perfection through Yoga?

38. Have they fallen both from this world and the world to come? O great Krishna, do they perish like clouds dissolved by the wind? Do they find themselves without support and deluded on their quests for God?

39. Please, my Lord. No one but you can completely destroy my doubts.

You advise me to practice all these fine things, he says. I'm ready to do so, and I will. But I don't think I'll be able to achieve all these things in this lifetime. I'm getting old. Suppose I don't achieve what is to be achieved while still in this body and I die? Won't all this effort go to waste? I'll be losing both."

"Both of what?" asks Sri Krishna.

"In the name of Yoga," says Arjuna, "I'm not having any fun. I haven't yet achieved the ease of spiritual readiness, nor am I enjoying the world. A bird in the hand is worth two in the bush. Here is all the fun and enjoyment. Why don't I enjoy this, at least? With this Yoga it looks like I'll enjoy neither this world nor the hereafter. Do you really want me to lose both?"

40. Then the blessed Lord said: Do not worry, Arjuna. There is no destruction—either in this world or in the next—for anyone who has embarked on the yogic path. O my son, know for certain that anyone who does good never comes to a bad end.

41. Those who embark on the yogic path—and leave their bodies before reaching their highest goal—attain heavenly states of the virtuous. They stay there a very long time and then take birth again in this world in a home of the pure and prosperous in order to continue their quest.

"Oh, no," Krishna says. "Please don't worry. If you have done meritorious deeds, you go to another plane, another level, which you may call heaven.

Here you will enjoy the effects of the meritorious deeds. Then when you come back, you are given a new body and birth in a better family—a pure and righteous family—so you will have a proper environment to continue."

42. Or they are reborn into families of wise yogis. Such births in this world are rare indeed.

It's called *Yogabrashta*, being born into a spiritual home. A birth like this is surely very difficult to obtain in this world.

There are two places, he says, into which a sincere aspirant will be reborn. One is the pure and prosperous. That means a rich, comfortable family. When you come into that family, you will have all the proper facilities, and if you still have the yogic goal, you will continue to progress. But if you are even more keen, you won't even be looking for a prosperous family, you will be born to a family of yogis. Why? Because the minute you're born, you see your mama practicing meditation and your dad doing *asanas*, Yoga postures. You will automatically go back into it.

43. In this environment, Arjuna, they soon recall the knowledge gained in former births, and strive for realization even more earnestly than before.

What a great comfort this is! But it's not given just to comfort you, it's a fact, also. When we know that this is not the only birth, not the end of it all, we have some confidence to practice. If this were the only life, why should we even bother about it? It's not that we can achieve everything in one lifetime, which is such a short span.

44. In spite of one's lapses, the Yoga practitioner is led onward by the strength of his or her former practices. Even a person who simply wants to know how to practice Yoga sees more clearly than those merely going through the prescribed motions of religious life.

45. By earnest and persistent effort—even over many lifetimes—a yogi becomes completely purified of all selfish desire and reaches the supreme goal of life.

At the end of this sixth chapter are two beautiful verses:

> 46. That [purified] yogi rises beyond the ascetics, those with psychic knowledge, and even those who do meritorious works. Therefore, Arjuna, be that yogi!

Maybe it sounds a little too much to say, but Krishna says it. By "those with psychic knowledge," he means those who study scriptures to gain certain *siddhis* (psychic powers). A person may have all kinds of *siddhis*, but a sincere yogi is far beyond this. He or she is also superior to ritualists. Sometimes people practice all kinds of rituals. They are even proud of having done this or that ritual. But Sri Krishna says the yogi excels all who act for their personal benefit. The true yogi acts without any personal motives, and is therefore above all the others mentioned.

> 47. Of all yogis [however], the very best is the one who continually worships me with sincere belief and becomes one with me.

In Yoga, selfless service by itself is good. But even that is excelled by the yogi who has sincere devotion and self-surrender. Doing service is fine and right. But when you have proper devotion and you love the work you're doing, then you just give for the joy of giving. That is even higher, yet.

Thus ends the sixth discourse of the *Bhagavad Gita*, the science of Yoga, entitled: "The Yoga of Meditation."

Chapter Seven

_____

The Yoga of Knowledge and Realization

1. The blessed Lord said: Listen, Arjuna, focus your mind on me; take refuge in me; and practice Yoga. Then you will surely unite with me and know me fully.

2. I will teach you wisdom which will lead you to directly experience the supreme truth. After that there is nothing else to know.

Later in the fifteenth chapter, all creation is compared to a tree. And life is compared to a tree, an imperishable tree with its roots above and branches below. Its leaves are *Vedas*, holy scriptures. *Veda* means knowing. One who knows it is a knower of the *Vedas*. It's the tree of wisdom. The only difference is that it's an upside down tree. Because it stands on its head, it is wise. The roots are above. That means it originates above. It expands here as *prakriti*, the manifest universe. We always refer to the infinite as above. And from that fullness this fullness here came to be. That's the tree of life.

Examples and stories have their limitations. We must simply go deep to discover the main purpose these stories have. In the beginning of the *Bible*, God speaks of a "tree of wisdom" with two kinds of fruits which he tells Adam not to eat. That means, "Don't reach for the good fruit." He doesn't even have to say, "Don't eat the evil fruit." The moment Adam wants what's good, automatically he doesn't want what's bad. Once you take one side, the other side follows. So God said, "Don't even reach for what's good. There's no evil or good in you. Stay away from those dualities." But if you begin to argue, "No, no, this is good, why can't I taste it?" then even as you do it, you'll be classifying something else as bad. When there is one quality, the opposite is always there. God asks Adam to remain above this good and bad, pleasure and pain, all the dualities. But Adam saw only the good, and he wanted to taste its fruit. So its counterpart, evil, arose.

All the different scriptures seem to have the same ulterior purpose, but each presents it in a different way, through different allegories. But if you keep that basic truth in mind, it's easy to solve all the puzzles from any scripture. All the stories are easily clarified. Then the stories aren't that important because you've got the truth—which was the reason for telling the story. If you want to keep the story, you can, but just for fun. You don't need it anymore. Until you get the truth, you need the story.

Such stories are like scaffolding. You need the scaffolding to construct the main building. Once you build it, take away the scaffolding. You can think of it like a lollipop. The stick is the scaffolding that holds the candy. Finish the candy, throw the stick away. This is all beautifully said by Sri Swami Vivekananda in the beginning of his book, *Raja Yoga*, which is a commentary on the *Yoga Sutras of Patanjali*. He says that all these temples, dogmas, worship services and different Yogas are aids, walking sticks, crutches. If you are limping, take any aid that helps. But remember that it's just a crutch. When you can really walk, throw the crutch away. It's a sort of insanity even to carry crutches when you walk well, which is why, at a certain level, you don't have to go to the temple or church. You don't have to do any worship. You don't have to stand on your head or practice any Yoga. You don't need anything.

3. There's scarcely one person in a thousand who truly strives for perfection. And even among those who succeed, rarely does one know me fully.

4. The eight aspects of my *prakriti* are: earth, water, fire, air, *akasha*, mind, intellect and ego.

5. Even these eight (including the more subtle manifestations) are gross, Arjuna, when compared to my higher *prakriti* which gives life to all the universe.

6. Everything originates out of these two aspects of my *prakriti*. I create and dissolve the entire cosmos.

7. Apart from me, there is nothing whatsoever. The entire creation is strung on me like a necklace of precious gems.

Remember, when Sri Krishna speaks in the first person this way—"I create and dissolve the entire cosmos .... Apart from me there is nothing whatsoever."—he is speaking as the cosmic essence in all beings, not just as one aspect called Krishna.

Instead of "strung on me like a necklace,"—as this *sloka* says—I would like to suggest a little different analogy because the string or thread is usually seen as different from the gem. I hope Sri Krishna will pardon me if I give a slightly different example. You may have seen a *mala*, a prayer necklace like a rosary. There is one kind made out of the same string put into knots. Take one long string, make a type of knot, leave a little space, make another knot, leave a little space and so on. If you pull it, the knots disappear and, ultimately, it all becomes one string. Have you ever seen that type of *mala*? Here's a knot and there's a knot; in between is the thread. What seems to be a knot actually is not a knot. It appears to be a knot, but it's nothing but the twisted string or thread. What you see is just string twisted.

The absolute essence, speaking as Krishna, says: "Whatever knot you see is nothing but me. I am the knot. I am the string. I am the entire *mala*." That's why there's nothing to worry about. Just have some fun. Because, ultimately, that essence is the One who is doing everything. The One became all these knots and in between the knots it is only essence. Then that One moves a knot this way, another knot that way. If this is understood well and applied in our daily lives, there will be no more knots at all.

Theoretically we may know this, but we don't always experience it in our lives. That's so important. We might have heard about the same Truth presented many ways. But, are we experiencing it? If not, why not? The reason is that when we become involved in actions, we forget. Maybe afterward we realize the truth: "Yes, I should have thought of this earlier." But, again, later we do the same thing, perhaps in a different way. Again we remember the teaching and say to ourselves: "Ah, I should have thought of it." Still, you can know it's all right. It's a good beginning.

8. Arjuna, I am the taste in pure water, the radiance in the sun and moon; in all scriptures, the sacred word *Om*; the sound in the silence; and the virility in men.

9. I am the fragrance of the earth, the brilliance in fire, the life in all beings and the purifying force in austerity.

10. Know me, Arjuna, forever present as the origin of all beings. I am intelligence in those who are wise, and splendor in all that is beautiful.

11. I am the power in strength, that is untainted by passion or personal desire. In fact, I am the desire in all beings, Arjuna, when desire is in accord with *dharma*.

12. The qualities of nature (the *gunas*) come out of me; they are my manifestations. Yet I am not contained in them.

13. Most people fail to look beyond the three qualities of My *prakriti*. People see only these changing qualities, and don't see me, the transcendent One. In the midst of all that changes, I am what doesn't change.

14. No doubt it is hard to see through this, my divine illusion (*maya*) comprised of the *gunas*, but those who take refuge in me absolutely pass over this illusion.

15. Others, still deluded by *maya*, lose their discrimination (*viveka*) and sink to their lower nature. Thus, they do evil things, feel no devotion to me and don't seek refuge in me.

16. Good people worship me, Arjuna, for four basic reasons: to be relieved of suffering, to understand life, to rise from poverty to wealth and just because they are wise already.

Here Sri Krishna speaks of four types of people who become devotees of God. All four worship God, but for different reasons.

The first is suffering. When everything else fails, then the seeker calls, "Oh, God!" That's one form of devotion. It's good. God doesn't criticize that. At least when everything fails, you turn to God.

The second is the person who seeks knowledge of worldly things: "I want to know this and that. God, please show me. Tell me the secret." Third is the one who is neither interested in knowledge nor in distress, but worships for worldly wealth. We see these three types in the world.

The fourth devotee is already wise. He or she worships just for the joy of worshipping. This devotee doesn't need to, but feels, "There's nothing else to do; let me just worship. Let me occupy myself this way."

17. Of these [four], the wise excel. Because their devotion is steady, they love me more than anything else, and they are my beloved.

18. All sincere spiritual seekers are certainly blessed with noble souls. Among them, however, those who know the truth and, with a steady mind, set me as their highest goal, soon identify with me; and I regard them as my very Self.

19. After many lifetimes, a person grows wise and takes refuge in me and nothing else. Then he or she realizes that I am all that is. Such a great soul is rare indeed.

20. Others still allow personal desires to lead astray their good judgment. [Thus] they follow their lower nature and worship lesser gods for their blessings.

21. Devotees may select any name or form as the object of their worship. But if they have sincere belief (*shraddha*), I make their faith strong and steady.

22. Then when they worship with steady faith the form they have chosen, they get what they want. But actually, I am the one fulfilling their desires.

Sri Krishna says, "Because they worship me, they get what they want, no matter which way they worship." He doesn't discriminate among devotees nor among their ways of worship. See the universality here. That's why the *Gita* is a universal scripture. Krishna, representing the Divine Essence, doesn't say, "You have to worship only this way or that way. It can't be otherwise." Instead he says, "Worship me in any form."

In India and neighboring countries, when you go into the countryside in the early morning, you may be surprised to see the lady of the house coming out and waving a camphor light and prostrating herself before a round ball. Look closely; you'll see it's nothing but a ball of cow dung which she herself collected from the backyard. Can you imagine that? Every morning she goes into the yard. Almost every family owns one or two cows, and, of course, there's cow dung produced overnight. She just selects a small piece and rolls it into a ball. The rest will go into a pit, but she brings that one ball to the front of the house. She puts a geometrical design around it, plucks a flower and sticks it right in the middle of the cow dung. For her, the dung becomes Lord Ganesh, God the Protector. After that's done, she immediately offers more flowers and then prostrates before him, offering the camphor light, and says, "Lord Ganesh, please protect my house the whole day."

That ball will be there throughout the day and night. The next morning it's put aside because it was worshipped as God. It won't go into the pit. It's separated. Every day for months they collect the balls. Then one day all of them are burned to ash. And it is this ash, which is called *vibhuti*, holy ash, that is applied across the forehead in some *pujas*.

The rest of the dung goes into the pit. She washes her hands as if she's touched something dirty. But the same "dirt" becomes God in that one little ball, and she worships that. And God bestows all the boons that she wanted. God doesn't say, "Can't you select something else? At least use a nice stone! That's at least better than this cow dung." No, God just accepts her sincere devotion and blesses her.

That's the greatness of the Hindu universality. But the truth is that God embraces everything. God doesn't negate. God doesn't say, "Only this, only that." You can just pick up anything and if you call it God with all your heart, it becomes God, because God is in everything.

There are many stories that demonstrate this, and they're not just made up. There are real people and true experiences behind the stories.

In a village there was a learned *brahmin* priest. As such, he was of the highest social level. The *brahmins* are mostly scholarly. Many think they must follow scriptures to the very letter. They perform extensive *pujas*, devotional religious services, every day. This *brahmin* was a devotee of Lord Shiva. He worshipped God in the form of the *Shivalingam*.

Do you know what the *Shivalingam* is? In Sanskrit, *lingam* means anything that symbolizes. So *Shivalingam* means the one that symbolizes Shiva. Shiva means auspiciousness and the Shaivites give the name Shiva to the absolute God, the nameless and formless One. But because it's very difficult to worship the nameless and formless, they had to choose something, more or less nameless and formless, but at the same time with a name and form also. So the *Shivalingam* is a kind of formless form, an egg-shaped stone taken from the river and placed on the altar to represent the nameless, formless God.

That's how the *Shivalingam* worship came about. They didn't want to give a specific shape to God. They knew God is beyond all names and forms and can't be limited to one shape. But their thinking was, "Unfortunately I am limited; I can't understand You as the unlimited One. For my sake, please, just come in a limited form." But because the *Shivalingam* is egg-shaped, naturally it must be put somewhere to keep it from rolling. So they made a circular seat for it. The seat is called *auwdi* which means something that holds something else in position.

Now, let's come back to the story. The *brahmin* worshipped the *Shivalingam*. Every day, he performed a two- or three-hour *puja*, or devotional ritual. And the important part of *Shivalingam* worship is *abhishekam*, anointing him, where you pour all the liquids—water, milk, honey, curd over the *lingam*. Shiva likes *abhishekam*. He likes whoever pours water over him because he's red; he's the fire. He's always hot. So when somebody pours water over him, he's happy. That's the idea.

The atomic energy is terribly hot, you have to keep on cooling it. And that's why if you go to a Shiva temple, you'll see the *Shivalingam* and a big pot filled with water out of which a drop of water is continually falling onto the *lingam*. The idea is that he's static energy. He's in constant meditation. When you sit in meditation, dynamic heat is produced and you have to cool off (which is why, incidentally, you should eat the proper cooling diet if you meditate extensively).

The *brahmin* used to pour milk *abhishekam*. He would get fresh milk and pour it during the *puja*. Of course he wanted pure milk so he had some cows. And because he had cows, he needed a cowherd boy also. So he found a young boy to care for the cows, taking them to graze, bringing them back and so on.

Every morning the cowherd boy would milk the cows and then give the milk to the *brahmin*. For a long time he didn't know what the *brahmin* was doing with the milk. But one day he happened to look through the window just as the *brahmin* was pouring all the milk on the head of the *Shivalingam*. The boy only saw a round stone there. Because he was illiterate, he didn't know what it was. But he was eager to know.

After the *puja*, when the *brahmin* came out, he asked, "Sir, I take pains to go and graze the cow in the beautiful pastureland and bring back so much milk. Why don't you drink that milk? You're pouring the milk on top of that stone."

"You low fellow! How can you say it's a stone? Don't say that again, you ignorant boy! That's not a stone."

"Oh, I'm so sorry! Would you tell me what it is then?"

"That's the *Shivalingam*, God Himself."

"I'm sorry, I'm sorry! I hope God won't punish me,"

"It's all right; you're illiterate. You didn't know what you were saying, so He won't punish you. But don't say that again!"

"Yes, sir. But please tell me, what will God give you if you keep on pouring the milk?"

"Well, God can give you anything—knowledge, wealth, health, everything."

"Oh, and that's why you're doing it?"

"Yes."

"Good. Can I do it, too?"

"Hmph! You are an untouchable. You can't do such worship. You don't even know scriptures, all the restrictions and disciplines. You can't do it. Don't even try."

But somehow, the moment he came to know a little of this, the boy became very curious. "What is this? The whole day I tend the cows. In a sense, I'm the one who gets all the milk, but he pours it and seems to be getting everything. Can't I do anything?"

One day the boy found a nice, small stone, and he placed it in a corner of the cowshed. Before he gave all the milk to the *brahmin*, he took a little and used that to pour over the stone. And he really felt it. He felt that something was truly coming from the *lingam*. So each day he poured a little more and a little more. And, of course, *brahmins* are quite clever. The priest noticed that the quantity of milk was less. One day he said, "Hey, what are you doing with the milk?"

The boy was frightened because the *brahmin* had told him not to do what he was doing. So he said, "Oh, I don't know. There is probably less moisture in the grass or something."

"Oh, you rascal. "You must be drinking it."

"No, sir, no, sir. I never drink it."

But the *brahmin* was still suspicious. "Probably he drinks it when he milks." So one day the *brahmin* spied on the boy. As soon as the boy milked the cows, he went to a stone and poured some milk over it. The *brahmin* caught him red-handed.

"You, you! I told you not to do that! Why are you wasting the milk like this? Don't ever do that again."

The boy apologized: "I'm so sorry." But he just couldn't stop. At the same time, he couldn't use the stone again. "What can I do?" he wondered.

You may know that one way to milk a cow is to bring the calf and allow the calf to drink a little milk. When the calf starts drinking, the cow will give more milk. After the calf drinks enough, it is drawn aside and tied to a small peg and then the cow is milked.

There is always a peg for the calf. Because it's for the calf, it's well-sanded and smooth, so the calf won't hurt itself there.

Looking about, the cowherd boy noticed the calf-tying peg and thought: "This also looks like a *Shivalingam*. If I bring another stone here, he will know what I'm doing. I'll just take a little milk, immediately pour it over the peg and then go."

And that's what he did. For a few days it was all right. But again the *brahmin* grew suspicious. One day as the boy was pouring the milk, the *brahmin* caught him again. "He's not going to stop," thought the *brahmin*. "He's gotten into a bad habit. I don't want anything here that will even look like a *Shivalingam*. I'll just chop off this peg." He brought an axe and started to chop the peg. But when he gave the first blow, he saw blood pour out!

Then he realized his mistake, cried out and fell at the feet of that little boy, "You should be my Guru. I have been worshipping all these years, but your devotion has brought God into this peg. Please tell me, what do you feel when you pour the *abhishekam*?"

The boy was frightened. At the same time, because he was asked, he had to say something, "Sir, I don't know. When I pour, I feel somebody stroking my head, somebody talking to me. I see visions. I see God coming to me. So that's why I was prompted to do more and more, again and again. Even with your strict words, I couldn't stay away."

Then the *brahmin* realized that his strict three-hour worship was nothing compared to this little, illiterate boy's worship. Even today there is a shrine at that place in South India. It's called Kandrapur, which means calf-peg village. It might be a little too much for our 21st century brains to accept: if you have faith, stones and pegs will talk to you. Haven't you heard of many great saints talking to pictures, to statues? Can you say it's all false? If you have faith, you can see God in everything.

God can manifest in any form, with any name. God is ready to offer us everything, bless and praise us, if only we have the proper devotion and faith. God is not just at one particular temple or church that's all decorated with gold, silver and velvet. You can worship God anywhere. There isn't just one place, or just one form for God. We should know that. Unfortunately, many people, and even some religious people misunderstand. Then they don't really experience that spirit. They simply read the scriptures and they take them literally. They miss the spirit of the teaching by holding onto the letter of the teaching. Letters have their own limitations. The spirit will reveal more to you than the letter.

That's why Sri Krishna says, "In whatever form a devotee wishes to worship me, I will make that devotee's faith steady."

23. However, those of limited understanding obtain limited satisfaction. Those who worship the gods (*devas*) go to the gods; my devotees come to me.

He distinguishes between the supreme God and the minor deities. At the same time, he says if you worship minor deities, it doesn't mean you'll get nothing. They are ready to give you what you want, but their capacity is limited. They can give you what they can, but that's not enough, not the goal. You may obtain some material pleasures, worldly benefits, but you won't be satisfied with that ultimately.

For example, if you worship Varuna you get rain. If you worship another deity for money, you can get money. If you have a personal wish, it's even easier to get those things from a minor deity. It's also like this in day-to-day life. Here's a mundane example: Let's say you want to get something done at an office. You brought your application very late. You want your application moved along, but there are already many people who have applied. Your application is the last, so it goes on the very bottom. You want to have your application on the very top so that you can be interviewed soon. There are two ways of doing things. You can become friendly with the superior officer and get that to happen, or you can just go there and be a little nice to the clerk, then ask that it be put on top.

Which would be easier? The junior officer will be happy with a little thing, an invitation to tea. Take him or her to a movie. You can become friendly with a lower officer in a shorter time, but it takes a long time to become friendly with the senior officer. This is a rough example, but in the same way you can go to little gods. They can give you a little something right away, but that's all they can do. They can't give you anything more. That's why they're called minor gods. They do have powers, but limited. And you have to go to each and every one for every little thing, from one office to another. That means you have to become friendly with hundreds. But if you become the friend of the boss, even if it takes some time, you won't even have to go and salute the others. The moment you walk in they'll say, "Oh, please tell us what we can do for you."

You see, seek that highest one first; everything else will be saluting you later. That's the point he's making. "My devotees come to me and they get infinite benefit. But people who worship little gods get little things, passing pleasures." Certainly you are not going to be satisfied with just those little things. You wanted something and you got it. Are you going to stop there? Don't you want something more? For the next thing you want, you have to go to another person and then another and another, and so on. Instead, you can simply go straight to the person who will give you all that you want. But to reach the top will take time, and most people aren't willing to wait. That's why Sri Krishna is explaining this.

24. Because their understanding is still shallow, many still believe that I, the unmanifested One, am limited to one particular manifestation. They have not yet seen my true nature which is unchanging and supreme.

No matter what you call it or in what form you approach it, if you see it as infinite and supreme, then that's all you need. It is the supreme God. Don't worry about the name. The minute you limit even the supreme God with one name, it's a limited God then. An infinite, supreme God should be able to take any name given. If the Supreme One says, "You shouldn't call me Shiva, I am only Krishna," how can you call that God infinite?

Anything that's infinite means all-embracing: "Even that is me, even this is me. Krishna is me. Lakshmi is me. Buddha is me. Jesus is me. Shiva is me. Moses is me. Allah is me. I am everything. I am God, I am dog, I am caterpillar, I am cockroach. Everything is me." Yes, if your mind really thinks the cockroach is the oldest and the infinite form of God, if you worship God in the form of the cockroach, you'll get the same benefit as the ones who worship God in the name of Krishna. Yet, I hope Krishna will forgive me for saying this, but it's not the question of the form of the cockroach or of Krishna. Behind the name, it's what you feel, what you're seeking. You're looking for something so vast, infinite. Simply because your mind is limited, you can't even call on the infinite without a name. So just give any name you want.

A great saint once said, "Lord, You don't have a name. You don't have a form, but we can't understand anything without a name and form. So we're giving you thousands of names and thousands of forms." The form you like may not be satisfying for me. Perhaps I would want to see the same God in a different form with a different name. Do all your children call you by the same name? It's not how you approach, not the name you use, not the form you give to God. Behind the names and forms, what you're looking for is the Infinite.

The same with holy scriptures. When you see Shaivite scriptures, they will say, "Shiva is the supreme God." If you read Vishnu Tantra scriptures, you will see, "Without Shakti (the Divine Mother), Vishnu, Brahman, Rudra, all these fellows can do nothing." It's your faith that counts, not the name and form. If you have faith in a stone and say, "This is my supreme God," that becomes your supreme God. What you perceive is important. Without this knowledge of the truth, many who talk of the supreme limit that with names and forms.

In fact, the great sage *Acharya* Shankara, while worshipping, said to the Lord, "Please forgive me. This is insanity. You are the whole world. I am making You sit here while I wave a little light." Even while doing so he said, "You have created all the sounds of the whole world and here I am ringing a little bell. But pardon me, please. Because of my ignorance and my limitations, I have to do this. Please pardon my ignorance." That's knowledge. Know your limitation. "I know my limitation, Lord, because of my limitation I am just giving You a name and a form, but please pardon me because I can't perceive even a little bigger than myself. You are infinite. How can a finite being perceive the infinite?"

If we know this truth, we will never discourage anybody from using any name or any form to worship that same God.

25. Not everyone can see me as I truly am, because I veil myself in *maya*. Thus deluded, the world does not recognize me as the one who was never born and never changes.

26. Arjuna, I know all about every creature in the past, present and even the future. Yet no one knows all about me.

27. People are deluded by attraction and aversion, which spawn all the pairs of opposites. These dualities, Arjuna, subject all to *maya* at birth.

That means deluded souls take birth with the same delusion. In a way, this shows that souls who are born with delusion must have lived before acquiring such delusion. In the beginning, babies don't show these delusions. But as they grow, their past *samskaras*, mental impressions, surface like germinating seeds that sprout and then bring up the old trees buried inside.

Chapter Seven

The delusion is caused by ignorance; opposites arise: likes and dislikes. If you aren't deluded, you won't have likes and dislikes. In a sense, you could say delusion causes likes and dislikes. But from what are you deluded? The truth. And what is the truth? Something permanent, never changing, always there. When we miss the truth, we look for the experience we might get from the truth. Again, what is the truth? Permanent peace and happiness which is always there.

The absolute truth is happiness, peace. When we are deluded we forget that we already have happiness, that we have peace already. Then we look for peace from things outside. If we think certain things will make us happy, we like those things. When we think certain things will disturb our peace or happiness, those we dislike. Likes and dislikes are caused either by wanting to get happiness or not wanting our happiness disturbed. But both of these attitudes are caused by the lack of knowledge that we have happiness always and it need not come from outside. Nobody can make us happy; nobody can make us unhappy. Happiness is always in us. The moment we forget the truth of our own true Self, we are deluded and begin to look for it from outside. That causes likes and dislikes.

Why did Adam reach out for the fruit? He forgot that he was the image of God, that he already was happy. Because he was the image of God, he didn't need the fruit to be happy. But when he forgot that, he thought, "Ahh, by eating this fruit, I'll be wise because it's the Tree of Wisdom." But you don't become wise by eating a fruit. Nothing on this earth can bring you what you have already. And nothing can take it away from you, if you don't let it go yourself. Letting it go yourself is delusion.

Stay away from anything that disturbs your peace until you realize that nothing and nobody can disturb your peace. Then you don't have to stay away from anything, You neither run after something nor run away from anything. Running after is liking; running away from is disliking. When you realize this, you stop running.

> 28. But people who do good free themselves from doing bad (sin), and thus rise above [the delusion] of these dualities. In this way their worship of me becomes very steady.

29. Whoever takes refuge in me—even as they are striving to escape the conditions of old age and death—will know *Brahman, Atman* and karma.

30. Those who see me pervading all the elements of nature; who realize me as the object of all worship, and who understand that I am the essence of self-sacrifice, will be conscious of my Presence continually, even at the time of bodily death.

Every soul is potentially divine. To realize that divinity is the ultimate goal. Achieve this by any of these aids. Use any label you want. Call yourself a Jewish boy or a Catholic girl, Christian, Buddhist or Hindu, Tantra Yogi or Mantra Yogi or an Integral Yogi. Use any label, it doesn't matter. But stick to it until you achieve the goal. Once it's achieved, drop all these affiliations and labels. If you want, just keep it as a sort of memento: "This is the crutch that helped me to walk." Put it in a golden case and keep it as a souvenir.

But you don't need it.

Thus ends the seventh discourse of the *Bhagavad Gita*, the science of Yoga, entitled: "The Yoga of Knowledge and Realization."

The Yoga of the Absolute Truth

1. Arjuna asked: What is *Brahman*, the Absolute? What is the supreme Self (*adhyatman*)? What is karma, Sri Krishna? What is this earthly realm (*adhibhuta*)? And what is the kingdom of Light (*adhidaiva*)?

2. What is the essence of self-sacrifice (*adhiyajna*)? How does one make such an offering? And how is it possible to control the mind during physical death in order to stay conscious of your Presence, my Lord?

3. The blessed Lord said: My highest nature is the imperishable *Brahman* that gives life to all beings, and dwells in individuals as the supreme Self (*adhyatman*). My offering that causes all beings to come forth is karma.

4. The perishable earthly realm (*adhibhuta*) is the physical body. And *Purusha* is the realm of light and object of all worship. I alone am the essence of sacrifice (*adhiyajna*) present in your very body, noble Arjuna.

5. If you are thinking of me at the time of physical death, you will leave your body and come directly to me; there is no doubt about it.

6. You go to whatever you are thinking of at the time of physical death, Arjuna, because your mind established that direction.

7. Therefore, think of me constantly and fight [for what's right]! If your heart and mind are given to me, then you will surely come directly to me.

Krishna has a clever way of doing things. Know that behind all the different reasoning, his aim is to make Arjuna face the situation, fight and not run away. If you read the whole *Gita* you keep coming across this hint: "Get up and fight." The underlying purpose is: fight your war.

We are all on the battlefield, constantly fighting to win the game. It's not just a one-time war. Don't think that if peace comes somewhere on the globe there is peace in your heart; the war is continually going on. The body and mind are a constant battlefield. Now and then he reminds us, "Don't give up. Fight with proper understanding; then you can win the war." Here again he says, "Always keep your heart and mind absorbed in me, then you will surely come to me." "It's certain," he says, "you will come to me."

Don't forget what this means. Krishna is not a person. He is an experience—the experience of peace and tranquility. That is God. It is peace that's telling you: "Remember the goal of perfect peace and fight your war, then you will ultimately be in peace." We can use all kinds of names, forms and symbols, but we should remember that peace is our God. We can't find it without facing life with the proper understanding. Sri Krishna is saying, "I can't fight your war for you. I can only guide you to fight." If Sri Krishna could do everything, he wouldn't be saying all these verses to Arjuna. If he simply wanted to win the war, he could have ignored Arjuna totally and just snapped his fingers: "The war is over." Certainly he doesn't need an Arjuna to fight the war. But it's not his war; it's Arjuna's war. Krishna can't fight Arjuna's war. If you eat something wrong and get a stomachache, should I go to the doctor?

Sometimes people think, "Ah, that person is all-knowing and all-capable. If he will just say I'm all right, instantly I'll be all right." It's like asking me to take the pill for you. We have to face our karma, our mistakes. If we made a mistake somewhere, sometime, we have to pay the price for it, and it takes time. It can't happen overnight.

If I had the capacity to change you overnight, I would do it. Sometimes I might have the ability. Still I won't do it. Does it sound like a contradiction? But if I do it, it's me doing it, not you. What you did, you have to undo. I shouldn't undo it. If I undo it, you won't learn the lesson yourself. And you can't continue that way. You have to earn your food. It takes time and patience.

Here true faith works wonders. But don't put a time limit on your faith. Sometimes a student comes and says, "Swamiji, I will have faith in you for two months. If nothing happens within those two months, I will look for somebody else." Is that faith? No, but this is: "I just have faith in you. That's all. You take your time. Even if I am not cured, I still have faith in you." If that kind of faith is really there, then you are cured immediately. Otherwise, it's not faith, it's a business. But with unconditional faith, nothing is difficult. All the impediments go away when you have that.

That's what is meant when Sri Krishna says, "With complete trust in me, get up and fight to achieve." You have to fight to experience the peace. Until then, wherever you go the war will follow you. Your karma is like your shadow. You can't escape it.

Many Hindus go to the Ganges. They have faith in the holy river, otherwise they wouldn't spend so much money and travel thousands of miles. After traveling all the way to Benares, they dip in the Ganges to wash away all their past sins. After the dip they should feel that all their sins are gone and that they're totally free. But when some people come out, they're still afraid of the same mistakes they made before. These people fear their past karma. Do you see? They commit terrible karma, then go there to bathe. After bathing they come out but still they don't have the confidence. This doesn't mean the Ganges is just ordinary. The Ganges *is* holy. The minute they step into the Ganges their karma stays out on the bank. As long as they're in the Ganges, no karma. But the minute they come out, their karma comes back again—just because they don't have that complete faith.

This is because the minds of such people still aren't clean. It's impossible to have good faith with an impure mind. Faith lives only in a totally clean mind. Otherwise the seed is sown in a field where it won't grow. What's wrong with the field? Doubt. Doubts nullify faith. Even a little doubt is enough to destroy faith. One must develop faith without room for doubt. "Even a little doubt is enough to ruin you totally," says Sri Krishna.

Our aim is great. If we're really spiritual seekers, we shouldn't think this is just a little fun game. We should take it as a very serious matter. Otherwise we'll simply waste time and keep procrastinating. "Therefore at all times remember me only and fight."

8. If your mind is not wandering or seeking anything else, Arjuna, because you made it steady and one-pointed through regular Yoga practice, then when you meditate on the supreme resplendent *Purusha* (the absolute Self), you experience that.

9. Think continuously of the Knower, the origin of all, the highest one, who is more subtle than antimatter, and yet upholds everything; whose form is beyond thought and who is beyond darkness and is self-effulgent like the sun.

10. Who thus meditates on this resplendent and supreme Self (*Purusha*) with devotion and a mind grown steady through Yoga, during the time of physical death will be able to direct all vital energy (*prana*) to the brow *chakra* and realize God.

11. Without many words, I will tell you about reality. This is corroborated by those who know the essence of holy scriptures. The eternal truth can be experienced by those who learn to control their minds, renounce all personal attachments and thirst only for *Brahman*.

12. This is the effective Yoga technique: At the time of leaving the body, mentally withdraw attention from the gates of the body into the heart area, and from there direct the *prana* into the head.

Close the gates of the body. Hindu scriptures say the body is a nine-gated city. You can come out or go in through these gates. Each opening is a gate: mouth, nose, ears, etc. Then he says withdraw into the heart, then into the head. That means, with all devotion raise the *prana* to the head.

13. Then say aloud or think of the sacred word, *Om*, which is the manifestation of *Brahman*; and you will leave the body and achieve the supreme goal.

If you could do this at the very last moment, it wouldn't matter what you did earlier, you would attain the supreme goal. But the trouble is, you can't just do that at the last minute unless you're prepared. You might say, "The Swami said I can enjoy everything until the last minute." But how are you to know when the last minute will be? Even if you do know, you might become completely disturbed at that moment. It's like Sri Ramakrishna's example of the trained parrot. You may be able to teach the parrot to repeat the beautiful mantra, "Rama, Rama, Rama, Rama." But even as the parrot repeats, "Rama, Rama . . ." if a cat jumps at it, immediately you hear the parrot screaming. What happened to Rama? Unless you cultivate the constant, conscious remembrance, you will forget it at that important moment. Many people repeat with their lips only. That's lip service. It doesn't come from the heart. It's just mechanical.

Another story well illustrates this point. Once "Mr. and Mrs. Shiva" were going for a joy ride in their jumbo jet. Lord Shiva and the Goddess Parvati were taking a pleasant flight. But Parvati looked down and saw a poor old blind man just walking along repeating the names of the God and Goddess: "Amba, Shiva, Amba, Shiva . . ." Amba means Mother. He was calling God as both father and mother. When the Goddess Parvati saw this, naturally with her mother's heart, she thought, "Oh, my poor son." And she said to Shiva, "Sir, didn't you see my poor child?"

"Yes," replied Shiva.

"Can we help him? He has been calling us constantly. Can't you give him his sight so that he can see the road and walk easily?"

"Well, dear, it's not that I'm a hard-hearted person. But it's not in my hands to give or take; he must be fit for that. In his previous birth, he never sympathized with people with disabilities, so he was born blind this time. He never used his eyes to look at the proper things. His eyes were always looking about at undesirable things, so he lost his sight this time around. Now he's purging his karma."

"Oh, that's all philosophy," said Parvati. "If you really wanted to, you could surely help him."

"Yes, honey, but I can't go against his karma. It's not in my hands. If you are destined for something by your own karma, even God can't help you. God's law is just to give you the result of your actions. Like a hard stone wall: if you go and lean on it, fine; if you go and bang your head, you'll certainly get a lump. Would you say then, 'Why did you give me a bump here?' The wall can't do anything. God is neutral like that. So I can't do anything against my divine law."

"Yes, that's all fine. But I'm really moved by his plight. My heart is aching. Please, do something."

As they were arguing, Parvati saw the blind man walking toward a deep pit. "Look! In another few yards he's going to fall into that pit. Please, either stop him or give him his vision. I can't bear the sight of it."

"Okay, dear, but you are the one who gives everything. You're the one who converts everything into energy. You're the mother. You have the kind heart. You have equal power, if not more, than I. You know that. You're the one to bless him. See, he's calling, 'Amba, Amba, Amba.'"

"No. You're just trying to get out of it. I can't do it without your permission. Even if I want to do it myself, I should get your counsel. Don't you know we're married? I don't want this to create any tension in our family later on. Unless you say so, I won't do it."

"Okay, honey. Let's compromise."

"Soon, soon! He's going to fall at any moment!"

"Don't worry. We can help him any second. Even if he's falling, we can save him. We have that capacity. Now he's saying, 'Amba, Shiva, Amba, Shiva,' both our names. Let's compromise. When he falls, if he says, 'Amba,' you go and catch him. If he says, 'Shiva,' I'll do it. All right?"

"That seems to be fair. Now, be ready."

Both of them carefully watched to see who would go to save the devotee. But as the man fell over he cried out, "Aieooooo." Neither "Amba" nor "Shiva." Shiva and Parvati just looked at each other.

"Are you 'Aieooooo'?"

"No. Are you?"

This is the test of a devotee. Prayers are like a mantra. When something is really disturbing, often people set aside their prayers and go to a lawyer or someone else for help. They never think of God.

Prayers must be sincere. They should come from the heart. Only then are they heard. That's why devotion must be totally one-pointed. If you say you trust God, then really trust God. Let anything happen; come what may, still you trust God. You have read the words of Tennyson: "More things are wrought by prayer alone than the world dreams of." Because in prayer you are meditating, you're one-pointed. You put everything into it. That's Yoga.

In these 12th and 13th *slokas* of Chapter Eight, Sri Krishna very clearly tells how to meditate, how deep you should go in and where to direct your *prana*. It should be upward. The breath should go up. It should seem to strike the top of the head. It's also important that the *Om* sound, or your own mantra, strike there at the top of the head, while the concentration of feeling should be at the heart.

14. It is easy to reach me, Arjuna, for the Yoga practitioner, steady in practice, who thinks of me constantly and has no greater attachments.

He says, "Yes, my dear Arjuna, whoever keeps me in his or her heart constantly, without getting distracted by anything else, always gets me easily."

It's a promise. The only problem is how to think of God constantly. The key is understanding what constantly thinking of God means. It's not that you just sit there in a corner and think of God constantly. Instead, involve yourself in daily activities feeling that all that you are doing is an offering to God. That's one way. Or feel that everything is being done by God through you as an instrument, which is a little higher level. With individual consciousness you might feel that you are doing things, but in the back of your mind you keep on knowing: "Without that higher consciousness, I can't do anything. So, I'm only an instrument being made to get involved in various activities." That's the best way to remember God constantly. Remember that higher consciousness.

Then you don't even think of offering everything to God. Such offerings come only after you think, "I did this. Now I'm offering it to You." You might think, "I made a delicious dinner, and I'm offering it to You." It's all right; you can do it that way. But it means there's still a little of your ego involved. The best way is to keep reminding yourself that even the capacity to make the dinner, to do anything, comes from God. Without God nothing moves. There is a beautiful saying in Sanskrit, and also in Tamil: "Without God not even an atom would move." That means even atomic energy, even the most minute movements in this cosmos happen only because of that Supreme

Consciousness. If that consciousness wasn't present, nothing would move. By remembering this truth always, we are remembering God always: "God, I'm not doing anything. You are making me do everything."

But if I say that without the Cosmic Consciousness things won't move, it leaves the impression that where there is no movement, no energy, there is no consciousness, as if it were a vacuum. Then how can it be called Cosmic Consciousness, Omnipresence? In reality even where there's no movement at all, there is consciousness, but it's not active. In a way, it's dormant, sleeping, potent. There's consciousness even in the inert particles of inanimate things. Only it's not functioning.

The great saint, Ramalinga Swamigal, used to sing, "Lord, You are feeding me; I am fed. You are making me sleep; I am sleeping. You are showing me; I am seeing. You are making me happy; I am happy. You are moving me; I am moving like a puppet. And not only me, the whole universe is Your puppet. Please grant me the boon to remember this truth always."

The advantage in remembering God this way is that it doesn't boost your ego. If you remember that everything you do is the act of God, then you won't be thinking, "I did it. That's my accomplishment." The "I, me, mine" gets completely annihilated, which is the very purpose behind Sri Krishna saying, "Continuously think of me, because I am the one doing everything." He doesn't mean, "I'm going to be happy because you think of me. And if you don't think of me, I'll feel terrible or I'll be disappointed." No, He's saying this for your benefit: "Know that I am the one working behind everything. I am the one who sent you here. I am the one who is going to get you back. And I am the one who is keeping you every minute. Even the air you're breathing goes in and out because of me. Remember this." That's the essence of this very beautiful *sloka*.

15. Those who come to me are great souls. They have so perfected themselves that it is unnecessary for them to be reborn again at this painful level of mortality.

16. Every creature in the universe returns to nothing, Arjuna, even Brahma, the creative function of myself. Only those who realize me transcend life and death.

17. Whoever understands the day of Brahma and the night of Brahma—each of which lasts literally for thousands of ages (*yugas*)—that person truly knows day and night.

18. As the cosmic day [of Brahma] dawns, all creation rises to manifestation out of the unmanifested state. And at the coming of night, all again merge into the oneness of the unmanifested.

19. Creation in all its infinite variety repeatedly arises, Arjuna, and naturally merges into oneness at the approach of night, then re-manifests as separate forms again at the dawn of another day.

20. Beyond these manifested and unmanifested states, there is yet another unmanifested, eternal reality which continues forever when all else appears to perish.

He talks of the manifested and unmanifested condition. One is dynamic; the other is potent, or unmanifested. In this *sloka*, Krishna is saying that even beyond the potent or unmanifested state, there is still much more. That means, mentally you can grasp something of the unmanifested state only to a certain degree, but don't think that's all. There's so very much more.

Not long ago, in the scientific world, a spaceship went up, took some pictures and came back. Then they saw that beyond this galaxy there are many more galaxies. For the first time they were able to prove it scientifically. Before this they were guessing. Now they have pictures of the new galaxy. It's appropriate for this *sloka*.

The unmanifested condition is a way of saying we can only grasp a limited amount because the mind is quite limited. Don't think that the unmanifested refers to just a handful more than that. There is so much more. In this *sloka* he's saying, "I am so vast, unending." Even when everything else dissolves, the essence, that eternal existence, never perishes.

What does it mean, "Everything else perishes while the eternal one never perishes?" At another place in the *Bhagavad Gita* he says, "What is, always is. What is not, never was." Any time something exists that means it is, it was, it will continue to be. Everything is immortal. Everything is non-perishing.

Chapter Eight

This book will never perish. The papers form into a book. If you tear the pages into small pieces, you don't call it a book anymore. The book becomes pieces of paper. Set fire and you get ash. In normal language we say, "The book was destroyed." But really you didn't destroy anything. Only the word "book" is no more. Only the form keeps changing.

That is the truth. The original essence is always there, you simply create a new form out of that, give it a new name. Once you dissolve that form, the name also goes. Form and name come and go, but the essence behind it is permanent. So you see the imperishable and the perishable, the indestructible and the destructible. What is perishable comes and goes. It is created and destroyed. In between, maybe it stays for a little while. So there's creation, preservation and destruction.

All these phenomena happen, in a way, superimposed on the essence. The whole universe is made of consciousness or energy, which takes various forms. To distinguish one form from another, you give different names. A mom and dad give birth to a few children. When the mother wants to call one of the children, can she say, "Child, come here?" How will the children know which one should come? She gives different names to identify them, just for convenience to call or pinpoint a child.

For our sake we give different names to different forms. But essentially they are all children. In the same way the entire cosmos is nothing but one vast consciousness—superconsciousness or super-energy. But if it just stays as energy, there's no fun in life. So the consciousness assumes various forms and various names for nice interaction. When we interact properly, we have fun. If we don't, we fight. Sometimes both are necessary.

The names and forms are perishable; the essence is imperishable. That's what this *sloka* is trying to teach us.

21. This unmanifested reality, which is infinite and indestructible, is my very nature; it is the supreme goal. The one who realizes this has come home, abides with me and need never again return to separateness.

22. You can experience this highest of states, Arjuna, with steady, one-pointed devotion to the Supreme One, in whom all creation exists and who pervades all beings.

23. Noble Arjuna, now I will tell you of the two paths of the soul at the time of physical death—one leads to rebirth, the other to liberation.

24. If yogis who know reality leave their bodies during the six months of the northern passage of the sun, which is the path of light, fire, day and the bright two weeks of the moon, they go directly to *Brahman* (absolute oneness).

25. If yogis leave the body during the six months of the southern passage of the sun, which is the path of haze, night and the dark two weeks of the moon, their souls pass through the light of the moon to physical rebirth.

26. These two paths of light and dark continue forever in this world. One leads to liberation; the other to rebirth.

27. Anyone who understands these two paths will never again be deluded. If you persevere in your study and practice of Yoga, Arjuna, you will attain this understanding.

28. Certainly there are many benefits from scriptural study, selfless service, accepting austerity and charitable giving. But if you practice Yoga and understand the light and the dark, you rise beyond all merit and attain the supreme and original Abode.

Thus ends the eighth discourse of the *Bhagavad Gita*, the science of Yoga, entitled: "Yoga of the Absolute Truth."

Chapter Nine

Yoga of the Regal Science and the Royal Secret

This chapter is the "Regal Science and the Royal Secret." That name is given to create an interest: "Oh, a secret! Please tell me." Anything secret creates curiosity. If I am talking to you, but I keep my fist closed the whole time, after a while you won't even be listening to me anymore. "Since his arrival he hasn't even opened his palm. What in the world is he holding?" It's a royal secret. That's why some scriptures are kept secretive also. You'll wonder, "What is it? I'd like to know, but I can't until I get initiated."

Many things are like that. In some cultures nobody sees the bride's face until she comes to the wedding hall. Then, for the first time, someone is going to see her face. Anything sacred should be a little secret, too. Sacred and secret go together, because anything that's valuable isn't simply dropped here and there. You can take out an imitation diamond anywhere and put it down, even on the bathroom sink, leave it there and go. But you don't leave a real diamond that easily, you don't even wear it every day, just on special occasions. You put on the ring, go to the party, come home, put the ring back in a velvet case and into the vault. Why? It has so much value. Something cheap is available on the road or on a park bench, but something of great value is sacred. The most valuable thing is the truth of wisdom. Such pearls are not to be just cast out to be trampled on. If there's something that has merit, keep it sacred. Even mantras are not just openly told to people. And that's why this whole chapter is called the "Regal Science and the Royal Secret;" it's royal. And the king doesn't come cheaply.

Now, should I talk about this openly?

1. **The blessed Lord said: Because your faith is not undermined by flaw-seeking, I will now reveal to you the most profound and secret knowledge. When you combine this knowledge with personal realization, you will be completely free of even the worst wrong-doing.**

2. This is the royal secret, the kingly science, the supreme purifier. Righteous and imperishable, it can be directly realized.

3. Those without sincere belief (*shraddha*) in this *dharma* will not realize who I am, Arjuna, and must therefore return to the mortal world of death after death,

4. Unmanifest, I pervade the entire universe. All creatures exist in me, yet I am not contained in all of them.

Sri Krishna talks about his true nature. He's saying, "Everything is My manifestation; everything came out of me, but there is still much more of me left. That's why I'm not contained by them. I am limitless. What you see is a fraction of me, a minute expression." Think of a potter who says, "Don't think all the clay I had has been used for these few pots. I haven't used up all the clay yet. I still have so much left over."

And, of course, we aren't able to see everything and then say, "Yes, I have seen Him." It's not possible. We just see one of His manifestations, sample that, and say, "By experiencing this small part, I understand the whole."

5. Now behold the mystery of my divine Yoga: All creatures in truth do not exist in me. Though I bring forth and support all that exists, I, myself, am not contained in them.

6. All the creation moving about abides in me, even as the great winds going here and there are actually resting in space (*akasha*).

7. At the end of a *kalpa* (cycle of eons), all creatures return to My *prakriti*. I generate them all again, Arjuna, at the beginning of the next *kalpa*.

8. By animating My *prakriti*, I repeatedly create the infinite varieties of all beings which are subject to the rule of my nature.

9. I myself am not affected by these actions [of my *prakriti*] because I witness it all with pure detachment.

10. Through My Presence, the elements of nature generate all that is stationary and all that moves. And thus, Arjuna, the world revolves.

Long before the scientists understood this, Sri Krishna said that the world revolves. And Sri Krishna explains that he is the cause. Yet at the same time he is a witness also. He is the cause of all the worlds and he is the witness of the manifested world, the one who keeps an eye on everything, an overseer. Normally the overseer is over it all and sees everything. He's not involved in it, though. If he were part of it, then he couldn't see it. But here, Sri Krishna is part of it, at the same time outside of it. He is in and out. Or he's overseeing himself.

Is it too much philosophy and theory? It's good to know that there's an overseer behind all this moving and unmoving nature. God is a big magnet—just there—while all the iron filings (representing nature) are running around. God is not moving, but makes every particle move.

We can copy God's example. Without losing our peace we watch ourselves running about. Just for fun. But in our cases, unfortunately, sometimes we forget that we are the pure, unaffected witness. Instead we identify with the part that's running about, the mind and body. And that causes all the problems. That's why it's good always to try to be the overseer of everything. Rise above everything and neutrally watch it.

11. Foolish people don't look beyond physical appearance. Thus they overlook my true nature which is the Lord of everything.

12. Thus deluded by self-preoccupation (ego), their knowledge is superficial; their lives are disastrously full of wrong-doing; and their works and hopes are all in vain.

13. But the great souls (mahatmas) have seen my true nature and take refuge therein. They realize I am the source of everything, and worship me with one-pointed devotion.

14. Because they strive for the highest with unflagging perseverance, their resolve is firm. They stick by their vows and humbly prostrate before me. Filled with devotion, they continuously sing my glory.

15. Others, on the path of jnana (wisdom), worship me by offering up the fruits of their knowledge. Thus they behold me both as the One and the many; wherever they look, they see my face.

16. In religious acts, I am the ritual itself, the sacrifice and the offering. I am the most potent herb and the sacred sound (mantra). I am also the pure offering, the fire into which it is offered, and he who receives it.

17. I am the father and mother of the whole universe, and also its most ancient grandfather. I am the one who gives you the results of your actions (karma). I am what is to be known. I am the purifier, the *Om* sound and I am the most sacred scriptures.

"The secret is that I am the father and the mother of the world. I am the dispenser and the grandfather. I am noble, the purifier. I am *Om*. I am also all the four *Vedas, Rig, Yajur, Sama, Atharva*. I am your father, mother, friend. I am a puppy. I am your Batman toy."

Don't always take it literally. The spirit of the *sloka* is: I am everything. I am father, mother, friend, brother, sister. If you call me enemy, okay, I am your enemy, too. Because I am the one who comes to you in various forms.

Rig, Yajur, Sama are the prime *Vedas*. "I am everything, all the elements. Fire, water, air, earth." It means "I am all the qualities, even a donkey, even a dog." All the qualities belong to God. God is the police; God is the thief. It's not just the most noble qualities that belong to God. If only noble qualities are God's qualities, who created the ignoble qualities? Where did they come from? Do they have a foundation without God? No. God is both the good and the evil. All the qualities are God's. Even in devotional scripture sometimes you see it says: "God in the form of lust, my salutations to You. God in the form of anger, my salutations to You. God in the form of the thief, my salutations to You." Even later in the *Gita*, he says: "Among gamblers, I am the superb gambler." Wherever you see excellence in any field, that excellence is the manifestation of God.

The less than excellent qualities are still God, but unmanifested. In the highest *Vedantic* understanding, God is called *Triguna Rahitam*, or beyond the three *gunas: sattva, rajas* and *tamas*. Everything is a combination of *sattva, rajas, tamas* and their intermixing. But God is above it all. *Sattva*—neutral. *Rajas*—might be loving. *Tamas*—hating, the opposite, like night and day. *Sattva* is the balance. While simultaneously expressing all these qualities, God is above all the qualities, yet not affected by any of them.

18. I am the goal. I uphold everything; I am the Lord, the witness, the abode, the refuge, the friend, the beginning and the end. I am the foundation, the infinite treasure house and the indestructible seed [of Creation].

19. I am heat. I am the one who holds back or sends rain. I am both immortality and death. I am also what is and what is not.

How is this possible? He says, "I am immortality and I am also death." Do you see the contradiction? "I am what is and also what is not." All this means that the one who is above these dualities expresses as the dualities. If God were only one-sided, there would never be anything else, because it's already conditioned. Think of a soft clay. Because it's completely unconditioned you can make it into whatever you want: toys, pottery, plates. But if it already had a form of its own, could you make it that way? No. Only the formless can be made into any form. Only the nameless can be given any names. Only the unconditioned can be brought into any condition.

That's why we say God's love is unconditional. It's not conditioned, so it all depends upon our approach. If we approach God lovingly, we get love. If we worship God as light, we get light and become enlightened. But if we say to the flame on the altar: "I don't like you here; I'll put you away in the attic near the roof," will the same light be blessing us? No, it will burn down your house. With fire, people cook and eat. With fire they also burn and kill. God's powers are neutral, like a zero. By breaking the circle, you can shape it into any letter or number that you want. All the numbers and letters are a broken zero. But originally, it was unbroken, beginningless, endless. That's the essence of this. That is the secret also: God is above all these things and it is God who manifests as all these things.

There was once a *siddha* (an accomplished yogi) who worshipped God as a young Goddess. He would sing, "Oh, my beloved Goddess, you came to me as a mother. Then you came to me as a wife. And then after some time, you came to me as a child, but it's always the same you." Normally we wouldn't say mother and wife are the same. But the accomplished ones don't see the difference between one and another. Both are God.

Of course, they have different functions to perform, different roles to play, according to our conceptions. But at the absolute level, it's just zero, neutral. By remembering this, we perceive God's names and forms, God's energy and God's expression as everything.

Two schoolchildren were having a conversation. One little girl said, "If you tell me the place where God is, I'll give you this mango." The other one smiled at her and said, "I'll give you two mangoes if you can tell me where God is not."

All seeking comes to an end when you experience this truth. Mere knowing of it is not enough. When they talk about the highest experience, the scriptures beautifully say, "Where to go, what to see, what to do." Really, you don't have to do anything. Sometimes by seeking it, you miss it. God says, "Not by doing, not by progeny, not by wealth, not by wisdom, not by education, not by scholarship; but just by renouncing everything, you experience this truth." Why? Because it's there already.

You have the pendant that you treasure on the necklace you forgot you are already wearing. Now you are seeking it everywhere. Then because it's so valuable and you lost it and can't find it anywhere, you cry and cry. At some point you go in front of the bathroom sink to wipe away all your tears, and looking in the mirror you discover: "My goodness, I've had it always. I have it now." Then you laugh at all your seeking. "Look at that. I've had it all the while."

A gentleman in Hong Kong once sang a beautiful song to me. "Where are you looking for God? In the temple, on the hilltop, in the sea? In the synagogue, in the church or in the scriptures? Why are you looking about? Are you insane, searching for God? The very searcher is God."

20. Those who sincerely perform religious rituals, continually sacrifice for me and take *soma* (a plant whose juice is used in *Vedic* sacrifices), in time will see their hearts purified and their lives free of the last taint of wrongdoing. They naturally rise to the high realms of the gods where they enjoy the pleasures of heaven.

21. After they spend their merits to fully experience the joys of heaven, they must return to this world again. Though they may

have been meticulous in religious observances, if they still want something, they are caught in the endless chain of personal desires, and thus must continue to take birth after birth.

22. However, I provide everything for those who want me above everything else, and constantly think of me. I add to what they already have and comfort them with absolute security.

What a great promise Sri Krishna makes. The last part is very pleasing to the ear, isn't it? God provides everything for you and protects you. When? Only when you worship God alone, thinking of nothing else. They call it *ananya bhakti*, devotion toward nothing other than this, totally one-pointed devotion. It's very hard to achieve, but worth it.

He says, "Want me more than anything else." That means you are worshipping your own peace, the true Self in you. But how can you do this? By constantly remembering, "This is the only thing that will save me, and keep me happy always. There's no other way." So keep an eye on it. Your own peace. Whatever you do, see that you are still maintaining your peace even as you do it. The moment you feel you're forgetting the peace or it's slipping away, immediately say: "No, I care more for my peace than anything else. Even if you could give me the whole world in place of my peace, I wouldn't trade that. I just want peace and peace alone. I'm worshipping my peace."

What is worship? You want to keep with you what you love the most. And that's your beloved God. You won't trade that. Anybody who trades his or her peace for anything else in life is foolish. Only a fool would trade the eyes for a beautiful work of art. Without your eyes how can you appreciate it?

That's why Sri Krishna says, "Worship me, follow me. I am the only one." Most of the scriptures say, "I am the only one. This is the only way." When it says, "Jesus is the only way," what does it mean? Peace is the only way. Jesus is another name for peace. Krishna is another name for peace. Jehovah is another name for peace. Buddha is another name for peace. When we forget what it means and only stick to the name, we fight even in the name of God.

Constantly ask, "Will this disturb my peace? Am I selling my peace to get this?" Sometimes you seem to be keeping your peace and still you're getting things. That means you had no expectations to receive anything. It's just coming to you. When you really go after something hoping that it will make you happy by getting it, you have already traded away your peace. Don't reach out to get something. If it just comes, then you say, "Okay, you've come. Fine." But you don't depend on that. This is what he means when he says, "Want me above everything else, and constantly think of me. Then I will give you more and still preserve your peace."

23. Even those devotees who are endowed with *shraddha*, true faith, using methods not prescribed in scripture, nevertheless are worshipping me, Arjuna.

There is an appropriate order for worshipping and doing the rituals given in scripture. Of course, there are people who don't know any of those things, and don't even know any scripture. An example is the Saint Kannappar, who, when he was a youth, was still known as Tinnappar, which means "hefty boy." As a child he was quite strong and solid, so his father called him Tinnappar. He grew up to become a hunter.

One day, he went hunting with two friends. At one point they were chasing a wild boar. Even as they aimed their arrows, the boar ran up and over a hill. Pursuing the animal they, too, went over this unfamiliar hill and saw a small shed. The animal seemed to have led them there. "What is this?" they wondered. "Who is inside?"

Tinnappar opened the shed and saw a *Shivalingam* there. "Look, this is a *Shivalingam*," said Tinnappar. "People worship this." Immediately past *samskaras* came forward in his mind. (*Samskaras* in Sanskrit means mental impressions or habits of mind; probably the saint was much devoted to Lord Shiva in a past lifetime.)

His friends continued on the hunt. But Tinnappar became madly attached to the *Shivalingam* and cried out, "My dear Lord, you are all alone here. Who takes care of You? Who feeds You? Nobody has bathed You, I can see. And You must be terribly hungry." See—all his past devotion rose to the surface. "Wait, wait," he said. "I'll give You a bath and some nice food."

He ran all the way to the bottom of the hill, searched for a big, juicy pig, killed it and began to barbecue it. As he roasted the flesh, he kept tasting it to see whether it was cooked well enough or not. Then he threw away the parts that were not good. He put the choicest sections on a big banana leaf, and started up the hill.

As he was holding the leaf carrying the offering, he remembered he should first bathe the deity before offering food. He didn't have any vessel for carrying the water. "What can I do?" he wondered. Then an idea came. He ran to the source of water there, carefully rinsed his mouth, then took a great mouthful of water, held it inside and began running up the hillside with the pork in hand, water in the mouth, back to the altar.

"God, God," he tried to call with the water in his mouth. Then he leaned toward the *Shivalingam* and poured the water from his mouth over the deity. In that way he gave a nice bath and then placed the pork on the altar.

Then he became very, very happy. He felt that he had fed God. He danced around and around in joy. "Every day I'll come and do this," he promised. "You won't be alone in the future. I'll be back tomorrow." And he went down the hill.

Tinnappar didn't know that on the other side of the big hill there was a village. And in the village lived a devoted *brahmin* priest who came every day to this hidden altar, worshipped there and left again. The next morning, very early, the priest arose, bathed and slipped away to the small hidden temple. When he arrived he saw the pork there and was stunned. "What devil is coming here and desecrating the temple like this?" he wondered. "My Lord, I don't know what to do. Who would dare try to pollute You this way?"

Disgusted and repulsed, he began to clean everything. He got fresh water to purify and sanctify everything. He came back and did a special, much longer purification *puja*, or worship, as prescribed in the scriptures (which he knew very well), offered flowers and said, "Please forgive me for letting this happen. I hope it won't happen again. Some vandals must have come here and done this."

Thus he worshipped with great sincerity and devotion. Then he returned to his village.

By noon, Tinnappar returned, saw the flowers and said, "My Lord, someone has only left You some flowers. They didn't give You anything to eat." (In fact, the priests do offer delicacies at the altar, but after worshipping usually they take it all home, because they know God isn't going to eat it physically.) But Tinnappar thought, "You must be really hungry." This time he was all ready with the pork. Again he poured water from his mouth to bathe the Lord and offered the pork before the *Shivalingam*. In his devotion he became so happy he just danced and jumped about in great joy.

Each day Tinnappar worshipped God in this fashion. And the next morning, Shivagocharya the *brahmin* discovered the temple "desecrated" again. He began to despair. At night he couldn't sleep. One night he only fell asleep as dawn broke. Then God appeared in his dream. "Don't worry, Shivagocharya," said the Lord. "You are a great devotee; but there is an even greater devotee worshipping me. He's a hunter. He doesn't know anything about fresh fruits and vegetables. All he knows to give is pork. He knows no rituals either, but I love his worship. I admire his faith and devotion. Tomorrow after your own worship, hide there and you will see true devotion."

Later that day after his own worship was finished, Shivagocharya was hiding and watching the small shrine. He saw the hunter arrive, pour water from his mouth and put the roast pork down before the altar. Then Tinnappar began to dance with joy. But as he was dancing, Tinnappar noticed something. In his devotion he didn't see the *Shivalingam* as a stone. Instead he saw God in human form. And as he looked he suddenly could see that one of the eyes of God was bleeding. Tinnappar stopped dancing. "God, what happened? You're bleeding. Did someone hurt You? What can I do? Wait, please! I'll bring some herbs."

He ran down the hill and picked some healing herbs, ran back, squeezed them and applied them on the bleeding eye. But the bleeding didn't stop. Tinnappar started to cry. He was completely out of his mind. He didn't know what to do. Then, suddenly, he knew.

"I know! An eye for an eye. That will take care of it," said the hunter. "You just wait, my Lord." From his quiver he took a sharp arrow. He applied the point of the arrow to the outside corner of his own eye, quickly pushed the arrow in and popped his own eye out of the socket into his hand.

Immediately he put that on the Lord's bleeding eye. The moment he took his hand away the bleeding stopped. He became so happy he didn't even think for a second about his own bleeding or the loss of his own eye. He danced around, jumping in joy for half an hour. "Oh Lord, oh my Lord! I'm so glad that this eye has helped You see," he cried happily as he danced about.

Afterward, he was ready to leave the deity, but to his surprise he saw that the Lord's other eye was bleeding. "My God, what has happened to You? Don't worry, I know the remedy now. I have one more eye for You."

Tinnappar drew the arrow out again and was about to push out his other eye, when he had a thought: "If I take this eye out also, I won't be able to see where to put the eye of God, because I won't have any eyes to see. Ah, wait, I can trace my way." He stood squarely before the Lord, lifted one leg high and put his foot on God's cheek.

Standing that way on one leg, Tinnappar said, "Now I can easily find my way to God's eye and put mine there." So he stood there and began to work out his remaining eye with the arrow head.

Now all the while Shivagocharya had been watching. When Tinnappar plucked out his first eye, the priest began to shake uncontrollably. "My God, what devotion," he said to himself. But when Tinnappar began to pull out his other eye, Shivagocharya literally fainted, and God appeared to him.

At the same moment, God appeared to the hunter in more grandeur than ever before, and called him Kannappar, which means the eye-fixer. "Kannappar, stop," said the Lord. I'm thoroughly satisfied with your devotion. I wouldn't have allowed you to go through this pain if not for this poor man who is also a devotee. You come every day to worship with true devotion. Certainly you will reach me." Kannappar's eyes were given back to him, and his sight returned—clearer than ever.

This is not just a story. There were sixty great Shaiva saints. Kannappar was one, a living person. He didn't know the procedures prescribed by scriptures, but with such pure devotion, there's no wrong method.

24. In truth, I am the object of all worship and the one who enjoys sacrifice and ritual. But until the worshipper sees me as I am, he must continually take rebirth,

25. Those who worship the *devas* go to the *devas*. Those who most revere their ancestors will become united with them. Those most fascinated with spirits will go to that level. But my devotees come to me.

26. Whatever is offered to me with true devotion—if only a leaf, a flower, a fruit or a sip of water—I accept it because it is given with love.

God doesn't worry about your pomp and show—golden chariots and golden plates, dozens of apples and oranges. Even one simple banana is fine. God is not worried about what you're bringing there, but with what feeling you bring it. If you just want to show off your position and wealth, God will know that also.

It is your pure devotion that God is accepting, even if you simply offer a handful of water or a leaf. God doesn't worry about your ingredients. Whether you come with a big golden plate or freshly picked flower, it doesn't matter. Once, a child found a withered flower near my house. It had been taken from a vase and dropped outside. The little child picked one up. "Swamiji, I brought you a flower." How sweet that was. Such things you cannot forget. You can't say, "One withered flower that we already threw out. What nonsense is this! How dare you bring it to me?" The love makes it something beautiful.

It's the heart behind the offering. People donated hundreds of thousands of rupees to Mahatma Gandhi for his project. But one day when his train stopped at a station and many thousands of people flocked to see him, an old lady there was trying to elbow her way through the crowd to come close to Gandhi. He noticed her and said, "Please, make way. Let that mother come close to me."

She came closer. "Oh, Babaji," she called, "Please wait a little." She opened her upper cloth and there was a bundle tied in a knot. She untied the knot. There was another knot. Knot after knot she untied. Finally there was a little bundle knotted. At last she untied it. There were a few copper pennies.

She said, "Babaji (dearest papa), I brought it for you. Please accept this."

Tears streamed from his eyes. He came down and embraced that lady. "With this I can perform miracles," he said. "Thank you, Mother."

It's not the amount or the elegance of gifts. It's the heart that God looks for. The same with your practices—chanting, devotion, mantras. How much of your heart is really there? What good if it's heartless? You can do hours and hours of meditation or mantra repetition, but in those thousands of times, if just once your real heart is into it, that's enough.

Here is a *sloka* I quote very often.

> **27. Whatever you do, Arjuna, make that an offering. Whether it's eating, sacrificing yourself, giving help or even your suffering (*tapas*), offer it to me.**

Then it's Yoga. It becomes worship. *Puja* or worship need not be done only at the altar. Whatever you do—even your eating—becomes worship if you do it with that feeling.

How can your eating become an offering of worship? Who's in the stomach digesting your food? In this very *Gita*, Sri Krishna says, "I'm the digestive fire in your stomach. So you're only satisfying me." Don't think that you're eating for your sake. See, you're doing this *yajna*, this sacred sacrifice of offering the food into the fire in the stomach. The food goes into this divine fire.

When you take a shower, think, "I'm washing God's temple." Everything becomes worship then. You don't need to think, "I'm just washing my bundle of flesh and bones." Instead say: "I'm washing God's temple. I'm dressing God's temple. God is seated here inside me, I'm feeding God." When you sleep, think: "I'm putting God to sleep." Then every act becomes *puja*. Your very life becomes an offering.

Doing things for others without expecting anything back is a form of worship. That's Karma Yoga. Sometimes people ask me, "When I go to work and get my own salary, how can I call it Karma Yoga?" It can be. What are you going to do with your salary? You are eating; you have clothing; you have a house to live in. The real question is why do you want to eat? Why do you want to dress? Why do you want a house? Why do you even want to live? To serve others. If you're living to serve others, then you need to eat. How can you serve without eating? You have to fill up the tank so that the car will go. You have to keep the engine greased and the car washed. You have to have a garage for the car. Can you do that without the salary? With that money you equip yourself with enough energy to give the energy back to others.

Then, even your eating, sleeping, drinking become Karma Yoga because you do it with the intention, "I'm only keeping myself fit to serve others. If I'm not going to serve others, I don't need to eat; I don't need to sleep; I don't need to have a house; I don't even need to live."

Live to serve others. With that attitude then if your salary isn't enough for day-to-day expenses, you can even demand a raise. "Boss, I'm serving you. But this money isn't enough. My family isn't provided for. You must give me more money." You can even demand more money and still be a *karma yogi*. Why? That money is not for your personal pleasures; it's not just to satisfy your senses. You're not overindulging in anything. You're just taking good care of yourself and others under your care. That's also part of your duty. With the proper attitude, even with the raise in pay, you can't say you are personally getting something for your work. It's all for others. Then the entire life becomes Karma Yoga. If you are living for the sake of everybody, serving God and the creation every minute with every breath, you are worshipping constantly. Your work has become worship and every act is a part of that worship.

> 28. In this way you free yourself from the bondage of karma and its good or bad results. Through this Yoga, you thus achieve true renunciation (*sannyas*) [of personal desires] and come to me in a state of liberation.

When he speaks of *sannyas* here he doesn't mean only monks who have taken vows of renunciation. Everybody should ultimately become so renounced. It means that you should renounce desire for the results of your actions, then perform them. Perform everything as your duty. Then you are a *sannyasi*, wherever you are. Always live for others, do for others, think of others. Automatically your needs will be fulfilled. You don't have to worry about it at all because you are living for others.

But don't expect that the minute you decide to renounce, everybody will immediately take care of you. No. You have to prove your sincerity first.

During my earlier years as a monk, I went about without anything in the hand—no money, nothing at all. I also made a vow not to ask anything from anybody. *You have no money to buy, no mouth to ask. If God wants you to have something, let God give it to you,* I told myself.

During the first few weeks I almost starved. But I said, "It doesn't matter. That's none of my business. If You want me to starve and die, You lose a boy. It's not my loss. If You want me to do some of Your work, You must fuel me. Why should I worry about these things?"

Then suddenly things started changing the other way. Wherever I went, there was an abundance of food around me. Piles and piles of fruit. Even at the railway platforms if I just sat there, from nowhere people came with trays filled with fruits. They put them down in front of me, so I would take some and distribute the rest to others: "Come on, everybody eat." Sometimes it even delayed the train. I was sitting at Palani Temple one day and a man literally brought a big bundle of coins, opened it and poured the coins over my head as an offering. I felt that God had put the money there and would distribute it as God wished. So I simply got up, walked down the hill, and left the money behind.

29. I am the same toward all beings. Before me, no one is hateful and no one is more or less cherished. However, those who lovingly worship me will realize that they are actually part of me and I live in them.

"By devotion you get more of me," says Sri Krishna. "Not that I choose to give more or that I choose not to give." It's like tuning. When you tune your radio well, you get better reception. If you don't tune your set well you might get all kinds of atmospheric disturbance. Then you blame the transmitting station, "Look at that! To my set God sends all this static but to yours God sends nice music. What kind of transmission is that?" You can also blame God, if you want. But if you're getting atmospheric disturbance, it means you haven't tuned in well.

30. Even if the worst sinners devote their lives to me with firm resolve, they will be transformed into saints.

How is it possible? If you have full devotion to God, that devotion itself will slowly take you away from a vicious life. We say you don't need to rise beyond all your undesirable habits before coming to Yoga. Just get involved with Yoga, and stick to that without fail. Then all those habits will drop away from you. If you are already a good *yogi* and *jnani* (full of wisdom), you don't even need to worship. It's a sinful person who should worship. And if that person worships well, their sins will be burned out.

It's the same point I made with some orthodox people in India and Sri Lanka who wouldn't allow the untouchables into their temples. We used to gather the untouchable people and talk to the temple authorities to make them open up the temples. In one town where there were many such orthodox people, they argued, "Why should God create untouchables? It means they should wait to take another birth before they can come into the temple. They can't come now. They're sinful people."

"Okay, are you free from sin?" I asked.

"Sure, we are great devotees. We are clean people, both physically and mentally. So we have a right to go into the temple."

I see. Now tell me, suppose there is a laundry. Which type of clothing goes there? Clean or unclean? You yourself say that God cleans everything. If you are already clean and you go to the temple, what is there for God to work on? You don't need the temple. It is they who need the temple. You stay out and let them go in.

"In your prayers, I hear you say, 'God, You are the one who is going to clean all the filthy matter from this heart and make me as pure as Shiva.' That is how you pray. So, if you are already pure, you are already Shiva. Why should you go to the temple? Let those other people go and get cleaned, you stay away."

Somehow we won with that argument.

Never think, "I'm unfit. I'm sinful and unworthy." If you are unworthy, then worship more, practice more Yoga. This opportunity is for everyone. Not even one person anywhere is an outcast. In a way a mother is more concerned with a sick child than with a healthy child. So God really looks for the unclean people who want to be pure in heart.

Now Sri Krishna concludes:

> **31. For soon, he or she becomes a person of *dharma* (righteousness) and discovers lasting peace. This is certain, Arjuna: my devotee cannot be harmed.**

What a guarantee he gives!

> **32. No matter your birth, race, gender or caste—even if you are scorned by others—if you take refuge in me, then certainly you will attain the supreme goal.**

Once a wonderful Catholic sister took me to a Trappist monastery to give a talk to the brother monks. But she wasn't allowed to come in. She had to stay outside while they received me. I was looking for a good opportunity to ask them about this. As they took me into the courtyard, there I saw a beautiful garden. In the middle of the garden there was a nice pedestal; and on the pedestal was a very old statue of Mother Mary.

"Sixteenth century statue," they said and showed it proudly.

I went to the Mother and paid my loving respects. Then I said, "Father, how could She come in here?"

"What do you mean?" he asked. "Don't you see, She's a woman!"

"Swamiji, don't tease us. I don't understand."

"Father, a woman brought me; you kept her out. But here is a woman you're adoring."

They looked at each other. "Swamiji, we understand what you mean. We hesitate to break the traditional pattern."

"Father, it has to be done one day or another. Why not today?"

Immediately they went into another room and had a board meeting. Within fifteen minutes they came back, "Swamiji, you won. We've already sent a Father to go and bring the Sister. She will come and attend your talk. But please don't force us to take her to our living quarters."

"There's no need for her to come to your living section. But this is a public place where I'm giving a talk. Actually, she is the one who invited me. Naturally she'd appreciate an opportunity to hear me."

Immediately the Father went to the door and invited the Sister to come in.

"What do you mean by this? Do you really want me to come in?"

"Yes, Sister."

"What a miracle. I think the Swami must have done something here."

For the first time in the Trappist monastery, a lady walked in.

> 33. Even the saintly kings and holy sages through devotion seek this very goal. Therefore, if you find yourself in this transient world of suffering, just turn to me.

Now an important *sloka*. He tells how to pray to God:

> 34. Think of me constantly; devote your life to me; offer all your actions to me, and bow down and surrender before me. Thus you become steady on your path to the supreme goal, and come unto me.

Your mind is to be fixed on God; your heart devoted, your works offered up; your ego bows down. See: body, mind, heart, ego—everything toward one goal.

Thus ends the ninth discourse of the *Bhagavad Gita*, the science of Yoga, entitled: "Yoga of the Regal Science and the Royal Secret."

Chapter Ten

Yoga of the Divine Manifestations

The tenth chapter is Vibhuti Yoga. *Vibhuti* means the Divine Manifestations, the same name connected with holy ash. In South India when holy ash is given, that ash is called *vibhuti*. You may wonder why they call the ash *vibhuti*. Is there a manifestation of the divine in the holy ash? To know that we should know what is meant by *vibhuti*, or how the holy ash is made.

Holy ash is made from cow dung. But even that dirt can become holy when it's completely burned. Cow dung is burned in an airtight chamber. When it's fully burned, it becomes pure, white ash. Immediately it gets the name, *vibhuti*.

So is there anything we should discard as dirty? Nothing is so low. If it's processed properly, even the dirtiest matter becomes the holiest of holies.

Even in dirt there is already holiness hidden. By burning out what isn't necessary you bring out the holiness, or the pure, Divine Consciousness. And that's *vibhuti*, the manifestation of the divine. In this chapter, Sri Krishna shows how the Divinity is manifested in everything.

1. The blessed Lord said: If you listen further, mighty Arjuna, I will continue my supreme teachings to benefit and delight you.

2. Not even the gods or holy sages (*rishis*) know my origin. The truth is that I am the source of the gods and the sages.

3. Among all people, those who recognize me as the unborn and beginningless lord of everything, know the truth and free themselves from wrongdoing.

4. Out of me arise the qualities of discernment (*buddhi*), wisdom (*jnana*) freedom from delusion, forgiveness, truth (*satya*) self-control, equanimity, pleasure and pain, birth and death, fear and also fearlessness (*abhaya*).

5. Also: non-injury (*ahimsa*), tranquility, contentment, austerity (*tapas*) generosity (*danam*), as well as honor and dishonor. Throughout the creation, all these different qualities come solely from me.

This means whether something is good or bad, painful or pleasant, God is the source. Without God, nothing can be. How can you even say something is bad or good? Nothing is bad if you use it for the proper purpose.

6. The seven great sages and the four ancient founders of humanity (*manus*) were formed in my mind, and from me received their vitality. The rest of the world's creatures subsequently evolved from them.

What is meant by the seven *rishis* and the four *manus*? They have various names with esoteric aspects. The seven *rishis* represent the seven planes of consciousness. Consciousness functions at seven different levels in this creation. This was long ago described by a sage who was addressing God and said, "Lord, I was in all those different levels and gradually evolved to the level of a human being. Please help me to go further and not backward." There are seven levels of consciousness in the creation. At the highest level are the *devas*, the gods. (It might surprise you to find that even the *devas* are part of the creation, which means they are not the Absolute Supreme Godhead. They also have different levels; there are higher and lower level gods.)

Number two is the human level. Three, the animals. Four, the birds. Five, the reptiles. Six, aquatic creatures. Seven, immobile things which are inanimate, stationary.

The creation is divided into the mobile and the immobile. Certain life forms have mobility. Others, such as trees, plants, rocks, metals, have immobility. They don't move by themselves—at least for the normal eye. But isn't it surprising that even thousands of years ago they recognized consciousness in the immobile things also. That's why immobile is one of the seven categories.

I have described it from the upper level down. But according to Darwin's theory, it can be seen from the lower level moving up. However, according to ancient Hindu scriptures, they are not intrinsically different. All are created equally; there is no superiority or inferiority. That's the difference between Darwin's theory and this understanding. All the *sapta rishis*, or great sages, who were in charge of creating various levels of creatures at various levels of consciousness, created them all simultaneously, not one after the other. It's a misunderstanding for the human being to look down on the so-called underdeveloped beasts, birds, plants and rocks. To say all are created the same way means the same consciousness pervades everywhere, at all the various levels.

Now the *manus*. *Manu* means law-giver. They decide who should do what, and how. Sometimes it's said that there are four *manus* who arrange the order of the creation. Don't misunderstand. They are all just different aspects of the one absolute God. They are not created like the rest. This means one and the same consciousness is functioning on various levels to create and give order to the different levels of creation. That's what Krishna is trying to explain in this *sloka*.

> 7. **Whoever truly understands my power and the glory of my many continuing manifestations is certainly established in unshakable Yoga (communion with the Infinite).**

> 8. **I am the source of everything. The wise understand this, and worship me with love.**

> 9. **Their minds always think of me. [Therefore] their lives are devoted to me; they have even dedicated their life-energy to me. When they talk, they always speak of me. Thus uplifting one another, they are ever content and joyful.**

> 10. **There are some who are sincerely devoted and worship me simply out of love. I bequeath them Buddhi Yoga, and through this they come to me.**

It's all Krishna's words. See—even to get Buddhi Yoga we need help from God. We can't even discriminate by ourselves. But we can acquire that Yoga of discrimination by real devotion, which means functioning with that devotional attitude. Worship isn't always limited to going to an altar, offering something and praying. The real meaning of worship is seeing God in everything. True devotion to God is doing something with the feeling that you are ultimately using and approaching the same consciousness, which is taking expression in different forms.

If we see God in everything, that implies containers or vessels full of that consciousness, as if the container itself might not be made of the same consciousness. But there's not even a single spot without that consciousness. It's all one: the contained is consciousness; the container is also consciousness. To feel and see everything as the expression of that consciousness is true devotion. Devotion is not simply prostrating and adoring and giving beautiful words of love. Devotion in daily life is seeing that everything is a manifestation of God. Devotion means seeing that consciousness, the same God in everything, or more accurately, as everything. Then however you relate with that aspect or manifestation, it becomes your worship. Your action or service is not for somebody else, but for the one consciousness. Devotion and worship go together.

That can happen every minute of our lives through everything we do. As that happens, automatically the Yoga of discrimination dawns. First, we do certain things to acquire a discriminating capacity—traditional devotion and worship. When you have *viveka* (discrimination), true devotion arises. Discrimination means you can distinguish between the real and unreal, the permanent and the impermanent. Actually, nothing is unreal. We may think some things are unreal or impermanent. Sometimes it seems to be a dilemma: remembering the ultimate essence while functioning in regular, worldly life.

All the different names and forms are temporarily given to modifications of the essential one consciousness, which is permanent. But, in truth, there really are no modifications. The original consciousness just appears to change. Water appears to be a wave. But the wave after all is nothing but water. If we see the wave only as a wave, and not as water also, then it's an illusion. We should discriminate: "Yes, I see it as a wave. Because it rises up, I give the name, wave; but it's the same water rising up." That's discrimination—seeing the same essence behind all the names and forms. We all may sit together using different names, appearing in different forms. This is good for functioning on the worldly level. But even as we notice the differences, even while doing different things, at the back of the mind we should be seeing it all as one consciousness: *Why it's all nothing but the same, expressing itself differently.*

But when everything is seen as only the same consciousness, then there is no fun in life. So for the sake of fun and play, just to delight us, we keep the changes and also see the superficial differences. But know that the changes are only there so we can play. If it goes a little beyond playing and we begin to fight, then we should stop and realize, "No, this is all nonsense. Ultimately we're one and the same." That stops the fighting. If we are carried away seeing the differences, we forget the basic truth.

This is discrimination, Buddhi Yoga. Always keep this in mind: essentially all is the same. Whether it's a piece of rock or a plant, a dog, a cat, a worm or a human being, we are all simply the same essence. Yes, it looks a little different, but the difference is really nonsense. If you want to make sense, there is only this essence. Duality is non-sense. Non-duality is true sense. See the essence and play with the nonsense. Then life makes sense: *viveka*.

Please keep this view always—particularly when you're getting into hot water, or a tough argument. At that point, use discrimination: "Oh, it's all nonsense! Essentially we're all one and the same. Why should we fight?" We can save ourselves with Buddhi Yoga, the Yoga of discrimination. This type of Yoga is not something to be practiced just in the morning or evening, but always! Let it become a steady part of your life.

How does Buddhi Yoga benefit devotees? Sri Krishna answers:

11. Because I am compassionate, I dwell in your heart, and from there remove the darkness of ignorance with the great light of wisdom.

Buddhi Yoga is the light of wisdom. When that insightful discrimination is present, there's no room for any darkness or ignorance in life, no problems. Some *Gita* commentators beautifully elaborated on the light or lamp of wisdom which is fueled by the oil of contentment. Its container is discrimination. Once you have discrimination, automatically you gain contentment, which is the oil. Discrimination is the container for contentment. And, of course, a lamp should have clean air to burn well. Foul air puts out the flame. That purity is the air of meditation, which should always be present so the flame will burn without interruption.

Chapter Ten

And the oil? *Brahmacharya,* which can be understood from two different levels. Awareness of the higher Self is the literal meaning of *brahmacharya.* But this can be practiced on the physical level also. That higher awareness is impossible without moderation in life. By conserving much *prana,* or vital energy, in the liquid form, awareness becomes keener; the mental capacity to remember is heightened. Often we get good ideas, but they slip by. They're not retained because there's no retention of seminal energy, the liquid form of *prana.* That's why celibacy is associated with *brahmacharya,* which may be translated either as celibacy or awareness of the true Self.

There is a beautiful connection between body and mind. Physical and mental are linked, bonded, fused, even welded together with the flux of liquid *prana.* When you want to fuse one piece of metal to another piece, you preheat them. Still they won't weld together without that flux. Those who know the welding process understand that. You need flux. It is this powerful, beautiful liquid energy that is the flux that fuses physical and mental, helping you retain the awareness.

You may often reach that higher awareness, but not be able to retain it. It slips away. The mind is weak. It doesn't have the capacity to hold that higher awareness. To put it plainly, the mind loses its strength by excessive sexual activity. That's why spiritual seekers who sincerely want to develop their awareness should conserve vital energy.

It need not be 100 percent. Of course, you don't expect a householder to live like that. But preserve as much as possible. Have limitation in your physical life. The maximum amount of *prana* is lost in the physical act of sex. But there are many other ways of losing *prana,* even by simply overeating or oversleeping; doing anything immoderately; overindulgence; talking too much; laughing too much; running too much. Anything in excess takes away your vital energy. Then both mind and body weaken.

Don't think the person is strong if you see some well-formed muscles. You may have all muscle, but one irritating word is enough to make you mad. Strong physically but mentally, a weakling. Call him a fool, and he'll go mad for a week. Is that strength? True strength is maintained by saving *prana* in every form to keep the awareness of the higher Self, which is the oil. If the oil runs out, there's no flame.

And of course there is a beautiful niche where you can always keep the lamp burning. That niche is your own heart. So let the lamp continue to burn and there will never be darkness in your life. All the benefit comes with Buddhi Yoga. It all begins with true devotion and worship in a higher sense, as service to the one essence. Work is worship. Let everything be worship.

12. Then Arjuna said: You are the supreme *Brahman* (Absolute One), the supreme Abode and the supreme Purifier. You are the eternal and divine *Purusha* (absolute Self or Consciousness). You are beginningless and your Presence is everywhere.

13. All the most exalted sages and seers have thus acclaimed you— including Narada, sage of the *devas*, Asita, Devala and Vyasa. And now you have also revealed this to me.

14. O Krishna, now I know that everything you have said to me is absolutely so. Neither the most powerful demons nor even the *devas* themselves, my Lord, fully grasp the truth of you.

15. You, and only you, know who and what you are, O Purushottama, master of the universe, source and lord of all.

16. Won't you please now, and without reserve, speak of your divine manifestations (*vibhuti*), in which you abide and through which you pervade all that is.

17. O great master of Yoga, how should I meditate to realize you? Which of your manifestations, my lord, should I hold before me?

18. Krishna, please tell me again—in detail—of your Yoga; I cannot seem to hear enough. Your words are the nectar of my life.

19. The blessed Lord replied: All right, Arjuna. I will now tell you of my divine manifestations, but only the most evident, because really there is no end to them.

20. I am the true Self in the heart of all creatures, Arjuna. I am their beginning, their middle and also their end.

21. I am Vishnu (the all-encompassing light) of the twelve gods of light (*adityas*). Of all radiant lights, I am the effulgent sun. I am also Marichi, lord of the wind and storm powers.

22. I am the *Sama Veda* of the *Vedas* (ancient scriptures). I am Vasava, leader of the *devas*. Of all your senses, I am the mind; and in living creatures, I am Consciousness.

This means that wherever you see something extraordinary, you are able to perceive God's Presence. It's not that God is absent from anything. God is present in everything. But in some places, you more readily see the brilliance. The same sun reflects on mirrors, but doesn't reflect on other things. This doesn't mean those other things don't have sunlight; they do. But there are certain places where everything excels.

Among Hindu scriptures there are four *Vedas*. Of those four, the *Sama Veda* is the most musical. It is said that whether you know its meaning or not, simply by listening to the *Sama Veda*, you are elevated. Snakes don't understand what you play, but they are enchanted by the music. The same with cows and plants. So it is with the *Sama Veda*. Whether you know it or not, simply by hearing, its musical vibration alone will elevate you. That's why Sri Krishna says, "I am more visible in *Sama Veda*." And, of course, he can be most easily seen through Vasava or Indra, lord of the *devas*.

23. I am Shankar (who does good) of all dispellers of ignorance (*rudras*). I am the lord of wealth, Kubera, of all nature spirits (*yakshas* and *rakshasas*). I am Pavaka, the purifying fire among the radiant spirits (*vasus*). And I am Meru of all the mountains.

24. Among priests, Arjuna, I am the divine priest Brihaspati (lord of devotion). Of military leaders, I am Skanda (god of war), and of bodies of water, I am the vast ocean.

Sri Krishna is explaining that wherever there is excellence, he can be seen.

25. Of all the great *rishis* (sages), I am Bhrigu. Of all words, I am the sound of *Om*. Of all sacrificial offerings, I am *japa* (mantra repetition). And of all that is immovable, I am the Himalayas.

He gives the excellent things as his special representations. This doesn't mean that all the other things are separate from God. But in the excellent things, you can see God more clearly.

Among all the mantras, *Om* is the superior one. And among all offerings *japa* (mantra repetition) is best.

That's why mantra *japa* (repeating a mantra) is the simplest and best practice for concentration. It can be practiced by anybody and everybody without any restriction. You don't need a special time. You don't need to carry anything with you, because your mantra is always in your heart. In the midst of work or when you drive, you can repeat it. When you cook, you can keep the mantra going. When you chew, you can chew your mantra with your food. *Japa* is very simple. At the same time, it is very subtle, because it is dealing directly with sound vibrations.

> 26 Of trees, I am *asvattha*, the tree of life. I am Narada of the *deva-rishis* (sages of the gods). I am Chitra-ratha of Gandharvas (celestial musicians), and of all *siddhas* (perfected souls), I am the sage Kapila.

> 27. Born in the nectar of immortality, I am the primordial horse Ucchaisravas, and also Indra's noblest of elephants, Airavata. Among all people, I am their king.

> 28. I am the thunderbolt (*vajra*) of all weapons. I am Kamadhuk, the wish-fulfilling cow. I am also the progenitor, Kandarpa, the love creator and the power of sex. Among serpents, I am Vasuki, king of snakes.

> 29. I am the cosmic serpent, Ananta. Of water spirits, I am Varuna, the god of water. I am the noble ancestor, Aryaman, and of all the governing powers, I am Yama, lord of death.

> 30. I am Prahladan (the prince of devotion) born into the demon race. Of all that measures, I am time itself. I am the king of the animals, the noble lion. And of birds, I am Garuda (the carrier of Lord Vishnu).

> 31. Of purification instruments, I am the wind. Among warriors, I am the supreme hero Rama. I am the shark of the sea creatures, and of the rivers, I am Ganga (the sacred Ganges).

32. I am the beginning, middle and ending also of everything created. Of all knowledge, I am the knowledge of *Atman*. And in controversy, I am reason itself.

33. I am the first letter: "A." I am the combining word: "and" (*dvandva*). Actually I am time eternal. Thus, I am the one facing all directions (Brahma). I sustain everyone as I dispense the fruits of all actions.

The first letter of nearly all languages is the letter A because that's the beginning of sound. Although we say "A" (rhyming with bay) in English, the most natural sound of the letter is "ah." All you need is to open your mouth: "ah," the very first letter. That is how sound begins.

In one form or another, all other letters also have this "ah." Without "ah" nothing else can come. You see that the "ah" precedes all other letters and words. That's why he says, "I am the letter 'A.'"

Of course, words and sounds have beginnings, but there is no beginning for consciousness. Consciousness is eternal: no beginning, no end; always there. Just the audible "ah" sound has a beginning. Beneath the audible is the inaudible "ah" sound, which you didn't create. It's already there. But you brought it out. You always have that silent "ah" going on within. Without producing any sound, if you just close your ears and eyes and listen within, you may hear the constant sound inside. That same sound itself has different levels. At a very deep level, it is not heard physically. Such a mantra—which is always vibrating—need not be repeated. But as it comes rolling through your windpipe, it is heard as "ah." So Sri Krishna explains, "I am like the letter 'A,' which runs through all other letters. So I am there in everything. That's why 'A' is the most important; it's my *vibhuti*, my manifestation." And of course all other letters and words are nothing but the multiplication of that beginning.

Time also never ends or begins. Time itself is timeless and comes from the timeless one. We create so-called sections of time and call those the present, past or future. But strictly speaking there's no past, present or future. They are our conceptions. Your present could be somebody else's past. For example, imagine a friend has come to visit us, but his wife had to stay home. Ask her, she'll say, "He was here." Ask us, we say, "He is here." Ask those who expect to see him later. They say, "He is expected to be here very soon. He will be here." See, from the wife's point of view, he was. For us, he is. For the other friend, he will be.

Time is all relative, like the flow of water that runs in a river. Imagine a log, floating on the water from west to east. Somebody in the west would say, "I saw the log." Now you say, "I am seeing the log." And the person further east might say, "I will see the log."

But the log is always there. Because you happen to see only so much, that becomes the present for you.

Understand this point. If you focus a telephoto lens, a small portion is all you see. Bring it to normal, you see more. Expand it to wide-angle, and you see much more. When you bring it back to telephoto, some of the pieces are lost. Past, present and future are just relative. It all depends where you stand and how you see. Space and time are unlimited. Thus, you more readily see God's manifestation, in space and time.

"And I am also facing everywhere, dispensing the fruits, bringing the results." In other words, God is the law-giver, who makes it the way it is. God is the law of nature: if you do this, you get that—action and reaction. God is the dispenser of the reactions for your actions; cause and effect. Nobody can do one and avoid the other. If you are the cause, you get the effect. In this again we see the *vibhuti* of God.

34. Yes, I am also death who devours everyone and everything. Yet in the same moment, I am the source of all yet to be born; I am the rich person's prosperity. I am the feminine qualities fame and fortune; eloquence and memory; mental brilliance, perseverance and forgiveness.

35. Of all the uplifting *Vedic* songs, I am the lovely Brihat in the *Sama Veda*. Of poems, I am the sacred Gayatri, I am the month Margashirsha at the beginning of the year, and of all seasons I am blossom-filled spring.

36. I am the intelligence of gamblers. I am the splendor in what is splendid. I am determination; I am victory. And in everything good, I am its goodness (*sattva*).

Why should he say he's the intelligence of the gamblers? If you gamble and win, what are you using? Your intelligence.

In one sense, right and wrong don't matter. Even right and wrong are our conceptions. Dirt and something clean are our conceptions. In their original state, there is nothing essentially dirty and nothing really clean. But from our viewpoints, we might say, "This is a good act; that is a bad act."

Even in so-called bad actions (according to our eyes), if we see something excelling, we see God working there. God is the greatest gambler among gamblers.

In essence, Sri Krishna is saying, "I am the goodness in everything good." God nestles in the goodness. In the same way, even in the bad, God is the badness. You see it as good or bad according to your understanding. What is terribly dangerous to you may be quite beneficial for another. Certain deadly poisons, for example, become lifesavers in the hands of doctors. It's all in the eye of the beholder. There is goodness in everything. If you use your Buddhi Yoga, true discrimination, you'll see the goodness in everything. That's God's *vibhuti*.

> 37. Among the Vrishni clan, I am Krishna. Of all the Pandavas, I am Arjuna. Among the sages, I am Vyasa, and of all poets, I am the poet-sage Ushana.

> 38. Among punishers, I am the scepter. Of instruments of leadership, I am statesmanship. I am the secret of silence and the wisdom of the wise.

The king holds the scepter. That means the law, the punishing rod. It's not a rod he hits with; it's the law. He's not punishing with anger or hatred. It's a correction, education. You do something, you get something. So he is the scepter of punishers.

The statesmanship of leaders, the secret of silence and the wisdom of the wise. Do you see a common thread here? Anywhere you see something beautifully done, something extraordinary, you are seeing the *vibhuti* of God. Realizing that, you won't condemn anything or anybody. That's the beauty behind seeing God's manifestations. Everything becomes a glorification of God. With this insight, you won't develop dislike or hatred for anything or anybody, which would ultimately affect your own mental balance.

39. I am the seed of all beings, Arjuna. For without me, whether animate or inanimate, nothing can exist.

40. Actually, Arjuna, there just is no end to my manifestations. Those described are but a few.

41. Whenever you see anything beautiful, prospering or powerful, know with certainty that these qualities arose from but a spark of my effulgence.

42. But, Arjuna, what use are all these details to you? Just know that I am (the I am), and that I support the whole cosmos with only a tiny fragment of my being.

Thus ends the tenth discourse of the *Bhagavad Gita*, the science of Yoga, entitled: "Yoga of the Divine Manifestations."

The Yoga Vision of the Cosmic Form

1. Arjuna said: Because you are so compassionate, you have taught me the most profound mystery of the Self, and I am no longer deluded.

2. I now understand the origin and dissolution of every creature which you have detailed for me, lotus-eyed Lord, as well as your own infinite Self.

3. Now I know that everything is just as you have said, and I long to see your Cosmic Form, O Purushottama (divine Self).

4. Lord of all yogis, if you deem me strong and steady enough to behold it, then I beseech you to show me your immortal Self.

5. The blessed Lord responded: Behold, Arjuna, you are about to see the multitude of my Divine Forms in their millions of colors and variations!

6. Look for all the celestial powers and spirits of nature (*adityas*, *vasus* and *rudras*), and so many other wondrous things, Arjuna, never before revealed.

In this chapter Sri Krishna shows his super-form. When you behold that, you see everything in the universe as part of his body.

7. Look at my body, Arjuna. You will see the entire universe there— all that moves and all that [seems to be] unmoving, as well as anything else you wish to see. And all are part of the same, which is me.

It's another way of saying that the same consciousness expresses itself as the entire universe. There is a beautiful expression in the Tamil language which translates, "God, You and You only are the one who has become the whole world. Without You nothing exists."

In his Cosmic Form he says, "See, the moving and the unmoving are all parts of my body. Normally you won't see all this with your eyes, so I will give you divine sight." The physical eye has limitations. Even our mental eye has limitations. Limited consciousness can't see everything.

Sometimes people who have a little more bile in their systems, sitting in a position for a long time in the hot sun will get up quickly, feel dizzy and everything seems to be reeling. Then they don't see people as people. Some chemicals go into the brain and derange it. Then they see from a different level. In the same way, you can't see the whole cosmos as one body, with the limited eye. You need a different eye.

8. But you cannot see my Cosmic Form just with your physical eyes. I will give you spiritual vision. Now behold my *Yoga Ishvara*.

Having heard of all these divine glories of the Supreme, Arjuna becomes very curious. "If all this is so," he says, "I would like to see your true Cosmic Form. You seem to be saying you are everything. Would you show me?"

"I appreciate your interest," says Krishna, "but unfortunately you cannot see that Cosmic Form with your physical eyes."

"Well, if you wanted to show me, you could also give me the eyes to see it. I would like to see that very much. Please give me the eyes and give me the show."

"To see the Cosmic Form of the Divine," he says, "you need a divine eye." It's not that you must be given a divine eye. You have it already. "I will remove all the temporary veils and let the real eye function. Only then can you see the Divine Form." It takes a divine eye to see the Divine Form. It takes a thief to catch a thief, because you have to possess that kind of eye.

When Arjuna wanted to see the Cosmic Form, Krishna said, "My boy, you can't do that with this limited, physical eye. And because you're interested and I know you're going to tell everybody afterward, I'll give you an opportunity to see the Cosmic Form to let others know also." He gave that capacity, but not just for Arjuna's sake. Through Arjuna, he is telling the world that there is a cosmic beauty, God functioning at a cosmic level. That's why he went to the trouble of giving that vision.

9. Sanjaya spoke: After saying this your majesty, Sri Krishna, the supreme Master of Yoga, revealed to Arjuna his Cosmic Form as God.

10. Everywhere, everywhere millions of faces, eyes seeing everything; countless mouths all speaking wonders; and visions too numerous to

describe. All this is he in a bejeweled heaven with infinite upraised arms revealing miraculous powers—a divine weapon in every hand.

11. Clothed in mantles of light and garlands of blossoming heavens— the infinite, wondrous and resplendent One—facing everywhere simultaneously. In the presence of divinity, an indescribable fragrance.

12. If a thousand suns were to blaze in the sky at the same time, their splendor would be [something] like the radiance of the supreme Self (*Mahatman*).

13. There in the body of the God of gods, Arjuna saw the manifold universe in its entirety with its many levels and divisions, all resting in their essential oneness.

In the cosmic vision, everything is seen as a little cell of that great body, just as we have millions and millions of cells in this body. In a way, we are all cells in the cosmic body. Certainly we can each be proud, because we're all cells in the cosmic body of God. And God needs every cell. Nobody is undesirable, nobody is inferior and nobody is superior.

Arjuna really saw everything then.

14. Arjuna's hair stood on end. Amazed and ecstatic, he fell in adoration before the Lord, pressed his palms together [near his heart] and spoke:

15. O Lord, I see all the *devas* in you. Your body contains every living creature and all levels of evolution, even the Creator, Brahma, seated on the lotus and surrounded by the ancient sages and celestial serpents.

16. I see you embodied in an array of countless forms wherever I turn: arms, bodies, mouths and eyes, on and on to infinity. You are everywhere; you have no end, no middle, no beginning. O Lord of the universe, your body is the entire cosmos.

17. And now I see you crowned with precious gems and holding the mace and discus, in the midst of a light so radiant that I can hardly stand it. You are like a fiery sun blazing out in all directions.

18. You are what is to be known—the supreme Imperishable Reality. You are the treasure house of the universe, the refuge of all

creatures and the eternal guardian of the *dharma* (timeless wisdom). Now I understand, you are *Purusha*, the ancient of ancients.

19. You reach everywhere; there's no place that you start or end, nor middle either. You wield infinite power. The sun and moon are your eyes. Your mouth is a burning fire that heats the whole universe.

20. From heaven to earth, every quarter is full of your Presence. O *Mahatman* (Supreme Self), the three worlds tremble before your terrifying and marvelous Cosmic Form.

21. It is true, the hosts of heaven (gods, angels, higher beings) actually enter into you, some so overcome, they extol you and bow before you with their palms pressed together respectfully. Hosts of sages and saints spontaneously praise you in songs sublime and [speaking for you] are saying: "Peace and peace to all."

22. When gazing upon you, even the celestial beings of all levels are astonished and overwhelmed.

23. The whole universe trembles, almighty Lord, on seeing your infinite strength and in the presence of your awesome form of countless eyes, that see everything, and infinite arms, legs, bodies and fearsome mouths with bared teeth. Lord, I too am shaking.

24. Seeing you like this—taller than the sky, your mouths open and blazing while waves of colors emanate from you, and your eyes, everywhere burning into me like fire—my heart is pounding with fear. O Vishnu, I've lost my courage and peace.

25. When I look into your terrible jaws with fearful tusks, I see the fires at the end of time. I've lost my bearings, and don't know where to turn. O Lord of the gods who upholds the whole universe, show yourself merciful!

26. I see all the sons of Dhritarashtra and all the earth's warriors, kings, and Bhishma, Drona and Karna, as well as our own mighty warriors.

27. All of them helplessly caught up in a torrent that's rushing into your terrible jaws and tusks. It's horrible! Some are being crushed between your teeth, their heads smashed to powder.

Arjuna just saw everything, including the war already being fought: Bhishma, Karna, Duryodhana and all beings destroyed. He saw the future as the present. He saw everything. He was flabbergasted!

After Arjuna gets the vision and sees everything, he gets frightened. "Please, please, I don't want it anymore. Come back down to normal. Take away these eyes. Give me the old eyes." Why? He got the vision prematurely. There is a natural maturity for everything. If you are forcing somebody to do something before the maturity comes, it creates more problems.

"Oh my God, what is this? I'm terribly afraid. Stop all this!"

When Arjuna saw the Cosmic Form of Sri Krishna devouring the world with a fiery mouth, he even saw his Arjuna personality there, Dharma and Duryodhana, too. He saw both armies already there fighting with each other, and many dying. Even as he stood with Krishna before the beginning of the war, he beheld the war in process. Why? Because he was also seeing the future as the present. And he wondered, "What is this? What am I seeing? Is it all already happening? Can nobody stop it?" At that level, there is no past or future. It's all here already, and he was seeing it at that level.

If Arjuna had maintained this cosmic view or remembered it well, this *Gita* would not have gone beyond this chapter. There wouldn't have been a separate Krishna to tell a separate Arjuna anything more. But he got this vision because the perception was temporarily granted to him. When that vision was taken away, most was forgotten. A glimpse of it comes, and then is forgotten because the world drama has to continue.

From a higher perception, everything has been ordained already. There is no future as such. Everything is occurring in the eternal present. But to read or hear this is only theory, you must experience it. Even though all is ordained, finalized, already finished, still we must function as part of the drama. In a drama, the future is already known to every actor. Ultimately the villain will disappear and the hero will be victorious. He will win his girl and they will live happily ever after. But in the middle of the show, if you are playing the part of the hero, when the villain seems to be winning, should you say, "Well, ultimately I am going to be victorious; why should I cry?"

Even if you know it, the director won't let you do that. She'll say, "Nonsense! Come on, do your job. Cry!"

Can we argue with the director: "Why should I cry? Everything is going to be all right." No, let us just play our parts here even as we realize it is all the same awareness; we are all equal.

> **28. Like a raging torrent roaring to the ocean, so are these warrior heroes rushing chaotically into your blazing jaws of death.**

> **29. Now I understand that all creatures, like moths to a flame, are rushing headlong into your gaping jaws of death.**

> **30. Your mouths are filled with fire. Wherever you turn, you lick your lips. On every side, you devour all that lives. O Vishnu, your radiance has set the universe on fire!**

It's frightening. In the cosmic light, you could see God devouring a few thousand people under the name of either natural or human-made disaster. You might want to blame somebody for that. But in the overall picture, it's all part of the game. It may sound a little hard-hearted, but the truth is that when God wants to eliminate something with simply one heavy breath, God makes the whole world shake; a planet is gone. Yes, it doesn't take much time. Like in our own bodies when we have some problems, what do we do? Sometimes we have to let the doctor cut it off or clean it out—perform operations, squeeze out all the things that are not helping the body. In the Cosmic Body sometimes God also does such things. Our bodies are the microcosm. God is the macrocosm.

In that light, we simply have to accept: yes, that's part of the way. God either uses the very nature, or uses some person. By accepting, we save our minds from falling into hatred. Otherwise we keep on blaming others for everything. It all depends on how we look at things. But we can rise above problems if we raise our awareness to a cosmic level and see as the whole. That way our minds stay balanced. We accept changing things.

As a devotee, it's easy to say, "It's all God's Will. I am Thine. All is Thine. Thy will be done." But if you come out and see your car with a big dent made by a passing car, in that moment you become furious.

What happened to "All is Thy Will. Thy Will be done"? You forgot to identify that view when you saw the dent. But if you really accept everything, you will think, "Yes, probably that's the will of God."

I'm not suggesting that you ignore the problems. Of course, take care of things. At least tell your insurance company, whom you are paying anyway. Let them take care of it. Or, if you saw the passing car, note the license number. Yes, do those things; but there's no point in getting depressed, excited or furious about it. That way you just lose control of your mind, and because of a disturbed mental condition, sometimes you make even more mistakes. So first—accept what happens peaceably. But don't just go to sleep. Accept it, and *then* do your part to correct the situation.

> **31. O God of such terrifying form, supreme Lord, you who existed before anything else, I prostrate before you. Be merciful. I must know who you are, what you do and why you do it.**

> **32. The blessed Lord said: I am all-powerful time, destroyer of the worlds and now I have come to devour this world. Whether you fight or not, all the warriors of the opposing army gathered here will surely die.**

Sri Krishna said, "I have come here to reduce the weight and to save the innocent from the wicked." Those are the two purposes. "Whether you are going to fight or not, Arjuna, it is already happening. Because you are my good friend, I am giving you some credit for valor. But it's already done. If you don't want the credit, forget it."

That is what's meant by, "Whether you fight or not, those warriors of the opposing army will not live." They have to go. It's part of nature's approach. Sometimes you do something with a goal in mind. If you attain the goal, you might think that you did it, and you might take credit for it. Actually, there's a still Higher Will which decides the final outcome. But does that mean the doctor should think, "There's no reason for me to do anything now. It's all decided." No, the doctor should operate, when necessary. He or she is part of nature taking care of you. But ultimately, whether you survive or not depends on the Higher Will. That's why no physician should ever think, "I'll save this life."

Don't worry, but do your part. We shouldn't stop doing. There is an old country saying, "When the temple keeper blows the conch in the morning, the sun rises." He shouldn't say, "Whether I blow it or not, the sun will rise." Then he'll lose his job. Just keep blowing your conch and let the sun come out when it wants to. But you do your part. That's why some feelings of individuality are given so you can do your part.

Even then, an enlightened person will continue to play the assigned part. He or she will act unenlightened in the midst of unenlightened people. When in Rome, behave like a Roman. When you are in the midst of the insane, don't act completely sane or they'll kill you before your job is finished. So act as if you also are insane. That too is enlightenment.

The saintly poet-sage Thiruvalluvar says, "Even if a fellow has learned everything, he is a useless fool if he doesn't know how to move with the world as it moves." That's enlightenment.

33. Therefore, Arjuna, stand up and be famous! Conquer your enemies and enjoy the kingdom uncontested. I have already slain the [enemy] warriors. You are to be my instrument, Arjuna.

34. Go ahead and slay Drona, Bhishma, Jayadratha, Karna and other brave warriors, whom I have already doomed to die in this battle. Don't worry or be afraid. Just stand and fight and you will conquer your enemies in battle.

35. Sanjaya said: After hearing these words of Krishna, Arjuna began trembling uncontrollably. He pressed his palms together over his heart, bowed before the Lord and with a choked voice he said:

36. Krishna, it is perfect that the world showers praises on you. Before you, all evil flees to the farthest corners of the cosmos, while hosts of saints and sages bow before you.

37. How could they do anything else but worship you, *Mahatman*? You are beyond everything else. You are the origin of all—even Brahma. O eternal Lord of the gods, you are the abode of the entire universe and you are indestructible. You are existence and non-existence. Yet, in the same moment you are that Supreme state beyond them both.

38. You are the *Adideva* (the original One), the most ancient *Purusha* (Self), the Supreme resting place and Refuge of the universe. You are awareness itself—the knower— and [still] you are all that is known. You are the ultimate home. O great being of infinite shapes and forms, you pervade the whole universe.

39. You are lord of the wind (Vayu), lord of death (Yama), lord of fire (Agni) and lord of water (Varuna). You are the moon and the creator of all that is born. Ultimately you are the great-grandfather of all beings. A thousand times I salute you and respectfully bow before you.

40. Wherever I turn, it is you! To my left and right I bow before you. In front and behind—my humble prostrations. You are boundless and your power is incalculable. You permeate all that is. In truth, everything is you!

41. Sometimes in the past, my lord, due to my ignorance and carelessness, and out of affection for a dear friend, I presumptuously addressed you casually, "O Friend," I would call, "Hey, Krishna," not realizing who you really are.

42. When we were playing or resting, sitting or eating, alone or with others, I must certainly have been rude to you by my manner that was too familiar. However I have been disrespectful, eternal Lord, I implore you to forgive me.

"Hey! Come here, do this, do that!" I used to talk familiarly with you," Arjuna said to Krishna, "Now I feel guilty about it. I didn't know your true nature." He really felt his mistake.

43. You are the father of the world and all that is in it, including the animate and inanimate. You are the supreme Guru. Certainly the whole world should adore and worship you. In all three realms, O mighty one of unparalleled strength, nothing is your equal.

44. Gracious Lord, I humbly bow before you and implore you to forgive me, like a father forgives his child, like a friend forgives a friend, like a lover forgives his or her beloved.

He uses these examples because the father should always forgive the child. Otherwise, how can he be called a father? A friend should forgive another friend; otherwise he or she is not a friend. In the same way, a lover should forgive the beloved. It is in forgiveness that you show your true affection.

45. I am thrilled to behold you as no one else has. But my mind is disturbed; I am terrified by your Cosmic Form. O God of gods and abode of the cosmos, mercifully show your more familiar form to me again.

46. I desperately want to see you as you were before—crowned with light, and not with thousands of arms displaying your powers, but with four holding the mace and discus.

47. The blessed Lord said: Through my yogic power, Arjuna, you have been blessed to see my Cosmic Form which is radiant, omnipresent and eternal.

He's just putting a little crown on Arjuna, making him feel a bit important. That's another way of handling things—by saying: "You are the chosen one. Remember, I'm especially giving this only to you."

And in a way it's true. Nobody else saw this manifestation. That's the beauty of it. Arjuna is the middle one of five brothers—neither too good nor too bad. The in-between was chosen. Sri Krishna could have chosen the eldest son, Dharmaputra, who is an enlightened and saintly person. He could have easily given *him* the *Bhagavad Gita*. Why not? He was too good. You don't select what is too good for such a thing. There is a trick here. The next brother, Bhima, was too wild. Arjuna was in-between. Krishna chose an average man, because the entire *Gita* is advice to the common person who should do his or her duty and, at the same time, know the ultimate truth.

That's the beauty of the *Gita*. It shows how to know the ultimate truth, while still doing your part, because you are still here.

48. Great hero, no one else but you can see me this way, not those who study sacred scriptures, nor those who perform ritual offerings, nor givers of charity, nor those who follow all the prescribed religious observances, nor even by the ascetics who embrace austerities (*tapas*).

49. There is no need for you to be afraid or confused any longer by looking at my awesome form. Let your heart be glad and your fears disappear. I will reveal myself to you again as I was before.

50. [Then] Sanjaya said: After saying this, Krishna reappeared to him in his gentle, more familiar aspect, and immediately calmed Arjuna's troubled mind.

51. Arjuna said: Now that I see your gentle human form, my lord, my mind is tranquil and I am returned to normal.

Of course, Sri Krishna calmed him down and came back to his natural form. And as he did, he withdrew the divine vision also, and Arjuna forgot almost everything he had seen.

"Hi, Krishna, how are you?"

See? Immediately he went back to his old relationship. That's human nature.

52. The blessed Lord said: It is certainly hard to see me as you have. Even the _devas_ long to see my Cosmic Form.

Sri Krishna concludes this portion with the next three _slokas_ which go together—one after another:

53. Though these produce much merit, the study of sacred scriptures, practice of austerities, gifts of charity and even self-sacrifice will not earn anyone the vision that you have seen.

Does it seem to be a contradiction? Earlier Krishna said austerity is important; practice is important; study and charity are important; and sacrifice is the most important. But here he says, "You cannot attain me even by all these things."

It sounds like total contradiction. The spiritual path is very tricky, but if you go deep, there is no contradiction. What he means is, "You can't see me in this form by study of _Vedas_, by austerities, by gifts or sacrifice. None of these are necessary to see me or to experience the peace."

I always try to put it in a yogic way. You don't need to do all these things to experience your peace. You don't need Yoga postures or breathing practices or mantra repetition or ritual worship or even self-surrender. None of these are necessary to make you feel the peace.

Then why do them? Not to achieve peace, but to avoid disturbing it. Please understand that by doing all these things you avoid disturbing your peace.

Do *you* bring light in by opening all the curtains? No, you don't need to bring in the light. The light is there already. Somehow you have been preventing it from coming in. Now you simply remove the things that prevented you from facing the light. This is what Sri Krishna is saying. All your study and practices are to keep you from disturbing your mind; they remove the things that keep you from seeing the light.

Look at a bowl of water, you don't have to do anything to make the water peaceful except stop shaking it. The same for your peace of mind. To stay away from shaking it, from disturbing the peace, you study scriptures, practice some austerities, renounce attachments and do all the Yoga practices.

All these practices are for self-refinement, not Self-realization. The Self is already realized. But the little self, the mind, must be refined in order to know this. To refine the self, just remove the de-fine-ments, the limiting definitions.

Keep this in mind: "I am fine already. What should I do? Just stay away from defining myself." Remember. Apply this in your daily life. Remember it constantly, which is what Krishna is saying in the next *sloka*:

> 54. Only by constant and steady devotion can I be seen in my true Cosmic Form, and known, Arjuna, and realized.

This means continually remembering, "I am fine. I don't *need* any definition. I can *use* some definition just for fun, but I shouldn't bottle myself up with definitions." Remember you can *use* some limitations, but always know that you are not limited. If your daily actions are based on this, you are already fine.

> 55. All who desire me above everything else, and [thus] completely devote themselves to me, and [thus] offer me all their actions, and [thus] shed all personal [selfish] attachments and feelings of ill-will toward any other creature—Arjuna, they surely enter into me.

Naturally, if you remain in your fineness, how can you bear any enmity? The minute you forget that oneness and mistakenly see the differences as the truth, then you create friends and foes. Instead, simply recognize the eminence of God, the peace personified.

Look at the example of soap and dirt. Why do you apply soap to dirty linen? Not to make the linen white. Soap will never make the linen white. What does it do? It takes the dirt away; that's all you need to make the linen white. Take the dirt away; and the linen is white. Soap cannot make it white. This sounds like a contradiction. The soap takes the dirt away and also takes itself away. Soap is also a sort of dirt.

That's why even all these fine studies, austerities, renunciation and ultimately everything else must drop away to keep you free. You can't even cling to the soap, which is all your good practices. Let them go like you let the soap go. But you can't discard these practices just whenever you want to; that is, with your own effort. Keep on refining yourself. Keep on washing until all the impurities are gone. Then even the cleansing practices will just drop away by themselves. Then you are ever free.

Thus ends the eleventh discourse of the *Bhagavad Gita,* the science of Yoga, entitled: "The Yoga Vision of the Cosmic Form."

Chapter Twelve

_____

The Yoga of Devotion

This twelfth chapter is really important. It has only twenty *slokas*, but they explain all of Bhakti Yoga, the path of devotion. Here Sri Krishna clearly paints the picture of a true yogi or devotee.

First, Arjuna asks:

> 1. Which devotees are better established in Yoga—those of steady devotion who worship you manifest in one form or another, or those who worship you as the formless and unmanifest one?

So far I have heard everything you've said, but I still have a little confusion, says Arjuna. One can worship the manifest or the unmanifest God. Which is better?

Sri Krishna answers:

> 2. Those devotees who continuously think of me with zeal, with sincerity and [thus] steadily worship me manifest in one form or another are perfectly established in Yoga.
>
> 3. And what of those who worship me in the unmanifest condition—beyond name and form, infinite and indescribable, beyond the grasp of the mind, yet everywhere present, unchanging, immovable and eternal?
>
> 4. [Through such worship] they quiet their senses, become even-minded, and naturally think of the welfare of all other creatures. Certainly, such devotees also come directly to me.
>
> 5. But those who seek me as the unmanifest choose a more difficult way, because it is very hard for one in the body to reach that goal.

"It doesn't matter, both are equally good," says Sri Krishna, but it's harder to worship the unmanifested, because it is unlimited. While you feel yourself to be limited, it is easier and better to worship something manifested. You are still within a body. It's hard to worship a bodiless, formless one. Your mind can't grasp it.

Then how should the embodied person prepare for the attainment of this goal?

> 6. The devotees nearest to me are those who renounce attachment to the fruits of their actions and instead offer them all to me; who desire me above everything else; and who, through yogic practices, meditate on me with a one-pointed mind.

> 7. Such devotees, Arjuna, whose minds are thus fixed on me, very soon experience me as their deliverer from *samsara*, the illusory drama of life and death.

> 8. Therefore, just keep thinking about me. Fix your entire mind (*manas*) on me. Continuously direct your discerning intellect (*buddhi*) to consider who I am, and you will soon know that we are united forever; there is no doubt about it.

There's no doubt about it. He has said it many times before: "Keep on thinking about me, and dwell on me." That's perfect Yoga, the higher form of worship. But how many can do that? That's why in the next *sloka* he comes down to a simpler level.

> 9. But, if you don't yet have the ability to fix your mind on me and keep it there, Arjuna, then you should learn to do so through Abhyasa Yoga (regular Yoga practice).

He says if you are not yet able to *fix* your mind on me, if you don't have that staunch devotion, then seek to reach me by Abhyasa Yoga. When the mind wanders here and there, again and again bring it back to me. That is what you call practice. At the higher level, there is no need for any practice. Your mind is already fixed. You are already doing everything in God's name. But if you can't do that, then practice to bring the mind back to God every time you forget. That is Abhyasa Yoga.

> 10. And if you have not yet developed the necessary self-discipline to practice Yoga regularly, in fact you can also attain perfection just by conscientiously dedicating all your actions to me (Karma Yoga).

If you find such practices too difficult, just keep on doing things, but while doing them say. I'm doing it for you, God."

11. And if you cannot even do that, you may still take refuge in me by surrendering your ego. Thus, you abandon the expectation of any personal rewards as the result of your actions—and your mind becomes calm.

See how much he dilutes it: "It doesn't matter if you do things for yourself. But at least when you get a result, give a little to me." See, you don't have to abandon everything.

In Eastern countries, when a farmer harvests something, he takes a little and says, "This is for God." The first bunch of bananas from the tree will be given to God. Anything that comes first will be offered. Even when a cow gives birth to a calf and begins to give milk, the first day's milk will be offered to God. You ask the farmer why he does that, he might say, "If we give it to God first, God will give us more." It's a kind of transaction, no doubt. But still, he has some connection with God. Instead of saying, "I'm going to devour everything; who worries about God?" at least he begins to think of God.

12. Knowledge (*jnana*) certainly is better than (mindless) practice. And meditation (*dhyana*) is above that knowledge. Even superior to meditation is renouncing attachment to the fruits of your life, because peace (*shanti*) immediately follows renunciation (*tyaga*).

This is an oft-quoted *sloka*, particularly the first portion, "Knowledge certainly is better than mindless practice." How many people just worship in a more or less mechanical way? They simply go before the altar, maybe light a candle or some incense and sit there. They don't even think of what they're doing. They may repeat some prayers with the lips, but the mind is somewhere else. In the beginning, probably they studied the prayer and said it slowly and thought about what it meant. But in time it became rote. The same goes for repeating a mantra, or sacred sound formula. When you began, you did it so intently. But now, the mind wanders all about while the mantra is repeated mindlessly.

That is what Krishna calls formal, ritualistic practice—without the mind applied to it or without even knowing the meaning. Sometimes you keep a sacred book with a nice velvet cover, open it, burn some incense and close it. You didn't draw anything out of it. It's the same type of mechanical practice.

Some Hindu *brahmins* will perform a *puja* (worship) morning, noon and evening. Many of them don't know the meaning of what they are doing. In the *puja* you are supposed to purify all the different limbs. With true feeling you touch the different parts with the mantra and feel that you are purifying yourself totally. Then you purify the inner self, the vital body, with your *pranayama*. When you inhale the breath, you repeat the mantra and feel that cool, sweet breath going in. All the movement is to be done with total feeling.

Once I was staying at someone's house with some students. I could see the person next door doing his prayers. I called some of the students and said, "See what he is doing." While saying the prayers, he was pushing his dog to one side and pulling his child on another side. In between he was calling, "I'm getting late for the office. Keep the coffee ready."

He was avid about saying his prayers. He believed in doing it every day, but he didn't know what he was doing. He didn't know the purpose behind it.

You might wonder if there is any value in doing daily practices without feeling. Better indeed is formal practice than doing nothing. It's better to be in an *ashram*, even if all you do is sleep, than to be somewhere on a street corner looking for your drug contact. So I don't condemn rote practices. Even if you keep doing them without thinking, one day you will say, "What is this? I'm just doing it. I don't seem to be gaining anything. My mind isn't here." Then you will search for the purpose behind it. In this modern age, when people don't understand the purpose behind a ritual, they tend to give up the ritual itself, rather than to look for the original intention. But the ritual is important. It should be there as a skeleton that reminds you of the purpose.

Still it's always better to know the principle than just to do the formal practice. Even if you don't practice, at least have knowledge of the principles behind it. And better than that knowledge is meditation. Sometimes you know what you are doing, but your mind is not *applied* to that doing. Mere knowing and doing are not enough. He's saying, put your *entire* mind on it: meditate on it. Do all that you do as a meditation. That's an even bigger step: perfection in action.

Knowing the purpose behind the action is knowledge. Perfection in action is the meditation. Whatever you do, have your mind totally on that. Such meditation is even better than knowing the purpose.

And better than meditation is renouncing the fruits of your meditation, your action and your knowledge. Renunciation is the highest practice, because peace immediately follows such renunciation.

Just as we saw the signs of the person of steady wisdom in the second chapter, here Krishna says who has true devotion and thus is dear to him:

13. Very dear to me are those devotees who hate no creatures; who are friendly and compassionate; who do not feel separate from others, and therefore do not think anything is their own; who stay calm in pleasure and pain; and who are forgiving.

14. I cherish those devotees who are ever content; who, through meditation, are steady of mind; who control themselves; whose convictions are consistent and strong; and who offer their hearts and minds to me.

Does he ever say, "Those who bring me the nicest bunches of fruits on a golden plate, or bring me heaps of gold?" No. Here are the qualifications of true devotees:

15. I cherish those devotees who do not disturb the world and are not disturbed by the world; who are neither excited by joy, nor are they victims of their own envy, fear or worry.

16. I love those devotees who are utterly detached from personal desires and whose minds [therefore] are pure and efficient; who are fair to all and never feel anxiety; and who selflessly renounce attachment to the fruits of their endeavors, even as they begin them.

17. I cherish those whose devotion has lifted them above the dualities; who neither rejoice over good fortune, nor run from pain; and who have transcended even desire and grief.

18. Very dear to me are those devotees who worship the same Self in friend and foe alike; whose minds stay balanced in the midst of honor or dishonor, heat or cold, pleasure or pain; and who are not attached to anything,

19. I love those devotees who maintain equanimity during praise and blame; who take refuge in silence [wherever they may be]; who are content [no matter what occurs]; whose homes are everywhere; whose minds are always steady; and whose hearts are full of devotion.

20. It is certain that those who take to heart this immortal *dharma* (eternal wisdom) that I am teaching you now and become full of faith and seek me as life's highest goal, they are my true devotees; and my love for them is boundless.

Thus ends the twelfth discourse of the *Bhagavad Gita*, the science of Yoga, entitled: "The Yoga of Devotion."

Yoga of the Field and Its Knower

This chapter begins with Arjuna asking:

> **1. Krishna, I would like to know more about *prakriti* and *Purusha*,
> the field and its knower, wisdom (*jnana*) and what is to be known.
> The blessed Lord replied: The body is called the field (*kshetra*),
> Arjuna. Whoever understands the field is said by sages to be the
> knower of the field *(kshetrajna)*.**

Prakriti and *Purusha* are terms which mean almost the same as *kshetra*
and *kshetrajna*. *Purusha* means the absolute Self or Consciousness;
prakriti, God's manifestation. Ultimately, they aren't different from one
another. We can never separate them; actually, they're one and the same.
Like dough and bread, one is unbaked; the other is baked. *Purusha* is
the unmanifested that we don't see nor can we make any use of. *Prakriti*
unmanifested is *Purusha*. In this chapter Sri Krishna describes these.

Kshetra can be translated as a house, place or field. *Kshetrajna* is the one
who dwells in the place. Holy places are often called *kshetras* and the
presiding deity, the *kshetrajna*. But here in the cosmic sense, *kshetra* is
prakriti and *kshetrajna* is unseen consciousness behind it all.

Another definition for *kshetra* and *kshetrajna* would be the known and the
knower. The most common meaning is the field and the knower of the
field. Nature, or that which can be known, is aptly called the field because
in a field you can grow anything you want. Whatever you sow, you reap.
If you sow good seeds, you get good growth; sow bad seeds and you reap
bad fruits.

> **2. And, Arjuna, understand this: I am the knower of the field in
> everyone. To distinguish between the field and its knower is what is
> true knowledge.**

Here Krishna seems to be answering Arjuna's unasked questions: "Are
there many *kshetrajnas* and *kshetras?*" Or, in simple language, "Are there

many souls as well as many bodies?" Sri Krishna says, "No, I am the Self or Soul in all the *kshetras*. The bodies vary, but I am life in all the bodies."

That is probably what is meant by "the image of God" in the *Bible*. God made *everything* in God's own image. Actually, the *Bible* doesn't exactly say that. It says, "God made *man* in His own image," not even woman. But the meaning is that God made everything in God's own image. If buffaloes could write a bible, they would probably say, "God made all the buffaloes in God's own image." Whoever writes does it this way. Usually they don't mean to demean others or ignore them. Probably a few people, all men, were sitting together and talking about these things, and they said, "God made man in His own image." I don't think they purposely omitted anybody.

"To distinguish between the field and its knower is true knowledge," says Sri Krishna. He's speaking of enlightenment and discriminative knowledge. *Viveka* is the capacity to discriminate between what the essence is and what its modifications or manifestations are. Never neglect this discrimination.

Two children go to a chocolate shop and see different shaped chocolates: round ones, square ones, globes, some made like elephants, some like cats or dogs. One picks out an elephant chocolate. His brother takes a dog chocolate. Will the shopkeeper say, "Give me a thousand dollars for the elephant and ten for the dog?" No; he's not worried about the names and shapes. He'll just put both together on the scale and say, "Give me so much per pound of chocolate." He doesn't care if it's an elephant or a dog, just how much chocolate it is. The seller looks into the weight of the chocolate; the buyer into the name and form. The child who takes the elephant might say, "Ah, the elephant is so tasty." The other one might answer, "No, no, the puppy is much tastier than the elephant." The children might even fight about it because they don't see the essence. But the shopkeeper knows that the reality behind both is the same chocolate. That's true knowledge: knowing that the ultimate essence and the names and forms are really one and the same, but in different levels. True knowledge is the ability to distinguish *Purusha*, the absolute Self, amid its manifestations which are *prakriti*, that is, to distinguish the *kshetrajna*, the knower of the field, from *kshetra*, the field.

When we stick only to name-and-form knowledge, it can be called secular knowledge. Knowledge of the essence is sacred knowledge. Secular knowledge without sacred knowledge always creates problems. But if you keep the sacred knowledge in mind, you can just deal with the secular conveniently while enjoying the whole world. That's what my master, Swami Sivanandaji, used to say in a simple way: "See unity in diversity." Then you can have fun with the variety or diversity. But if you miss the unity and just see the variety, that's a sort of lunacy.

Here we can see the similarities and the differences between the scientists and the yogis. In a way, our material scientists are also yogis. But they only try to know about the manifested universe. It's one-sided knowledge. They apply the same methods as the yogi does. In a way, they even practice the study of yogic posture and meditation. Scientists sitting in the lab may even forget to move their legs for hours and hours. They may forget to eat and sleep. What great *tapasya*, or austerity, they are performing. See, the practices are almost the same. How many scientists lose their marriages and families. The spouses complain that they forget their families. In a way, they have renounced personal life. It's almost the same thing with the spiritual people. But the spiritual renunciate's main interest is knowing the essence. He or she is trying to know "that which is to be known, by knowing which you know everything."

> 3. Listen to me and I will tell you in brief what the field is and how changes take place in it. I will also show you who the Knower is and what the Knower's powers are.

> 4. Over the ages this wisdom has been chanted and sung by the *rishis* in many different ways—artfully using words and reason that effectively point to reality.

In these next two *slokas*, Sri Krishna talks about the components of the field, the manifestation of the essence:

> 5. Arjuna, the field is a combination of the following: the [five] great elements; the egoistic sense of individuality (*ahamkara*); discerning intellect (*buddhi*); as well as *prakriti* (in its unmanifest state), out of which everything else evolves: the ten senses and the mind (*manas*); and the five sense objects.

6. Arising in this field are: desire and aversion (love and hate); pleasure and pain; the physical aggregate that holds all these together (the body); intelligence and perseverance (will).

You may wonder why nothing more concrete is mentioned here. How can pleasure and pain, emotions and intelligence be the *kshetra* or field? In the ultimate sense, even mind is a subtle form of matter, a manifestation. Intelligence and egoism are part of the mind. In yogic terminology they are called *manomaya kosha* (mind sheath), *vijnanamaya kosha* (intellect sheath) and *anandamaya kosha* (pure ego sheath). They are all different sheaths or dresses for the soul. They change because the mind is constantly changing.

You don't always have the same emotions. Intelligence waxes and wanes. Sometimes you seem to be extra intelligent, and sometimes your intelligence is distorted. Whatever is constant and never changes is the *Purusha*, and anything that changes is part of *prakriti*. So that's why all these elements—desire, hatred, pleasure, pain and so on—are said to be part of the manifested *prakriti*.

The next few *slokas* are more practical; they are not just high philosophy. It's all right sometimes to speak of the spirit, the Self, the essence, but it might just sound like so much talk. It is so subtle that it's beyond our mental grasp. Even to speak of it, the speaker must use *prakriti*, and so must the listener. *Prakriti* talks and *prakriti* hears. We are all at the level of *prakriti* (the manifested), trying to think and talk about the essence, the unmanifested *Purusha*. It's something like a little grandchild trying to fathom the grandfather. The finite is trying to measure the infinite with its finite instruments. A drop cannot measure the depth of the sea.

Knowledge of that essence, or *kshetrajna*, is possible only through its realization. That's why it is called *realization:* you have to go into that reality. But on our ordinary level we are all in a *real-Lie-zation*, it's all a "real lie," and that is what we call *maya*, or illusion.

Here again we should understand what is meant by illusion. It is said that all the different things and phenomena are illusory, *maya*, not truly concrete. What, then, is illusion? This book, for example, is illusory. What I call a book is not really a book in essence. It was not a book awhile ago, and it's not going to be a book later. It's paper pulp made into sheets and cardboard and put together, printed and called a book. When the paper goes through the press, ink is printed on the pages, you make sense of all those marks and create words and meanings. Together all these things make the book.

Suppose you take the book and start tearing out each page and leave the pages there in a pile. Is it still a book? No. What happened? You didn't destroy anything. All the parts are still there. You just changed the *shape*. So immediately you cease calling it a book. You call it a heap of paper. Set a match to that, and you call it a heap of ash.

Things constantly change their names and forms. Constant changing of names and forms is the outer illusion. Even the value of these relative things changes every minute. If you buy a book and the next minute decide you don't want it, immediately the price drops fifty percent. It's a used book now. It depreciated.

Everything depreciates. Nothing is permanent. Your body, your beauty, your materials, even your money depreciates. All these things that constantly change are called *maya*. But that doesn't mean these things are useless or that they should be ignored or thrown out. Use them, but don't think they're permanent. Just know they are changing.

Sri Krishna's point here is that knowledge of the essence, with which all these things are made, is necessary for us to live peacefully through all these constant changes. But to understand this truth we have to begin from where we are—at our normal day-to-day level. How can we approach it? We use our minds. We refine our minds. We should become more cultured. That's why in the following *slokas*, Krishna talks about the mores of self-culture. What are the qualities that the mind needs to arrive at the level of understanding the truth?

Can we understand by just hearing of it? No. We may know, theoretically, but that won't satisfy our hunger. We might know how to cook, but that doesn't mean we know all the pages of the cookbook by heart. Krishna says, "Let's get cooking." He gives a beautiful list of what qualities your mind should develop to make it fit to experience the truth:

7. Those who have wisdom are humble and do not hurt others. They are forgiving and upright. They serve their spiritual teachers (Gurus) with devotion. Their minds are pure and steadfast. They are loyal to their convictions and they [can] control their own minds.

8. They have seen the evil of identifying with their own bodies and minds, the field that continually undergoes the painful cycles of birth, suffering, old age, disease and death. In the presence of the sense objects they have *vairagya* (dispassion) and are free of *ahamkara* (the egoistic feeling of separateness).

9. They have no personal attachments because they do not mistakenly identify themselves with their own homes, families, husbands, wives, children or parents. Thus, unencumbered, they enjoy continuous equanimity in the presence of [so-called] good or bad fortune.

10. They enjoy the Yoga of steady devotion to me, without interruption and naturally seek out quiet places away from the hubbub of society.

11. In this way they develop continuous realization of the Self, which they recognize to be the essence of knowledge of the truth. I declare this to be wisdom. Seeking anything else is ignorance.

In those days, when they wanted to tell you something about the positive truth they would also mention the opposite at the end. We see another example of this in the simple words of the saintly South Indian poet Thiruvalluvar in his *Thirukkural.* He asks, "What is Yoga? What is righteousness? What is spiritual life? Make the mind clean; that's Yoga." Then he adds, "All the rest is the opposite."

Sometimes when I tell people, "This is all there is to Yoga," they say, "Is that all? You make it so simple. We thought we had to practice ten hours of *pranayama* a day, stand on the head and all kinds of things." See how simple it is. Just keep the mind clean, and you don't even have to worry about staying calm.

A clean mind will be calm always. You don't even need to make it calm. What kind of mind becomes restless? A dirty mind. You may know the saying, "Cleanliness is next to godliness." It doesn't matter whether you dry clean it or wet clean it, just keep it clean. And if you read Sri Krishna's list again, the qualities he names are all based on that cleanliness and calmness: humility, modesty, non-violence, forgiveness.

If you aren't going to forgive, your mind will be restless. If somebody said or did something to you and you dwell on it, your mind will simply be bubbling. I don't need to explain each of the qualities. The aim of each is the same: purity. Keep that aim in mind and all these qualities will automatically come. Maybe we can touch on one or two, for instance, "service of the teacher." What has that to do with purity? In this case, your "teacher" means the one who guides you on the right path. You should submit to him or her with all humility. If you aren't going to be humble to that person, with whom are you going to be humble? Normally, we don't want to submit ourselves to anybody, but we have to if we go to the doctor. "Doctor, I am at your mercy. Do anything you want. Cut anything you want." You may even allow the physician to make you die in a way. She gives an injection and you are "temporarily dead," anesthetized.

In the same way, if you can't be egoless, devoted and submissive to your own spiritual teacher, you won't be that way with anybody. Let your mind be free and clean from egoism, at least in this relationship. Let this be the beginning. If you get free from the ego, even for a minute, you get a glimpse of the light. Then gradually you will see not only that one person as your teacher, but everything will be a teacher to you. You will begin to learn from everything and everybody.

It's like looking for something in the pitch dark and suddenly light comes. You now see not only what you were looking for, but many other things also. You may have turned on the light to see the refrigerator, not to see all the other cabinets, but when the light comes, you see everything. In the same way, at least for the moment you are rid of egoism, and the mind gets a glimpse of the truth of the teacher. And, at that time, you may see other things in that light too.

This is where you begin to free yourself from ego. At all other places the ego comes forward: "I know everything; who are you to tell me. I am great! I did this. I did that." All this "I, I, I," normally comes. But at least with one person you say, "I don't know anything." It's very difficult to say, "I don't know, and that's why I have come to you." When you really mean that, you become humble and devoted, and you are open to learn more. You are clean then.

Here, Sri Krishna describes the supreme *Brahman*, the Absolute:

> **12. [Now] I will tell you what is to be known. You will live forever when you know the supreme and absolute *Brahman*, who has no beginning and can be called neither the truth (*sat*) nor the untruth (*asat*).**

Sat means truth. *Asat* means untruth. You cannot say that *Brahman* is real. Nor can you say *Brahman* is unreal. What does it mean? It means you can't say anything about it. It can't be put into words, because if you say one thing, its opposite is possible, too. *Brahman* is to be realized, not talked of.

He uses the word "supreme." All that we can say about God is less than the truth. The Supreme is not to be talked of, not even to be thought of. It's beyond the grasp of mind and speech, because they are finite things, part of *prakriti*. Finite instruments can never describe the infinite One. The only way to experience or realize this is to become it. If you become that, where is the "you" to explain? Like the drop who wants to fathom the sea and tell you how deep it is: if that drop jumps into the sea, no matter how long you sit and wait for an answer, it's not going to come. But it has understood the sea—not as a drop, but by becoming the sea. So the supreme *Brahman* can never be expressed or expounded; it can only be realized. Still, Sri Krishna says:

> **13. *Brahman* is all-pervasive—present in every hand and foot; *Brahman* sees through every eye, speaks through every mouth, hears through every ear. Every head is *Brahman*, enveloping all.**

I just said you can't say anything about it, so why does he say this now? He has to say something. That's the dilemma. We say we can't talk about it, but still we must somehow satisfy our minds. Thus we slowly widen our limited understanding, more and more, until one day it becomes unlimited. Instead of thinking, "God is only here in this statue or that church, or works with two hands only, or twelve hands," we see God as the Cosmic Form. All heads are God's heads and hands; all mouths are God's mouths. Literally, it is so, because God becomes everything. Naturally, it is all God.

Sri Krishna continues:

14. Though the senses are irrelevant to God, their functioning shines with God's splendor. *Brahman* is independent, yet is the ground of everything. Though God has no *gunas*, yet it is God who experiences their play.

15. God is inside every being and yet outside too. God is far away and right here now. God moves and yet doesn't move. It is so subtle, it is incomprehensible,

Thank God, I am just passing along what Sri Krishna said. If I alone were saying all these things, you would probably bundle me up and take me to a psychiatrist: "What is this, far away and close, thinkable and unthinkable? You are always contradicting yourself." In a way, it is still better to talk about all this than to waste our time gossiping and getting into trouble. That's one benefit of scripture study. As long as you are studying this, you are saved from so many problems.

16. God is indivisible, yet appears to divide into different creatures. God is seen as the Sustainer of all, yet devours all beings, even as God simultaneously generates them all anew.

"God is indivisible, yet appears to divide into different creatures." It's like the waves and the sea. The waves are nothing but sea water. The same sea water takes different forms, which we call waves. The waves seem like divisions, but are they not actually the undivided sea?

17. Deep in the hearts of all, there is the light of all lights, forever beyond darkness. This is wisdom, the goal of all knowledge and what is to be known. Know this to be the absolute *Brahman*.

18. Thus, I have briefly revealed to you the nature of the field (*kshetra*), wisdom (*jnana*) and what is to be known. Any of my

devotees who understand this will rise to my state and realize their oneness with me.

"Rise to my state" means the devotee is prepared for that realization or absorption. He or she is fit to become one with God.

Now Sri Krishna says:

19. Understand that both *prakriti* and *Purusha* are without beginning, and know also that the qualities of nature (the *gunas*) arise from *prakriti*. And from the interplay of the *gunas* arise all the modifications of the field.

It is not that the natural universe was created by something or somebody. There is no beginning and no end; it's a continuity. Both are always there, but when something comes into our experience we say, "It has begun." It's similar to speaking of the beginning of a day or its end. Which is truly the beginning or end? Simply for our own convenience we set limitations and say, "This is the morning; this is the evening; the sun is rising; the sun is setting." If you take a plane and travel along with the sun, there's no setting or rising. If you could develop the proper speed, you could travel with the sun constantly and be always at 12 noon eating lunch.

Now Sri Krishna says:

20. Though *prakriti* is the cause and the effect of every action, and also the instruments of action [through the body and the senses], it is *Purusha* who experiences all pleasure and pain.

21. *Purusha* (the unmanifested), resting ever present in *prakriti*, experiences the play of the *gunas*, which are the manifestations of *prakriti*. However, attachment to any of the *gunas'* pleasing experiences veils the *Purusha*, which then takes birth in good or evil circumstances.

Here Krishna speaks of the *Purusha* as if he were taking birth and then dying. But all this delusion of birth and death is dispelled by knowledge of the truth. *Purusha* means the absolute Self, absolute Consciousness, the essence. And *prakriti* is the nonsense, or the manifestation of the essence. The entire cosmos is *prakriti*. Everything that has been created is *prakriti;* Creator is the *Purusha*. Again, they are not two different things. They are not separate from each other. The Creator has created Itself as creation. I say "Itself." It is the One become many. And whoever knows this truth, together with the functioning of the *gunas,* knows immortality.

The *gunas* are the three forces or qualities in the world. Actually, there are only two forces, not even three. Though we call them these: *sattva, rajas* and *tamas. Sattva* is tranquility; *rajas,* too much activity; *tamas,* inaction, or non-activity. *Rajas* and *tamas* are the extremes. *Sattva* is the balance of them both, neither extreme, one way nor the other. The *gunas* are part of the cosmic vibrations, movement functioning on three levels: action, inaction and equanimity or serenity.

Everything in this cosmos is moved by this vibration, this moving energy. Call it wind if you want. All the forms are changed and get new names by the *gunas.* Our moods change by the *gunas.* Sometimes we're all happy, beautiful, wonderful and saintly. Other times we are the worst crooks. Another time, good-for-nothing. It's all different ways the wind of the *gunas* blows on you. Because of the different play of the *gunas,* everything happens.

Even in nature, sometimes it's all beautiful and serene, particularly at moments when day and night meet, early morning and early evening. There is natural serenity then, neither too much action nor inaction, dusk and dawn. Daytime is predominantly *rajas*—activity. Night is predominantly *tamas*—inaction. But the *sattvic* times are early morning and late evening. So remember to take advantage of the naturally *sattvic* period, which is the best time to meditate.

These are the three *gunas,* moving everything. If we know that ultimate essence and the creation with its changing names and forms—and the cause of their changes—then we know the whole picture of the entire creation, the Creator and the cause. And once we know this truth, we naturally identify with the unchanging principle. We feel we are the unchanging principle, and whatever change comes is part of the creation, a variation of the three *gunas.* Identifying with the pure Self, we become immortal. That is, we know we are immortal. We know that we are never born and we never die, though simultaneously because of the *gunas,* the elements keep changing.

22. The Supreme is present in your body and mind. There God may be recognized as the witness, the permitter, the ground of being, the experiencer, *Maheshvara* (highest of the high) and *Paramatman* (the supreme Self).

23. Whoever understands the true nature of *Purusha* and *prakriti* together with the *gunas*—whatever his or her calling may be—is free from the cycle of births and deaths.

Birth and death are nothing but the elements coming together or separating by the wind of the *gunas*. By knowing this truth, we feel our immortality, and, as such, we don't have birth and death. The *sloka* says, "Knowing this, you are never born again." But, of course, words have their limitations. It means there is no need for birth.

In another sense, with this enlightenment we have no more personal desires. It is desire that causes birth and death. No desire means no need for a body. If we don't feel like going anywhere, why do we want a vehicle? No car, no bicycle; nothing necessary. But if we desire to go somewhere, then we are given vehicles. And, in the same way, when the mind wants to achieve or experience something, it will be given a vehicle, which is the body. Those bodies come and go. That's what we call birth and death.

In *slokas* 24 and 25 Sri Krishna talks about the different Yogas.

24. Some realize the true Self by meditation (*dhyana*), others by the path of knowledge and still others by Karma Yoga (the path of selfless service).

Meditation is Raja Yoga. The Yoga of knowledge is Jnana Yoga. Then he mentions Karma Yoga, the path of selfless action.

25. There are yet others who don't know any of these paths. Still, if they but hear of Self-realization from others and are moved to worship with true devotion, they too achieve immortality.

Bhakti Yoga, the path of devotion, is also accepted. Just begin where you are. If you don't know how to meditate or do Karma Yoga, simply choose a symbol and worship. Fine, begin there. Something is better than nothing.

If you just take hold of any link of the chain and keep pulling, you'll get the entire chain. In the *Bhagavad Gita*, you see, there is equal importance given to all the different Yogas: Karma, Bhakti, Jnana and Raja.

But you'll notice then in certain places Krishna will say, "This Yoga is better than that," or "This is the best." That's because it's more effective to say that the one you are talking about now is the best. It creates more interest in those with aptitude for this one. Your host may feed you with delicious desserts every day. Each time he or she will say today's is the best. When you are eating something, you should enjoy that totally. The supreme place should be given to whatever you are hearing now.

In this sense you can understand the Hindu system. For example, the *Shiva Purana* (scriptural tales of Lord Shiva) talks of Shiva as the ultimate, supreme God. The *Vishnu Purana* (scriptural tales of Lord Vishnu) says Vishnu is the ultimate one. The *Shakti Purana* (scriptural tales of the Supreme as the Goddess Shakti) says that Shakti is the greatest one whom even Vishnu and Shiva come and serve. When they speak of one, they give primary importance to that. You can go toward whichever attracts you more. But if you do go close, you may see the Shakti devotees singing salutations to Lord Vishnu and Lord Shiva. You might wonder, "What is this? I'm worshipping Shakti. Why am I using Vishnu and Shiva mantras?" And if you worship Shiva, you will also say salutations to Shakti. It is just to get you focused on one path that it is said he or she is best, the only one. Eventually, you should see that they are all best; that all are one and the same. Otherwise, it's fanaticism.

In a way, I have to say that a combination of all the Yogas is really the most beautiful. They are all supplementary and complementary. Karma Yoga makes us efficient; Raja Yoga strengthens the mind. Bhakti Yoga unifies us in sweet relationship with the Divine. Jnana Yoga sharpens the intellect and makes it luminous. We should have all these great qualities.

26. Whatever comes into existence—whether animate or inanimate— does so through the union of the field and the knower of the field.

Without these two, there is no room for these names and forms of birth and death.

27. Whoever perceives the supreme God *(Parameshvara)* the same in all beings, who recognizes the eternal one amidst those who appear to be dying, that person sees the truth.

Who is the one who is really seeing? The one who sees the ultimate principle behind all these changing and unchanging manifestations. Others see, but they aren't seers. They are blind because they see only the superficial.

If you want to see everything, go to the seers. That's why spiritual aspirants are called seekers. They seek to see. They see something already, but they are not seeing the right thing. In a sense, they're still blind. One who has really seen is a seer. That person can help others see. Otherwise, it's the blind leading the blind.

Who is the genuine seer? Who is the true person of knowledge? The one who knows what is to be known. Having all kinds of degrees with letters before or after your name doesn't indicate real knowledge. It's all right. We don't condemn that knowledge, but it will be useless without the basic knowledge which is the key to use worldly knowledge well. Otherwise, it's like putting a sharp sword in a monkey's hands.

Once a king had a pet chimpanzee. It was always near him like a watchdog. One day the king felt sleepy while he was walking in the forest. He didn't want to be endangered while he slept so he told the chimp, "Take care. See that nobody hurts me. Here, keep this sword in hand."

The chimp was very happy. It took the sword and kept it ready. He walked around with the sword like a bodyguard while the king was sleeping. After a few minutes, the monkey saw a little fly. It flew about and landed right on the king's nose. Zip! The monkey certainly took care of the fly. It's life flew away immediately. But, unfortunately, not just the fly but the life of the king also flew away.

And that is why we don't put the right thing in the wrong hands. All modern problems are caused by having the right things in the wrong hands: war, pollution, competitions, arms races and so on. By themselves, they're not bad. Nuclear energy isn't bad by itself, but in the wrong hands problems are created. It's beyond our capacity to handle it. Probably, we let too much come out of the jar.

Do you know the story of the little boy who was playing on the beach, and he found a big antique jar? It was very beautiful and well corked. He became curious. "What could be inside the jar?" He really worked hard to open it. The moment he opened it—whoosh! Out came a cloud of black smoke. Then the smoke condensed into a wild genie who said, "Sir, thank you for releasing me. I was bottled up here. I can do many things. What can I do for you? I am your servant now because you released me. However, you must keep giving me work. If you don't give me work, I will have to devour you."

The boy said, "I have many wishes. I can give you lots of work."

"Come on, come on! I'm itching to work."

"Good! Build me a castle."

Whoosh! In an instant the castle was there.

"Bring me a car." Immediately the car was there.

"Bring me servants." And they were there. Before he even finished his commands, the thing happened. Whoosh! Finished!

The genie didn't give the boy time to think. "What next? Come on! Hurry, hurry!"

Soon the boy got so tired that he said, "Sorry, I don't know what to tell you anymore."

"No? Then I must swallow you!"

Fortunately, the boy ran to a wise teacher, who gave the genie a curly hair to straighten. The genie couldn't do it, but he kept trying. In that way, he stayed busy and didn't harm the boy.

Humanity is running today for having opened that jar. We are so proud. We think we know many things. We can split the atom. We can break down the neutron. We know the secrets of DNA. Yes, we can create everything. But now we are about to be swallowed. We have created so many Frankensteins.

We are really tampering too much with nature without knowing how to handle the energy. That's literally the situation today in the world. We have opened the jar, and the demon is running around. Now we don't know how to keep him occupied. It is all due to the lack of fundamental knowledge of the spirit and its unity. Even though we have eyes, we are blind. Even though we have intelligence, it is perverted. Certainly, now it is time to open our eyes and see what is to be seen and know what is to be known. Whatever it is, large or small, everything else can wait.

The fundamental knowledge is worth the seeking, because then you experience that peace and enjoy the whole world. Everything else can wait—and should wait, because without this you aren't going to be happy with other things.

> **28. Because you recognize the one God (*Ishvara*) equally present in every being, you naturally avoid harming any living creature, including yourself. And in this way you attain the supreme goal.**

> **29. The one who sees reality perceives that all actions are done solely by *prakriti*, and that *Atman* is not the doer.**

This is a beautiful *sloka*. In simple words, your true Self is the actionless witness, you are not part of all these actions. It is the *prakriti*, the manifested part of the real you, that performs all the actions. When you wake from a deep sleep, you know you have slept and you say, "I slept very well." How can you know that? Because you're the constant knower, the witness. Everything else is the known. Being that knower, you are changeless, you know you are happy or unhappy; you know you are restful or disturbed; you know you profited or you lost. You know you are angry. If the real you were angry, how could you know that? The knowing part isn't angry.

Does this make sense to you? It's very subtle, but if this is understood, you will never need a psychiatrist. You wouldn't go to one and say, "I'm unhappy; I'm disturbed." Instead: "I'm not disturbed, but my mind seems to be disturbed." If you can't repair the mind yourself, you might just put it in someone's hands and say, "Please fix it. When can I come back to get it?" Or, if you don't want to leave it there, just stay while the doctor makes the repairs and take it back with you. But you needn't be affected by the problem.

If you *really* understand this with your heart, you can always be happy and peaceful. Even in the midst of calamity or terrible sorrow, you can say, "Ah yes, poor mind, so sad. Well, what can I do? You have made some mistake and now you are facing the result." At that point, you can tell the mind, "I told you not to do that. You were mad for it. You were attached to it. Now you say you lost it and you're disappointed. I told you what would happen."

Yes, you can talk to the mind like that. Suppose your mind says, "I'm disappointed. I'm disturbed." Then you say, "Why? You were running after it. I told you not to run after anything, but just to be where you are and let things run after you if they want. But you ran after him (or her, or this or that) and the more you ran, the more it ran ahead of you. Now you are tired and say, 'Oh, I didn't get it. What can I do?' At least you should listen to me in the future." You can do this under any circumstances. Even if you have lost a dear friend or a million dollars, you can always rise above these dualities created by the mind.

That's Yoga. Just put yourself in a different position. That position is what people call being "high," and it's not just temporary relief or self-hypnosis. It's the truth. Or, for the sake of argument, even if it were just temporary, or even completely false, it doesn't matter. When you're crying that you don't have even a single dollar, simply say, "I'm the king." At least as long as you feel you're the king, you won't worry about that dollar. Put that positive suggestion into your mind.

See, even this one idea, one-half of a *sloka*, one word is enough to take care of your life. We don't even need hundreds of *slokas*. Just learn one thing and enjoy the benefits. The saint Sri Ramakrishna said, "If you want to kill yourself, a small pin is enough. But if you want to kill others, you need a big machine gun." In the same way, if you want to experience something for yourself, one word is enough. But if you want to help others to experience it, then you read all the books and references and charts.

30. Whoever perceives the whole variety of creation resting in the oneness (unity), and knows that all action is the evolution of that oneness, that person has realized the absolute *Brahman*.

31. The Self has no beginning nor any differentiating qualities (*gunas*). Though it dwells in the perishable body, Arjuna, it is deathless; it is not the doer, nor is it at all affected by anything that is done.

32. Just as the all-pervasive *akasha* (etheric atmosphere) is never tainted because it is so subtle, so is *Atman* present throughout the body of every creature, forever untouched and immaculate.

The *akasha* means "atmosphere"—not the lower level above New York, Chicago and Los Angeles, but the outer space above that. It is not tainted or polluted even though many particles roam around in it. Pollution can reach only up to a certain level. You can throw any junk into real space and it will orbit, but it will not taint the space. In the same way, the real Self is not tainted by anything. It is always pure but temporarily looks tainted. If you bring a rose near a crystal, the crystal will look rosy. Bring a blue flower and the crystal assumes the blue color. The crystal doesn't really turn blue. Because of the proximity of your happy mind, you assume that happiness and say, "I'm happy." When the mind becomes unhappy, you assume that color and say, "I'm terribly sad." Step away a little from the disturbed mind and you are fine again. Take the flower away from the crystal and it's colorless and pure again.

Always assert that purity. Know that you are That: "I'm not the body, not the mind. Immortal Self I am." Any time you feel you are getting near your mind when it's dirty, assert yourself: "No, I'm not the mind. It's the mind that's dirty. It is the mind that's crying, the mind that's restless. I just am." The minute you detach yourself, you will just laugh at that mind. "Foolish mind! Again and again I tell you not to be naughty, not to do all these things. But you don't listen and now you come crying." Try this technique, you will see how happy you can be. Then nobody can make you unhappy. What else do you need in this world? Just that *nityananda*, that eternal bliss.

Now Sri Krishna gives us an example:

33. Just as one sun lights this whole world, Arjuna, so does the Lord of the fields (God) enlighten all creation.

In modern language we can say it this way: just as the same atomic energy pervades all the things you see and don't see, just as one and the same electricity runs through different gadgets to come out variously as music or color or heat or motion or shock or light, so does Sri Krishna illumine the whole *kshetra,* the whole field, the whole universe, you don't have different electricities for different purposes. *Atman* is like that. Atom and *Atman* are more or less the same. Scientists call it the atom; yogis call it *Atman;* the *Bible* calls it Adam.

34. If you have uncovered the eye of wisdom and can distinguish between the field and its knower, between the path of absolute freedom and the bondage of nature's illusions, then you have attained the Supreme.

Thus ends the thirteenth discourse of the *Bhagavad Gita,* the science of Yoga, entitled: "Yoga of the Field and Its Knower."

Yoga of the Three Qualities of Nature

In this very useful chapter, Krishna divides nature into three *gunas*. We don't have an exact English word for *gunas*, but the rough translation would be "qualities."

Krishna begins by saying:

1. **I will tell you more about the supreme wisdom (*jnana*) by which the great sages and saints went from this world to a state of perfection.**

Again, in this chapter, wisdom, which is the basis of all other types of knowledge, is expounded and glorified:

2. **Those who rely on this *jnana* feel themselves at one with me. Thus, they do not see themselves coming into being at the time of conception; nor are they disturbed at the moment of [so-called] death.**

It sounds a little mysterious: neither born nor dying. He is talking about that which is eternal, without beginning, ending or changes.

Even though he says that those who rely on *jnana* are not disturbed at the time of death, in the next *sloka* he begins to explain how the cycles of birth continue.

3. **My womb is *prakriti*, the great creator. Therein I place the seed, Arjuna, and thus all beings are created.**

4. **Everything that comes into being does so from the womb of nature.**

The entire manifested nature becomes the womb. The supreme *Purusha* (the absolute Self, unmanifested) is the one who plants the seed, which is a ray of Itself, into *prakriti*. That is how the birth of all things begins. We saw this before in the "Yoga of the Field and Its Knower."

You may wonder, "How does a *jiva*, or individual soul, take birth?" The *jiva* is qualitatively the same as the cosmic *Purusha*. In simple language, we can say that the *jivatman* is the individual consciousness or individual soul, and that *Paramatman* is the Cosmic Consciousness or Supreme Soul. So it is the *jivatman* that is planted into the Goddess who is all manifested nature. That is how to understand birth and death. Birth means we get a body; death means we lose the body. That's all. *We* exist even before the birth. If we were not already there, who would it be who would get the body, and who would lose it?

That's why even in our everyday talk, if somebody dies we ask, "Where is she? What happened to her?"

"She's dead and gone." Gone? If she's dead, how could she have gone anywhere? She lost her body and went away. That's the idea. Then, where did she go? Maybe in search of another body, or maybe she didn't need another body, so she just went on. How simple it is to be born and to die. And we make such a big fuss over it.

Now the question is, when the *jiva* (the individual soul) comes into the *prakriti* (the world), how is the *jiva* affected by this? It's here that the *gunas* come in.

5. Mighty Arjuna, the forces of nature are harmony, restless activity, and inactivity (*sattva*, *rajas* and *tamas*). They arise from the creative energy (*prakriti*) which binds the indestructible one fast to the physical body.

We have to understand that when Krishna says *sattva*, *rajas* and *tamas* arise from *prakriti,* that *prakriti* is not different from them. It's just like the flame and its heat—they are inseparable. We cannot determine which belongs to which. The *gunas* are the very nature of *prakriti.* They are her motivating force. They cause the constant changing from one shape to another in this world. These three *gunas* are something like a tri-colored picture. When three colors are printed one over the other, they can give a whole range of different colors. The printer mixes these three colors in different ways to give *all* the different colors. When you print with three colors, sometimes you see seven or eight on the final sheet. They are all different combinations of the original three. So *sattva*, *rajas* and *tamas* are the three colors, but they give multifaceted hues. All the forms, visible and invisible, are the result of the modifications and combinations of these three *gunas*.

Now, Sri Krishna describes their characteristics.

> 6. Although the *sattvic guna* is pure, luminous and without obstructions, still it binds you by giving rise to happiness and knowledge to which the mind readily becomes attached.

We think very often, "The *sattvic guna* is really good. It won't obstruct us in any way, because it is stainless, pure and luminous." But for the final and highest experience, even *sattva* must be transcended. *Sattva* is better than *rajas* and *tamas*. *Sattva* is a good fellow. Good company is better than bad company. You can get rid of the bad company by getting into good company. But even good company will not be conducive to that final experience.

If you are feeling sleepy in a noisy crowd, you would be better off in another crowd where everybody is sitting and listening to soft music or talking very quietly. But when you really want to sleep, even nice company should be left behind; you can't stay with them and experience sleep. So *sattva*, too, can become a sort of bondage. How? Your *sattvic* quality creates an attachment to joy: "I want to be always happy." When you are always in light, you are happy. You don't want to be unhappy. You are still not quite free then. Pleasure based on outside things is caused by *rajas*. However, pure happiness is the outcome of *sattva*. But even that can bring a binding attachment.

> 7. The seed of passion is *rajas* (restless activity), Arjuna, which gives rise to [sense] thirsts and thereafter the bondage of [selfish] attachment. This in turn leads to compulsive behavior.

The thirst to know is caused by your *sattvic guna*. When you are predominantly *sattvic* you feel like reading scripture, meditating or doing selfless work. That's all caused by *sattva*. But *rajas* binds you to passionate, selfish action for your own pleasure or personal benefit.

> 8. But know that the quality of *tamas* veils the mind in ignorance [of reality]. This in turn deludes and binds all embodied beings through carelessness, laziness and over-sleeping (dullness).

Sometimes we feel negligent and indifferent: "Oh, I'm not interested in anything." It's a kind of heedlessness. Sometimes it might *appear* like a beautiful, *sattvic* quality, because it's so still. But, no, it is based on *tamas*. There is a South Indian proverb, "He's so lazy, you have to peel the banana and put it in his mouth." The easiest fruit to peel is the banana. That shows the epitome of dullness, the quality of *tamas*.

Knowledge of the *gunas* is very useful, because you can see that a person is not always *sattvic, rajasic* or *tamasic*. The *mind* is tossed by all three *gunas*. We should know that we are just sitting in the midst of it. Unfortunately, we tend to identify with the movements of the *gunas*. The correct understanding is: "My mind (not I) is in a beautiful, *sattvic* state. And other times it's revolutionary. It creates all kinds of problems. It's *rajasic*."

Whenever you are disturbed or worried, or whatever the condition, immediately sit back and analyze. Is my mind *tamasic* or *rajasic?* By knowing this, you separate yourself from the colored mind and see what's really happening. It will help you not to blame yourself totally or blame someone else. Just know it is all part of the dance of nature.

Here, he puts it in a little different way:

> 9. *Sattva* binds you to happiness; *rajas* binds you to compulsive behavior; and *tamas*, by veiling your mind, binds you to confused thinking and bad judgment.

So, by observing our moods, we can understand which *guna* is predominant in us at the time.

> 10. Sometimes, Arjuna, *sattva* arises above *rajas* and *tamas* and predominates. Sometimes, *rajas* is above *sattva* and *tamas*, and *tamas* sometimes is above *sattva* and *rajas*.

When *sattva* is predominant, *rajas* and *tamas* stay away. But when *rajas* comes, both *sattva* and *tamas* stay away. And when that last fellow, *tamas* comes, both *sattva* and *rajas* leave. It is not that one is always *tamasic*. When you see people who are *tamasic*, don't condemn them completely. At that point, *tamas* has taken over in their minds. Dominated by *tamas*, the other qualities have temporarily subsided. If you allow yourself to be dominated by *tamas* most of the day, you'll be labeled a *tamasic* person.

So, the greater percentage of the qualities determines which label you get. It's like an equilateral triangle. If you put the base toward you, the other two recede. Any one can be the base. When one leads, the others follow.

Here is a beautiful indication of the *sattvic* person.

> **11. When the light of wisdom shines through all the gates of the body, this is a sign that *sattva* is dominant.**

"All the gates of the body" means the senses. Every sense is sharp and clear. Your observation is superb; your taste, superb; your smell, superb. Nothing is dull or sluggish. You are alert all over. You see, hear, taste, smell and feel exceptionally well. When you feel this way, know that you are filled with *sattva guna*.

If you use your senses perfectly and intelligently, at least most of the time, then people can say you are a *sattvic* person. When *sattva* is predominant, all the senses function in a pleasant way. That is perfection in action. Action doesn't mean just when you are doing something. Even when you look, you don't miss anything.

Occasionally, you'll see someone walk up and down the same street fifteen times. Ask them, "Did you notice what happened there on the corner?"

"Oh no, I didn't see it." That is a lack of observance. But when all the senses are alert, that is the quality of a *sattvic* person.

Now, the characteristics of a *rajasic* person:

> **12. Whenever you see greedy behavior, restlessness or continuous thirsting after one thing or another, Arjuna, these are signs that *rajas* is dominant.**

"I want this; I must have that." That kind of longing for things predominates. There will be greed and excessive activity. Don't confuse the activity based on *rajas* with activity based on *sattva*. In *sattva* there's also activity, side by side with tranquility—like a spinning top you don't even see the movement. It appears to be standing still, but there is dynamic activity going on. As the top slows down, you see restless rotation. That's *rajas*. When even that is gone, it's still similar in appearance to its height of movement. Would you call that *sattvic?* No, total absence of all activity is *tamas*.

13. And when *tamas* is dominant, ignorance, sloth and indiscriminant thinking arise.

In this next *sloka*, Sri Krishna speaks of the connection between the predominant *guna* and the soul leaving the body at the time of death.

14. If the mind is predominantly *sattvic* when the body dies, then the soul goes to the pure realms of the wise who know the Supreme.

This could bring a certain idea to the mind. "Ah, I can be *rajasic* and *tamasic* always. Just at the time of death, I will be *sattvic* so my soul will leave the body in a *sattvic* state. It will take its next birth in a *sattvic* womb where its environment will be conducive to continue Yoga practice. Therefore, why can't I do whatever I want and, at just the last minute, become *sattvic?*"

Unfortunately, you can't be that way. Sri Ramakrishna gives a beautiful example: A man taught his parrot to repeat a holy name, "Ram, Ram, Ram . . ." It was always repeating "Ram."

One day a cat saw the parrot and jumped on it. At that moment the parrot simply screamed. It forgot to say "Ram." It was screeching. Where did "Ram" go?

We can't express a beautiful quality just at the last moment. In those final minutes we seem to lose most of our strength. Whatever has been dominant in our life will predominate at the last minute. Unless life is filled with *sattva* most of the time, you can't have *sattva* at the end.

Moreover, you probably won't know when the end is coming. It doesn't give notice. When you're a tenant, at least the landlord gives you a quit notice a month ahead, otherwise you can take him or her to court. But this landlord never gives you any notice, but simply says, "Time to go." Actually, this landlord doesn't always tell you that. The doctor might say, "Her heart failed." Those are the doctor's words. But the landlord simply took away the key—without your even knowing. Any minute you may be asked to get out. You can't say, "No, no, let me bring in some *sattva* before I quit, because the other day the Swami said that if I die with *sattva* I can go to a better place." So be prepared.

15. If the mind is predominantly *rajasic* when the body dies, that soul, in time, will be reborn among those attached to compulsive actions. If the mind is predominantly *tamasic* at such time, that soul is later conceived by parents who are ignorant [of the truth] and deluded.

The baby comes to a family of sleepy, deluded, inert people. We can see the truth of these two *slokas*. How beautiful are the children born to spiritual couples! Why should such souls choose those parents? It's not that the couples decide to have such babies. In a way, a baby's previous actions make it select that womb. Don't think you create the babies. They're not even your babies. The baby takes you as its parent.

In the *Gita*, these children are called *Yogabrastha*. As Sri Krishna mentioned earlier, these are the ones who did spiritual practices and had to quit the body. Wanting to continue, naturally they chose spiritual couples to be their next parents.

Concerning the fruit of the actions inspired by each *guna*, Krishna now compares the *guna* to its fruit.

16. The fruit of good actions is a pure and *sattvic* mind. The fruits of *rajas* ultimately are pain and suffering. And the fruit of *tamas* is ignorance (mistaking the unreal for the real).

We can express it the opposite way, too: the fruit of *sattva* is good action. We can't say which one brings the other. If you consciously perform good actions, you develop *sattva*. If you have developed *sattva* already, naturally you'll always be performing good actions.

And the fruit of *rajas* always causes pain, because *rajasic* actions are based on passion and selfish motives. It may be a little difficult to understand why performing selfish actions always causes pain. You might think, "Many of my selfish acts bring me joy." However, fear arises, and that is painful. Because you are reaching for some joy just for yourself, then you don't want to lose it. The anxiety or fear over losing it is painful. You want the joy to continue always.

But in *sattvic* action, you don't want anything. Things just come to you. When they come, you say, "You have come, fine. Be here, if you want to."

Then they might say, "Sure, go ahead, see you later." But if you have gained something from a selfish act, you won't even allow the fruits to just be there. You will lock them in your safe immediately because you are afraid of losing them.

Not only the desire and effort to get an object cause pain; fear of losing it and the effort to protect and guard it are also painful. Sometimes getting it is easy. If you buy a lottery ticket for $1, you might win $100 or $10,000 easily. Or, without expectation, you may inherit some property. The earning may come easily. But the minute you acquire it, you don't know what to do with it. Where should you keep it—in the bank or invest it somewhere? Worries about investments arise.

That's why I say *rajas* always means pain. If you are *sattvic*, you think, "It's come. Probably God gave me something and God will tell me what to do with that through somebody. Something will happen. I don't need to worry about it."

In simple language, every selfish action is *rajasic*. It may bring some excitement, but it has its own depression later on. Excitement is the mind swinging to the plus side. You lose your neutral position. The pendulum loses its zero point, where it was just resting peacefully. But you can't be out there on the plus side always. You have to swing back. And you won't just return to the original peaceful state without first swinging to the other side. If you swing 30 degrees into the excited, positive side, certainly you will have to swing 30 degrees to the negative side of pain and depression. That's why excitement (*rajas*) causes pain and depression.

Constant tossing and changing is the outcome of *rajas*. If, unconsciously, you begin to do something like that, know that *rajas* is predominant in you and is moving you to do that. Arrest it. You can use your will over all three qualities. Develop that will and cultivate the *sattvic* part by controlling *rajas* and *tamas*. That's Yoga. All yogic customs are based on this—to keep your mind always *sattvic* or tranquil.

"Tranquility is Yoga. Equanimity is Yoga," as Sri Krishna says in the second chapter. Keep yourself always high, but not the high caused by some action. That excitement is an artificial high. It's not natural. If you look for artificial heights, then you will also have to face artificial depths. That's like soaring up on a big, beautiful "trip," then crashing down. There's no gentle landing because you didn't take off gently.

But please remember: Though *rajasic* actions bring pain, they are better than *tamasic* ones, because in *tamas* you don't do anything. There is no hope for a *tamasic* person. At least do something *rajasic*. Then you'll face the painful results and learn something. You can learn from *rajas* but not from *tamas* because there you are just inert, sleeping. That's why I say it's even better to do some mischief than to just sit there dully doing nothing, because the resulting pain will be a beautiful training ground for your growth. A sensible person should know this secret: With pain, we nourish our souls to grow high; it teaches us lessons. Every time we are hit, we learn something new. So let's not try to run away from suffering; it's the best classroom for us.

Sometimes, in your work you might notice a degree of *tamas* even in the midst of activity. For instance, you might neglect to notice something important while building something. It's a combination of *rajas* and *tamas*. If you analyze it, you might see that you still have about 15 percent *tamas* and maybe 85 percent *rajas*. It's much better than pure *tamas*, because with activity you soon face the results. If you perform right action, you see good fruit. Wrong actions soon show you bad fruits, and you know you have done something wrong. That's the only way to learn.

In a way, the entire world is going through this now. You see the *rajasic* tendency predominating around the globe in all these wars and calamities, racial tensions and riots, and the attitude problems of "I and mine." "My country must survive," "My community must be topmost," "I must use this and not you." It really hurts me so much to see these things. This is all based on *tamas* and *rajas*, and it is bringing a great deal of suffering to teach us the necessary lessons.

17. Wisdom arises from *sattva*. Out of *rajas*, greed arises. And from *tamas* comes carelessness, errors in thinking and ignorance.

18. Those whose minds are normally *sattvic* are uplifted. Those in *rajas* stay where they are. But those in *tamas* lose ground.

Chapter Fourteen

19. Whoever sees that all actions are done by the forces of nature, which are the *gunas*, and knows the One who is beyond the *gunas*—surely that person is a seer and rises to my state.

The Seer is you. As you become the Seer, all the rest becomes the seen, and the process of seeing happens because of the *gunas*. It's called *Triputi:* the Seer, the seen and the seeing; or the Knower, the known and knowing.

When the Knower has understood all that is to be known, there's no need for any further knowing, and that is the end of the process. As long as you want to know, then you need all the faculties in order to know. Knowledge is what comes to you without any obstacles. A ledge is something that stops you. When there is no ledge, you have knowledge, and you don't worry about knowing anymore.

Know *that* by which everything else is known. As it is said in the *Bible*, seek that by which everything else will be added unto you. Seeking that, you have sought everything, because everything will be added, whether you want it or not. What a beautiful saying! Whether you want it or not, it will be simply added on for you. The *Bible* might have read: Seek that and you will *get* everything. But no, it's even easier. You don't even have to bother to get it. It just comes to you. Why? Because you got what's to be gotten, then everything likes to get you. Everything comes to you: "Hey, you got the most precious thing. We love you, we want to be with you. We want to have you with us."

Instead of your trying to get everything, it all comes running after you. And what is that kingdom you are seeking? It's the kingdom of not seeking anything; you have realized that even seeking a kingdom is bondage. Yes, even wanting the kingdom of heaven is bondage; it's ignorance. Why? You are already in that kingdom. And where is the kingdom? It is already in you. So why seek outside for it? Just stop seeking. The instant you know that it is already in you, you stop seeking because seeking itself is a sickness. Some of the great sages have said, "Don't do anything. Just be quiet. You have it already. Just realize that."

And by simply knowing that you already have what you are looking for, then you have everything.

This is another way of saying, "Renounce everything." Renounce even the desire for the kingdom—that means renounce all your desires. Become utterly desireless. Liberation is there already, the moment you stop desiring anything for yourself. Then all those things that were so proud because you were chasing after them will come chasing after you. Money is very proud because it thinks, "You see, without me she can't survive. She is always running after me." Power and position are also proud because they think you are a slave running after them. "Look," they say, "We're tossing this fellow here and there because he's after us."

But everything is radically changed when you say, "I don't care anymore for you fellows! I don't need any of you! I'm happy by myself!"

Then they wonder, "Hey, what is happening to this fellow? He's not after us anymore. We'd better not leave him. Let's run to him."

Everything will be "added unto you." Now all the things you renounced are after you. That's why the scriptures say that a true renunciate will be served by both the Goddess of wisdom and the Goddess of wealth—Sarasvati and Lakshmi. If you are a true renunciate they will be sitting beside you, massaging your feet. Money itself will be saying, "Master, just command me. Is there anything I could do for you?" And wisdom also will ask, "Is there anything you want answered?" Perhaps you will say, "Yes, someone has asked me a question, You answer the question." Immediately the answer comes through, you don't even have to read books to answer, because the Goddess of wisdom is always there. The question itself presses the button, and immediately the answer comes.

If you ever think this Swami is giving a beautiful explanation of the *sloka*, you should know it is not the Swami who is giving. It is Sarasvati who is serving the Swami. All you have to do for that is say, "I don't want anything anymore."

> 20. Because the *gunas* give rise to the physical body, those still
> embodied ones who transcend the *gunas* also leave behind the cycle
> of birth, pain, decay and death, and attain immortality.

He speaks here of the *jivanmukta*, one who is liberated while still living in the body. At this point, the individual understands that all the afflictions are in the mind and body, which is *prakriti,* and not in the real Self, who is just there watching the whole thing. It is the light in the midst of everything, like the sunlight that comes through a beautiful stained glass window. The colors are not part of the sun. The sun's rays pass through the colors and appear to be colored. Actually, it's the same light on both sides. When we realize that, we are liberated from actions and reactions. We see them objectively as separate from us. One who sees that is said to be beyond or devoid of the three *gunas.*

Next, Arjuna asks a question similar to the one he asked in the second chapter about a person of steady wisdom.

> **21. Lord, what are the signs of those who have passed beyond the three forces of nature? How do they conduct themselves? And how did they get beyond the grip of nature?**

> **22. The blessed Lord replied: When nature's qualities are present, such people neither become attached to, nor do they reject the light, activity or delusion born of the *gunas*. And when these qualities are absent, they are not missed.**

You don't need to hate *rajas* and *tamas.* If you see *tamasic* people, don't judge them. Probably, you were once like that before. Now they are growing just as you did. The one who has gone beyond the *gunas* neither likes nor dislikes. You see everything as part of nature's work. You are above all that. Even *sattvic* people are attached to pious learning and spiritual practices. Those caught up in *rajas* are always up and doing. What seems good to them they execute devotedly, and what seems bad they abhor and avoid. They like some things; they dislike other things. That's part of *rajas.* However, *tamasic* people are lethargic, sleepy and they welcome those qualities very much. They are even annoyed if their sleep is disturbed by others. (It's good to know that if you are annoyed when somebody wakes you, at that moment, your mind is controlled by *tamas.)*

But the *jivanmukta,* the liberated one, who is the knower of the Absolute, is beyond all three. He or she is like a mirror. The mind of such a person reflects whatever quality or color is brought before it. It *seems* to accept the different colors, though in reality it doesn't. The mirror knows it's a mirror, though the onlooker sees different colored objects reflected there. The mirror's understanding is true knowledge. If you are a *jivanmukta*, you know that you are not affected by what is being reflected in your mind. You don't worry about what others say. Others don't see you directly. They see you through your mind.

But if you would like others also to see the real Self in you, keep the mind clean. And with your clean mind, you can also see them well, because you see them through the same glass. If I put a blue glass between you and me, I could say you are wearing a blue shirt and you will say I am wearing a blue robe. Neither is correct. But if you see your Self correctly, you needn't worry what I say. Even if I say you are wearing blue, you'll think, "Probably he is seeing through his *tamasic* mind. I know I'm wearing white."

We don't have to fight when others see us in their own way. It all depends on what color glasses they are wearing, what *guna* controls their minds. Before you label other people as this or that, beware of your glasses, the color of your mind. Clean the mind well and you will have the correct vision.

23. Because they perceive that the *gunas* are the sole doer, they stay centered and remain unmoved by the winds of nature.

24-25. Those who maintain their equanimity in the midst of pleasure and pain, friends and adversaries, praise and blame; and those who identify with the true Self, thus perceiving the same essence in a clod of dirt, a stone or a nugget of gold; and those who let go of every selfish pursuit; it may be said that such people as these have gone beyond the forces of nature.

Here is further description of the qualities of those who know what is to be known. Sometimes, totally *tamasic* or dull people don't worry about praise or blame either. They will just smile. Extreme *sattva* and extreme *tamas* look alike at first. But they are at completely opposite poles. You should not delude yourself thinking, "I'm above all these things." And again, because *jivanmuktas* or liberated ones look on clay and gold equally, this doesn't mean they are going to throw everything out. They are not *attracted* by gold, nor are they going to reject clay. In regard to their relationship with things, they're equal—but they will use them properly. They will use clay as clay should be used, and gold as it should be used. What they are free of is the *attachment*.

They don't personally undertake anything, so there's no funeral for them. They just enjoy life as it comes. They don't plan anything. Sometimes it might look like they're planning when a *sattvic* force functions through them. But it's not they who are planning. Things happen. Plans unfold by their mere presence. They won't say, "It was my plan; I did that," because, in fact, they are not the doer. Their minds do things. Because of the purity of their minds, however, they are unaffected by that. They don't want to take the credit for themselves.

You might wonder, "Do only harmonious, *sattvic* ideas come through such minds?" They might *allow* other thoughts into the mind. But since they have separated their identity from their minds, the mind doesn't receive so much force to do these other things. Normally, you don't arrive at that *jivanmukta* state unless you have consciously developed a *sattvic* mind. But sometimes, it is true, such a liberated state might be attained while the mind is still *rajasic* or *tamasic*—due to the person's *prarabdha* karma, certain acts of his or her previous births.

Sometimes you see certain yogis or *siddhas* (accomplished ones) who just lie in a ditch like a buffalo. For example, years ago, I met Sri Swami Nityananda, a great *siddha*. When I saw him, he was lying in some muddy water like a buffalo. His action looked *tamasic,* but behind that there was a *jivanmukta*. I met another great *siddha* in a small village in South India. I knew he was there, but he was hard to reach because he didn't want to be discovered by anybody. He was dodging me. I followed him, and, at one point, caught up with him. He pretended to be a blind man. Quietly, I walked behind him. Suddenly, he turned his head and said, "Why are you following me?"

"How do you know I'm following you, if you are blind?" I replied.

"You rascal." He lifted his cane and turned around to strike me.

"Yes, please give me that at least. I can't go without some blessing from you, by any means."

"Ah, you are a clever man. Did you bring a bottle of brandy for me?" As an offering, he asked for brandy.

"Sorry, I don't drink."

"You don't drink, but don't you know I drink brandy and eat meat?"

He did eat meat and drink brandy. Can you label him *rajasic* or *tamasic* as you would most others? It's hard to say. *Jivanmuktas* know they are liberated, completely free. But *you* can't always tell. It's hard because you note only the physical body and mind. Unless your own body and mind are so clean that you can see through their exteriors, you will simply see them as ordinary men and women. You might even avoid people like that, thinking, "You call this person a Guru; that person a *siddha*, a saint? You don't even want to be near them."

It's hard to see the true caliber of such people. There are *jivanmuktas* who don't want to reveal themselves. They roam about like insane people, fools or children. Why would they do that? They just want to choose the right students who really want something genuine. If they come across a sincere and serious student, then just one or two words is enough. Even then they won't keep the disciple nearby. They chase him away. "That's enough. Go work with what I've taught you." Even today there are such teachers. You can't simply go and live with them. If a hundred people seek him out, he may talk only to one person. Sometimes they even take stones and pelt the people who come. When I went to see Sri Swami Nityananda, he started throwing stones at me. Somehow, I was introduced as "Yogiraj Swami Satchidananda." The minute he heard the name, Nityanandaji said, "Yogiraj, Yogiraj, ah, Yoga, Yoga—*siddhi, siddhi*, be careful, be careful."

I understood what he meant and said, "Please bless me, Swamiji, not to get caught in those things. You are the right person to bless me for that, because I know what you underwent."

"What's that? What did you say?"

Few people knew the previous part of his life. But I happened to know a little of where he had been before and how he came to be here, because I also knew his Guru.

Chapter Fourteen

When I was a young boy, I met Swami Nityananda's Guru, who used to come around to our village and neighboring villages. Nityanandaji was his disciple. When Nityanandaji started practicing, he accomplished certain *siddhis* and started demonstrating them. He would stop the running of trains, for example. He also produced currency from his empty pockets, and other things.

His teacher chased him away. "Don't even stay anywhere near me." That's how he came to Bombay. There, also, he began demonstrating his *siddhis* and attracted a lot of people. Then, at a later stage, he calmed down and started advising others, like me, "Don't get caught in *siddhis;* they puff up the ego and block you from experiencing peace of mind."

That's why I said, "I really need your blessings because you are certainly the one who would know these things." He immediately understood.

I tell you this because there are so many great people hiding behind many faces. That's why you can't easily say who is a realized *jivanmukta* and who is not. Don't put all so-called yogis into one category. Some may be duping you. Some may be blessing you. The minute you see any strange Swamis, don't immediately criticize them, because you don't know what's underneath. You have to vibrate on the same wavelength to really know people. Otherwise, don't judge them. You can simply say, "I don't know everything. I'm not ready. If I'm not drawn to this teacher, I'll just stay away."

It's hard to decide who is a real saint or a realized person, who is a *jivanmukta,* and who is not. Some may reveal themselves by their actions. Some do not care to. Some may purposely hide it. If a student has a real keen interest, the teacher might say, "You seem to be okay; come on. Do this and go away." If they let a few people stay with them, then it becomes an organization. Many purposely avoid organizations.

26. And whoever serves me with steady devotion, that person also passes over the *gunas* and is well prepared to experience the absolute oneness of *Brahman.*

27. For I am the home of absolute oneness, of *Brahman,* who is immortal and unalterable. I am the eternal *dharma* (truth) and infinite bliss.

He gives these beautiful descriptions to show indirectly that the Absolute can be understood through its various qualities by the different yogic paths. "Whoever serves me with steady devotion . . ." refers to Bhakti Yoga, the path of devotion. "I am the home of *Brahman,* who is immortal and unalterable," indicates Jnana Yoga, the path of wisdom. "The eternal *dharma*" would indicate the goal of Raja Yogis (on the royal path) who completely conquer and purify their minds.

I believe it's always better to have some of everything, all the paths— Integral Yoga. You are not always in the same mental state. If a little *rajas* comes out, some restlessness, just convert it into divine *rajas* by doing some beautiful actions. This is Karma Yoga, the path of selfless service.

Even your *tamas* can be converted. If you want to sleep, all right. Sleep with God's name in your mind, which is Bhakti Yoga, devotion. That kind of sleep will be much more beautiful than the sleep that follows TV "thrillers" or horror stories. All the qualities or *gunas* are quite normal. Just divert them into the proper channels to reach your goal.

Thus ends the fourteenth discourse of the *Bhagavad Gita,* the science of Yoga, entitled: "Yoga of the Three Qualities of Nature."

Yoga of the Supreme Self

This whole chapter is quite beautiful. It has very few *slokas*, but they speak of the Supreme *Purusha*. In India at many *ashrams* we used to repeat these *slokas* in Sanskrit while meals were being served. It took just a short time. By the time we had finished, the food was served. That was the tradition.

Chapter Fifteen speaks of the tree of life and how to cut through it to get to liberation. It all begins with a beautiful allegory:

> 1. **The blessed Lord said: The wise speak of an eternal *Asvattha* tree (sacred fig) with its roots above and its branches here in this world. Its leaves are the *Vedas* (holy scriptures). Whoever understands this tree knows the most sacred wisdom.**

It's an upside-down tree—a tree in a headstand. Speaking esoterically, the microcosm of the body itself is an upside-down tree. Your roots are your hair and head. Some roots are long; some curly. And the trunk is the *meru dhanda,* the spine. The branches are the arms, legs and subtle nerves (*nadis*). The joints are the glands. So the roots are the head; that's why the head comes first at birth, just as the roots are the first part of a tree to grow.

Actually, this isn't the true beginning. For the microcosm, which is the physical body, the roots are present. But their contact with the macrocosm, the entire cosmos, is even further up. In the beginning we have an opening at the crown of the head to communicate with the cosmos.

The whole skull is soft. But gradually we harden. The opened portion closes. The head, unfortunately, becomes a heavy nut.

That is the *Asvattha* tree. The literal meaning of *asvattha* is, "that which is not today as it was yesterday." It was one way yesterday, another today and it will be different again tomorrow. It is constantly changing, like a river. It appears to be the same river each day, but it's not the same water. There is a constant flow.

2. Nourished by the *gunas*, its branches spread above and below. It buds forth all the sense objects, and its roots reach down to this world, binding people to one action after another.

3. The true nature of this tree—its form, origin, end and even its presence—is not perceived at the level of worldly awareness. Just cut down this deep-rooted *Asvattha* tree with the sharp sword of non-attachment.

What should you do with this tree? Cut it down. Get *moksha*, liberation. That doesn't mean you literally cut it down, but detach yourself. Know that you are not involved; you are at a different level of consciousness. Ultimately, even this body and the entire cosmos are all the same substance. They aren't different, but they are at different states.

4. There is a place from which none ever returns. That is the goal. Seek it by vowing: I take refuge in the original *Purusha*, who is the source of all, the Absolute, from which streams forth the eternal energy.

He is saying that once you really understand the absolute truth and submit yourself to that truth, then there is nothing for you to obtain or fulfill in this world; all your so-called duties are over. You realize that you don't have any duty of your own in this world. You have been brought in by that absolute Consciousness, made to perform some duties, and then when the job is over, you are fired. So all these things—coming and going, taking birth, annually celebrating birthdays and then celebrating the death anniversary—none of these make sense anymore. As part of that absolute Consciousness, you realize that you were never born, nor are you ever going to die. When people experience that reality, they have gone to the place that every soul ultimately should go. On reaching that state, they don't come back again. That means no birth, no death. That's the grand finale. And that's the meaning of this *sloka*.

By taking refuge in the Absolute, you need not come back. That's encouraging, because coming and going is not so easy. The seers and sages have called birth and death a disease. There is pain in coming and in going. Others might enjoy your arrival—"another addition to our insane asylum." But not you, who arrived crying. And after staying for some time, you became completely blinded by ignorance and don't even want to go. So when death comes, you cling to the body. Coming is painful, and going also is painful. In fact, one should be happy to say goodbye to this body when the proper time comes. It's ever a nuisance, always looking for doctors, every day into the kitchen ten times, constantly things oozing out through all the holes. Don't think it's so pretty and enjoyable. How much you must clean up every time you wake up. And yet, we say, "Such a beautiful body."

Thiruvalluvar says the relationship between life and the body is like that of a little bird inside an egg. When the bird grows enough and pecks to break through the shell, it doesn't cling onto that. It just feels relieved to be out of the shell. The body is not really so enjoyable; it's a prison, even though people spend so many hours fixing it up.

Life is more beautiful out of the body. We have many more capabilities. Yet, people don't want to go. I remember an old fellow who was constantly coughing and sneezing. He was so sick even his children asked him to sleep outside on the veranda, because inside he was a nuisance to everybody. He was so disgusted that he said, "Lord, why am I still alive? Don't you want to come and take me away?"

The Lord happened to hear his prayers and suddenly appeared. "Yes, did you call me, sir?"

"Who are you?"

"I'm the Lord of Death. You called me. Are you ready?"

"Oh sir, I wasn't serious. I still want to see my grandson be married. It's my responsibility."

How we cling to life in this body! But if we realized the beauty of living free without this prison, we would never want to come back into this sort of life. That happens only when we realize the immortality of the soul, when we realize we are that *Purusha*, the Supreme Consciousness. We are not the body; it's simply a house, even a dilapidated house. Although we change our cars every few years, still after even eighty years we want to keep living in this same vehicle, the body, though it constantly needs repair, new parts and new paint.

That's why Sri Krishna says if you really take refuge in that absolute truth, you experience a grand stage in life, at which point you will never even consider coming back to this.

But who can cut down this tree? Who can become detached?

> 5. Fortunate are those seekers who are no longer deluded [by that tree] and thus are liberated from pride. Because they have conquered personal attachment, they ever abide in their true identity, which is the Self. No longer disturbed by personal desires, which have completely abated, or the pairs of opposites, such as pleasure and pain, they attain that eternal goal.

What a beautiful *sloka*! Who will reach the eternal goal? Here are the qualifications: "liberated from pride and delusion," because pride and delusion are part of the mind. You must be free from your body, ego and mind. It's the mind that takes pride. It's the mind that becomes deluded. It's the mind that becomes attached to things. Who enjoys pleasures or dislikes pain? Again, the mind. Who is happy? Who is unhappy? The mind. But you—the real you who is the Self—*know* this.

That's why you say, "I know I was happy yesterday. I know something happened to me this morning and I know I'm unhappy now." What's common here? "I know." If something had really happened to *you*, you wouldn't be able to know it. Certainly, you would have lost the capacity even to know. But see this: your "knowing" is unchanged.

Then what happened to whom? The mind was happy yesterday until something came into it this morning and disturbed it. But you say, "I know both." See, as the knower you are not affected by the mind. If you—your real Self—were unhappy, how would you know you were unhappy? It's as if an insane man were to come forward and say he's insane. Immediately, you're certain that he's not insane. No insane person will say, "I'm insane." Instead he'll argue, "Who says I'm insane?" He's insane, so he can't see his condition accurately.

But in your case, the knowing is correct; you know you are unhappy. But can the knower really be unhappy, or does the knower just know something else is unhappy? That's how to constantly analyze. Even during Karma

Yoga, or selfless service, keep asking yourself: "Am I doing this?" As you lift a log, you ask, "Am I lifting the log? No. My mind wants it lifted and my hands are helping. The real one is just watching. My mind has a desire to do this; it directed the body here and said to the hands, 'Come on, lift the log and put it there.' And the body is obeying the mind." It's true, literally, you are the eternal witness.

And that is the eternal goal. It's not that you are literally *going to* arrive at that state someday. You are already there, but somehow you don't seem to recognize it. You are already rich. You have eaten a big lunch. You're not hungry at all. But you fell asleep and in your dream you feel yourself to be poor and hungry, running and sneaking into someone's kitchen. It's all a dream. Really, you have had a sumptuous lunch. Now you wake to find yourself lying in your comfortable bed. And you say, "My goodness, my stomach is still full."

In the same way, you seem to have forgotten your real nature. You have slipped into a kind of sleep. You assume all these qualities: rich, poor, full, hungry, happy, unhappy. That's why we say, "Wake up." It doesn't matter whether you are doing Karma Yoga (selfless service), meditation or just eating. Whatever you do, keep this in mind constantly. Think: "Who is doing this?" Or ,"Who is eating now? Who is hungry? Who knows who is hungry? Who is enjoying the taste of this food? Am I doing it or is it my mind or body?" If you keep on questioning—even in the midst of heavy work—you separate your identification from the body and mind. That separation is liberation. You have liberated yourself from the body-mind clutches and you remember your true nature.

Then *you* become the master, because you are able to see your mind and body as separate things and slowly you get a grip on them. You can say, "Now do this, do that." Sometimes you can say, "I don't want you to do anything. Keep quiet. I'm going to rest. Everything must be silent." And the mind becomes silent.

You can train the mind well. Just know that without you, the mind cannot do anything. The mind has no power by itself. It's the mind and body that function, and you are the witness. Suppose you could go away from them. Would they keep working? No. And when you are here, who is it that works? The mind and body. You are not working. So even though you are not working, your presence is necessary for them to work. Do you understand? Without your presence, they can't work. But in front of you—the witness, the knower—they can function.

It's similar to a magnet that is just there doing nothing while all the iron filings run about. The magnet doesn't move, but it gives enough force for the filings to move. When it's not there, the filings become inert; they have no power of their own. Or, we could compare this to a plain, clear light inside a many-colored globe. You see all the different colored lights. But if you take the clear inner light away, no colored light shines out. You are that clear light; you are simply there. By your presence, everything happens and you know it. Being and knowing are the only two things that you do, nothing else. And because of your mere presence, the mind and body get the necessary energy, or magnetism, to function.

But how is this understanding helpful in your day-to-day life? When you are troubled or excited, just sit back and analyze, "Hey, who is troubled now? Who's excited? Not me. I simply know the mind is troubled because I have been watching it. It did a few things without even listening to my advice. Now it has gotten caught and is troubled." You treat your own mind as a naughty child. But you are not affected by it. The moment you separate the mental problems from you and say, "I'm different; it's the mind that's suffering," then all the suffering is gone. Try and see. Why should you feel sorry for the mind when it suffers? It's done something wrong; it has to suffer to learn. *You* needn't worry.

That's liberation. When you are really free from identifying with your own body, mind and egoism, you are always happy. You are an eternal witness, you just see and enjoy everything. Sometimes the mind functions as a hero—all right, enjoy the hero act. Sometimes, it's a villain; then enjoy the villainy. Enjoy the mind. "I see you really play the part beautifully; all right go on!" But *you* are not affected by it.

Most people don't see this separation. They still see your body and mind functioning and say you are doing this and that. It doesn't matter;

let them think so, because they can't see the separation. To others it may *appear* that you are doing things, but really you are not. The real you isn't doing anything; only the reflected you is. This is action in inaction. You are active and, at the same time, inactive. You know that the real you is inactive, but others see you as active. They might even praise you. But you will just laugh at them. Such a person is called a *jivanmukta*. You have your freedom from all bondage. You are just you. That's the eternal goal.

> 6. *That* is beyond the light of the sun, the moon or fire. That is where I am. When you reach this goal, you will never again fall back to a feeling of separateness.

This means that once you experience this eternal goal, you never come down again. You are there. You are really victorious then. That is the real victory. You have achieved what is to be achieved. You have conquered what should be conquered. It's called *Atma jayam,* Self-victory. It's not sport victory, beauty victory or money victory, but Self victory. You have attained your own *Atman.* In any other condition, it can be said that you have lost your Self, lost your soul. You are ignoring it. It could be said that you have murdered your soul, or killed your real Self.

Of course, you can't literally kill what's eternal and indestructible. But when you totally ignore your true Self and identify with its reflection, it's as if you killed it, because you are not enjoying its beauty.

> 7. A part of my Self, which is eternal, comes down to this world and attracts nature's qualities. The mind and senses are animated by the individual *jiva* (soul), which is part of me. Thus, I move about and perceive in this world of nature.

> 8. The true Self, who is God, enters and leaves a physical body as an individual soul; when the soul goes on, it takes with it the mental and sense capacities, as the wind carries fragrances from flower to flower.

A small portion of the Cosmic One (*Paramatman*), which is beginningless and endless, jumps out as a *jivatman,* or individual soul, and then expresses itself through the body, senses and mind. It just plays around and then goes back. This *jivatman* and *Paramatman* can be compared to the water inside a pot and the water outside. It's the same water. If you dip a pot in the sea, the water that is inside may be called pot water. Outside is the same water, but you call it sea water. Break the pot, it's all sea water again.

This is an example from scripture. But I would like to suggest another analogy: a pot made of ice. If you put it in the sea, there is water inside it, water outside, and what is the pot itself? Also water. So inside, outside, and in between, all are water, but at different densities. That is the difference between *Jivatman*, *Paramatman* and what separates them. That which separates you and God again is the same God.

All you have to do is melt! Apply a little heat. That means accept a little heat whenever it comes. Don't always look for a cool situation. In Sanskrit this is called *tapasya*, austerity. *Tapas* means to heat or burn. A gentle roasting will make the ice pot melt. When that happens, you no longer see yourself as apart from others. All the barriers have melted.

That's why the *Upanishads* say, "*Brahman*, the Absolute, is the Truth; the world is false." But you don't have to read all the *Upanishads* if you just keep this one point in mind. God is all there is. There is nothing else. The *Bible* puts it: In the beginning there was God and nothing but God. Only God could say, "There is only me and nothing else but me."

> 9. The ears, eyes, nose, senses of taste and touch, and even the mind, come to life only by God's Presence. Thus, it is God who actually experiences and enjoys the sense objects.

Now Krishna talks about the eye of wisdom.

> 10. Deluded people do not realize who it is that quits the body [at the moment of physical death]. Nor do they perceive that living presence that dwells within, giving life to the body, enjoying the senses, experiencing everything and doing things through the *gunas*. But those with intuitive insight see and understand.

Those who have intuitive wisdom will see who is born, who lived, who died, who was happy, who was unhappy, and so on. That's what people call the third eye. It's not one of these physical eyes which see physical objects. It is the third eye to see spiritual truth.

But how to obtain this eye of wisdom? Probably, Sri Krishna will have some good ideas. Let's see what he says.

11. Those who strive to perfect themselves through Yoga discover the *Atman* within themselves. However, those who seek, without refining their minds and character, are unable to perceive the *Atman*.

Two types of people strive to see the truth. Those who are immersed in Yoga and those who haven't refined themselves. The second type of people are not blessed with the spirit of Yoga, though both are trying. What, then, is the spirit of Yoga? You will find the answer in a small sentence from the *Yoga Sutras of Patanjali*: *Yogas chitta vritti nirodhah* (Book 1, *sutra* 2). Yoga means a mind free of all turbulence—calm and clean. "Equanimity or purity of mind is Yoga." You don't need any other definitions. In Chapter Two of the *Bhagavad Gita*, Sri Krishna defines Yoga as "perfection in action." But that comes only if you have a clean, calm mind. If your mind is restless, you can't be perfect. Perfect action is directed only by a calm mind. The simplest and best definition of Yoga is "a calm and clean mind." If you want it even shorter, say Yoga is a clean mind, because a clean mind is a calm mind. A dirty mind can never be calm.

Purity of mind, or purity of heart is Yoga. Blessed are those who are pure in heart, for they shall be yogis, and, yes, they shall see God. "They shall see God" means they shall find peace, that's all. Peace is our God. God is absolute joy, unending peace. God is not an image. If you have unending joy, that's God. If you have permanent peace, God is that.

That's why all the scriptures say *shalom, shanti,* peace and so on; they all have different words for this same experience. And every scripture speaks of purity of heart or peace of mind. Jesus was a great yogi. Probably, he didn't know the word Yoga, so he just talked about purity of heart. If you are endowed with the yogic attitude, whatever act you do will be perfect, and you will see the truth.

Because this is "Yoga of the Supreme Self," Sri Krishna gives a few ideas of its eminence:

12. There is sunlight that fills all the world; there is moonlight and also firelight. Know that all these lights are of one light, which is my light.

13. With but a drop of my *ojas* (energy), my Presence in the earth sustains all living beings. And my Presence in the moon, as the life-giving fluid, *soma*, nourishes all plant life.

He is just expressing a little of God's glory. God is the energy behind everything and is the nourisher behind all your nourishment. Behind your vitamins A, B, C, D, and E, there is a vitamin "G" (for God). Remember to take plenty!

14. I enter and abide in all creatures as the breath of life. And as *prana* and *apana*, the life currents within, I am also the digestive fire.

He says, "I am the digestive fire in your stomach. Even to digest your food, I am there as the digestive energy. I am there as the food; I am there as you; I am there as your energy, and I am the one who digests myself." Do you remember what Krishna said earlier? "The fire is myself; the offering into the fire is myself; the one who accepts the offering is myself; the offer also is myself. It is all ultimately myself. So I am playing all the parts."

God seems to have a monopoly. God doesn't have anybody else to play with because probably there is no one else but God. God is certainly the poorest and loneliest one, because apart from God there is nobody. Maybe for this reason, God appears to multiply into all of us.

15. I am present in everyone's heart. Thus, I give rise to memory and understanding—or take them away. In fact, I am that which is to be realized ultimately: I am the goal of all sacred scriptures. Indeed, I am the author of the *Vedanta*, the end and essence of holy scriptures. And I am also the Consciousness that understands them.

16. There are two aspects of *Purusha* in this world: that which is subject to change and that which never changes. All created beings are of the perishable aspect of *Purusha*. But the essence of every creature (*kustasha*) is the imperishable *Purusha*.

17. There is yet a Supreme *Purusha*, the highest Self, infinite and eternal, who pervades and sustains the three worlds.

Again, *Purusha* is the Supreme Consciousness. But the *sloka* speaks of two different aspects of *Purusha* in the world. One changes; the other never changes. He's presenting the same idea in a somewhat different way. Even the so-called creation is essentially an expression of the *Purusha*, the same Supreme Consciousness. But that's called perishable because the expressions of that essence are subject to change. Consciousness itself is imperishable. And all this entire creation is part of consciousness. So how can we say the creation is perishable and the absolute *Purusha* is imperishable?

It means *Purusha* taking expression as many is perishable. It might be clearer if we say the names and forms are perishable; the essence is imperishable. The creation is nothing but names and forms. We can put everything in the creation into two categories: names and forms. Nor are they truly categories. Everything with form has a name. The creation is the universe of name and form. If we simply ignore the name and form, then all we see is the essence: consciousness. For an analogy, let's just say that water is imperishable. But the waves, foam, spray, bubbles and icebergs are all perishable. If you go to the Arctic, essentially you see the imperishable water and simultaneously the perishable waves. They're constantly changing form. They come and go. Icebergs and bubbles are also perishable. A little wind or a touch of anything is enough to burst the bubble. It's gone, perished. But actually there never was a bubble. At essence it was always the same water, before and after. The water took a different form, which we called a bubble. Thus, we can understand the imperishable in the perishable.

In what way is a drop of water different from the sea? Essentially, they're one and the same. In this analogy the drop is separated from the sea. But the *Purusha* is never separated from itself; it's indivisible; it's always together.

Even if we are all sitting together in a room, we could say we are separate. We say this because we see bodies with nothing in between. But sometimes you can actually see the vibrations here also. Everybody is nothing but a mass of vibration. Many have experienced this at one time or another. It's true. So, in reality we aren't separate people sitting apart from each other. We are all a mass of vibration, which is consciousness. So there is consciousness here, consciousness there, and, in between, also the same indivisible consciousness. But somehow our lack of realizing the truth makes us say, "You're there. I'm over here. And there's nothing in between." That's why whatever we put into words is a falsehood from the perspective of the absolute. Truth cannot be talked of. The minute we begin to talk, we are in the perishable realm of duality, which, ultimately, is a lie. Even scientists agree, nowadays, that there's no place where there is nothing.

18. I am that *Purushottama*, the Supreme Consciousness, described in scripture (the *Vedas*) as the one who is beyond both that which changes and that which is unchanging.

"As the *Purushottama*," says Krishna, "I transcend the perishing and the non-perishing, the forming, dissolving and changing." The *Purushottama* is the one who cannot be confined to this changing world. It is the unchanging. We don't know how big it is. What we see as changing, forming, dissolving and reforming is probably a minute part of the vast whole. Probably God just took a small piece of Itself and said, "Now you can go and change, take birth and die and create yourself again and again," while the rest of God is still sitting there somewhere. All these millions and billions of solar systems in the macrocosm are probably just a small part of the whole, which is God. God just took a part of Itself and said, "Now you can go play, while I watch."

19. When people are free of delusion, they recognize me as the Supreme Self. Those who realize this know everything, Arjuna, and worship me with their entire being.

The minute you realize that everything is nothing but God, who is to worship whom then? That's the problem with words. When you begin to put things in words, you confuse people. Sometimes it's better not to read many books. The more you hear, the more confused you get. Saint Ramakrishna beautifully said that if you really want to attain realization soon, forget all you have learned. Children have better realization than the so-called educated people. We muddle things up by trying to say things that can't be put into words.

A beautiful passage in the *Upanishads* says that the Supreme Self is beyond speech and mind. The supreme reality can't be grasped by the mind and spoken with words.

Then why do we have this book speaking of the truth? First we say, "Please listen," and then, "I have no tongue to talk." Still we speak of it: "My mother is the one who never had a child." Such descriptions are found in the *Upanishads* also: "See the track of the serpent in the sky." What does it mean? A serpent never flies. And even if it flies, it won't leave tracks. This is just another example. It means we speak of something that can't be described in words. All the great sages have clearly said you can't know it by reading; you can't talk about it; you can't even think of it. The *Mandukya Upanishad* says you can't grasp the Supreme Self; you can't even describe it; can't even think of it.

What should we do? Stop talking and try to experience it. When the experience comes, we don't talk and we don't *have* to talk. If you are really happy, your face will glow with light. Everyone will know you are happy. I don't have to tell you that experience is the best way. So all talking is just nonsense. But until we experience it, instead of talking about other things, it seems to be good to talk about that which cannot be said. That way we avoid a lot of problems.

So we do all these Yoga practices to make our minds clearer. Then we recognize this truth that cannot be understood with the mind. The mind should say, "I have no capacity to understand it." Then it stops its egoistic approach. For the mind to accept its incapacity, it must be free from the ego. That's why we first move the mind away from unwanted things. Then it becomes calmer, steadier and stronger, and it realizes the ultimate truth.

Sometimes, it's better to ignore all the *Vedanta* and just do Karma Yoga (selfless action) which cleans the mind and frees us from the ego. Then just one *sloka* is enough to elevate us to that height.

> 20. And now, pure-hearted Arjuna, I have passed on to you this most sacred and profound science. When you truly comprehend this, you become enlightened, and you have accomplished all that there is to accomplish in life.

Thus Sri Krishna ends the "Yoga of the Supreme Self." It makes us seem so little, doesn't it? Compared to that Supreme Self, who are we then? So minute, so minute.

Thus ends the fifteenth discourse of the *Bhagavad Gita,* the science of Yoga, entitled: "Yoga of the Supreme Self."

The Yoga of the Divine and the Demonic

The sixteenth and seventeenth chapters are very important because they give so much practical advice to the spiritual seeker. Some of the other chapters are mainly theory and philosophy. But I feel we should look more for practical hints. The important question is, "What should I do in my life?" We all know there's something higher to be achieved. We don't have to worry about its name, where it is, or whether it's a he or a she, or one or many.

Mainly, it just creates problems trying to give names and forms to the nameless and formless one. God is something beyond name and form. But we have to perceive that infinite One in some name and form. There is nothing wrong in doing so. Unfortunately, many people want others also to choose the same name and form they prefer. There's the problem. They say, "I like this name and form, so everybody should like it. And if you don't, I don't like you!" That's the reason I don't bother much with the name or form. I just say stick to one thing. Any name and form is okay. All names are God's name; all forms are God's form.

The real question is how to perceive or realize *that*. What should I do to get a glimpse of it? I want to experience it instead of simply playing with words. That's the important thing.

Sadhana is the actual practice of Yoga. Without *sadhana*, there's no accomplishment. Here in the sixteenth chapter we see some of the divine qualities that every seeker should develop if he or she wants to reach that great accomplishment.

1. The blessed Lord said: Arjuna, these are the qualities of one who will attain a divine state: fearlessness (*abhaya*); a pure-thinking heart; staying on the Yoga path of wisdom (no matter what happens); always giving generously (*danam*); control of the senses; a life of self-sacrifice (*yajna*); a desire to study scriptures; acceptance of austerities (*tapas*); straightforwardness;

At the very beginning, Sri Krishna gives a beautiful quality: fearlessness. A true spiritual seeker who is after the truth should know no fear. Fear is a result of lack of faith. If you have total faith in that Supreme Power, you won't be afraid of anything.

> 2. Not causing pain to others (*ahimsa*); truthfulness (*satyam*); never angry; always peaceful (*shanti*); renunciation of the fruits of your actions (*tyaga*); never speaking falsely or maliciously of others; compassion for all beings; not coveting what others have; gentleness; modesty; never fickle;

> 3. Full of vigor; always forgiving; courageous in adversity; pure of body and mind; no hatred toward anyone; and never puffed up with pride. These are the characteristics, Arjuna, of a man or woman destined for a divine life.

Even though the list is a long one, if you develop even one of these qualities to the fullest extent, automatically you see the other qualities coming. It's not that you have to practice one at a time. Let any one lead; the others will follow because they are all links in a chain. You can't be truthful without being non-violent, without being pure, without being modest.

And the basic characteristic to develop, which underlies all the rest, is selflessness, or renunciation. When I say renunciation, please don't immediately misunderstand and think, "Someone is a renunciate because he or she wears particular clothes, or has a special name or lives in an *ashram*." These are not the true signs of renunciation; you can live in an *ashram* but still be very much attached to your own room, your own mat, your pillow or your own altar.

Real renunciation means freedom from selfishness, you renounce your selfishness. Once that is achieved, you won't be bothered by anything. Wherever you are, you're at home. Nothing will disturb you. A true renunciate won't be angry at anybody, won't hate anybody, won't be afraid of anything. It's the attachment that causes fear. Because of attachment, you want to possess things. Anxiety about trying to get something is in your mind. The doubt whether you will get it or not is there. People often say, "I'm afraid I'm not going to get it."

Sometimes you get something, and then you are afraid of losing it. You have it, but now you think, "How can I protect it? Suppose somebody takes it away from me?" Even before you got it, you were afraid of losing it. Both fears are due to attachment.

Renunciation doesn't mean that you negate everything, that you're indifferent and run away. No, it's just being neutral. Simply love everyone and everything and do everything without attachment. It's like taking photographs on uncoated film. Imagine, if instead of putting sensitive film in your camera, you put an ordinary micro-sheet and start taking pictures. You won't get any impression. It's the sensitive coating on the micro-sheet that keeps the impressions. Then, when you develop it, the impressions get "fixed." It's simply photography.

If the film in your mind isn't so "sensitive," you can enjoy taking pictures, but nothing will get "fixed" there. But if the film is very sensitive because of your attachment, you will get a lot of snapshots. Some people are too sensitive. If they see something for even a second, they can't forget it. They go home and "develop" it: "I must get it. How can I get it? Oh, how I would love to have it."

It's all a darkroom business, you take the picture in a dark place, the camera. Then you develop and fix it in the darkroom. Once it's fixed, even if you bring it into the light, it remains fixed. Then you are really in a fix. And it's all caused by the minute coating of sensitivity, which is composed of selfishness—"I want it. I must get it. I come first." It's ego sensitivity.

When that ego is gone, all the divine qualities are automatically there in you. The ego is the root cause of all the troubles. But sometimes when a tree has grown too big, you can't immediately uproot it. So you put up a ladder, climb up and chop off the branches, one by one, to remove most of the tree. Then, cut the side roots, dig a big trench around it, tie a rope to it; ask somebody to pull from the other side; then finally cut the taproot, the ego. That's why Krishna says here that if you can't go immediately to the very root, then chop away little by little, until you get to it.

Here he gives the demonic traits that should be chopped off.

4. On the other hand, Arjuna, those destined for a demonic state are ostentatious, arrogant, conceited— and ignorant of the truth.

And what are the effects of these two lists of traits?

5. The divine habits lead to *moksha* (freedom); the demonic habits, to bondage. But don't be alarmed, Arjuna. You are destined for the divine state.

He is telling all this to Arjuna. At a certain point he must have thought, "My goodness, as I am enumerating all these demonic qualities, what will Arjuna be thinking of himself? He might even wonder if he was born for a demonic state." So Krishna says, "Please don't worry, you are born for a divine state."

Sometimes if you keep hearing about undesirable qualities, you get doubts about yourself. It's like reading about so many disease symptoms; you begin to feel you have them all: a little cough, a little sneeze, one day's absence of bowel movements, a little sleeplessness, and immediately you buy all the pills available. Most people have some undesirable qualities. Sri Krishna knows the human tendency and says, "Don't worry; you have divine qualities. You have only temporarily been deluded." Thus he elevates Arjuna.

6. There are two types of people in this world: those predominantly with divine qualities and those predominantly with demonic qualities. I have already described at some length those with divine qualities. If you listen now, Arjuna, I will tell you of the demonic.

7. Demonic people do not know right from wrong. They do what should not be done and will not do what ought to be done. You will not find purity or truth in them, nor upright behavior.

8. They insist that there is no God, nor truth and no moral order anywhere in the universe. Instead, they say: "Everything is just the result of lust and sex; what else is there?"

This is the philosophy of such people. Even in the Hindu tradition there was the *Charvakas* school of thought. They said, "It's all a part of nature. Why speak of God? It's just positive and negative joining together through lust." Does it remind you of some schools of Western psychology? In their minds everything is connected with sex and lust. Thousands of years back, the *Charvakas* said the same things.

The trouble with the philosophy of these people, whether 5,000 years back or today, is that they don't go to the very root of the matter. They simply snip away at the twigs, here and there. They think that nature simply functions without any force or consciousness behind it. Those with demonic attitudes are not awed by the Cosmic force. They think, "I can do anything I want. I'll just eat, drink, make merry and enjoy life at any cost." They are not afraid of committing crimes for their own satisfaction.

We see this nowadays in many places. Many people are just interested in money; they don't care how they get it. Whatever way they can, they do it. Money is their God. If such people trusted in some sort of intelligence behind everything, they couldn't do many of the things we hear about.

For example, look at the cigarette industry. There are so many big factories, so many thousands of people working on cigarettes, and millions of dollars spent promoting and producing cigarettes. Millions and millions of dollars are spent educating you to smoke while schools and colleges are closing for lack of funds. Compare the amount that is spent to make you smoke with the amount spent finding a cure for cancer, a product of smoking. Not even one-hundredth the amount. For every dollar spent to cure cancer, at least $100 is spent to produce it.

And, certainly, the people who spend millions of dollars educating you to smoke know that it's not good for the health. Nobody needs to tell them that. Probably, they don't allow their own children to smoke. They themselves, in fact, may not even smoke. What does it mean if they know it's poison and they themselves don't want to use it, yet they spend billions educating others to do so? What for? To make money. Little by little, day by day, they are murdering their fellow men and women. You should label them "Public Enemy Number One." If they had even a tinge of divine quality—the fear of some Higher Intelligence—they would never dare to do some of these things.

9. Because they have so little *buddhi* (discerning intellect), they rise up as enemies of the world. They are cruel to others and bring about suffering and destruction.

How apt his words are now. He has clearly predicted the current state of affairs. We know without doubt that many of the wars are created by the people who sell arms and ammunition. If there were no wars, they would have to close their factories. So, to sell their arms, they want wars. The next few *slokas* describe such people.

10. Filled with insatiable desires, they are hypocrites who strut about with pride and arrogance. Because they are deluded, they cling to their evil ideas and pursue their unclean ends.

11. They are weighed down by one anxiety after another, which ceases only at the moment of death, and still they cling to the belief that satisfying their lusts is the greatest goal of life.

12. Bound on all sides by ever-present attachment to one scheme after another, they have given themselves over to greed and anger. Thus, they strive to amass vast wealth—by *any* means—hoping in vain to satisfy their insatiable cravings for sensual pleasures.

Sri Krishna had excellent foresight. Five thousand years ago he clearly saw what is happening now. He uses accurate words to describe these people. He quotes their own words:

13. They say: "Today I got this. Tomorrow I will have that. This is mine, and that wealth also will soon be mine."

14. "I have already killed that person, and I will kill others also. I am God, and I do as I please. I am a powerful *siddha* (a perfected one). And I am satisfied with myself [just as I am]."

15. "I am rich and well-born. Who is my equal? I will sacrifice and give charity as I choose—and take pleasure in my own generosity."

It's the very image of ignorance. I don't even like to read these things.

16. Thus deluded and out of touch with reality, they go on and on. Bound by their own greed, they are trapped in false perceptions. And so, addicted to lust gratification, they sink to a foul and hellish state.

17. Blinded by pride and intoxicated by wealth, they obstinately cling to their self-conceits. Their so-called religious offerings, if any, are simply ostentation, never performed in the spirit of the scriptures.

18. They have given themselves over to the ego's selfish and insatiable lust for power, sex and wealth. Arrogant, violent and easily angered, they cruelly abuse my Presence in themselves and in others.

19. Malicious, cruel and filled with hatred, these are the worst of humanity. Birth after birth, I cast such self-degraded evildoers into the wombs of those with demonic natures.

20. They are so deluded, Arjuna, that again and again they are reborn with ingrained demonic habits. And failing to reach for me, they continue to sink even lower.

Here, in the twenty-first *sloka*, he gives the three gateways to hell. It's better to know what the gates are so we can stay away from them.

21. Hell has three gates of self-destruction: lust, anger and greed. Therefore, renounce them.

As with the divine qualities, one follows the other. Lust means craving for all sorts of sensual gratification; it need not be just one sense alone. It can be lust for money, for power or for name and fame. And if that gratification is interfered with, the person gets angry. If it is satisfied, he or she is greedy for more. There's no end. The more you fulfill lust, the more greedy you become. If anybody prevents you from getting what you're lusting after, you're angry. Lust, anger and greed are all coworkers.

It's very important for a seeker to know what is conducive to his or her development. Even before we attempt to know the truth, we should first know what is untrue. It's easier to see what is false. Truth is very subtle sometimes. God is very difficult to know, but we can easily know what is not God. That's why even when scripture tries to define the supreme *Brahman*, it uses negative language: "*Neti, neti* (not this, not that). *Brahman* is not this, nor this, nor that." It is always easier to know what is not true first.

You become a good seeker once you know well the nature of the world. If you know it well you won't want it anymore, because usually the world, or nature, tries to pull you down. It is quite hard to bring a boulder up to the top of a hill. But to get it down needs only a small push. It will just keep rolling down. That is nature's tendency, to pull you down.

You may say, "God created me as well as nature. Why should God create a nature that constantly pulls me down?" It's here that we see the great importance of a human birth. Until its human birth, the soul passes through many other lives with many bodies of lesser intelligence. Gradually, the intelligence evolves and expands. It's like a seed slowly sending up its roots, sending small branches out, then opening up and unfolding, growing up and up until it brings forth another seed. And as intelligence opens, side by side you see the free will developing. At the human level, free will is completely unfolded. That is, you have been raised to a height where you don't need any more help. You've been taught all that is to be taught in your previous births. You have been given all the experiences that nature could give you, from the small blade of grass to a unicellular animal and up and up.

After achieving the human level, that Cosmic Intelligence, or God, says, "Okay, now I have taught you everything. I'm going to test you." Isn't that fair? During the whole year your teachers teach you in the classroom. At the end of the year, will they simply pass you along to the next class? No. To see if you have grasped what they taught, they test you in the examination hall.

Human birth is God's examination hall. And how does God test us? Through nature. "I have given you free will," God says. "It's easy to fall down, but I have taught you to climb. Let me see whether you are using your intelligence or not. I'm not really working against you. I simply want to test your capacity."

In an example from the *Bible*, God created Adam and Eve. God could easily have left them in the garden undisturbed. They would probably still be living happily there. Why would God create the snake of temptation? Sometimes I think God is very mischievous. God could have just left them in the Garden of Eden to roam about happily. But then, they would not have had the opportunity to prove their education.

To prove what you have learned, you must be tested. Every seeker is an Adam, whether male or female. Everybody who wants to be elevated up and prove his or her knowledge is an Adam. And the entire world is acting as a snake. It just sneaks into your room and tempts you: "Come on, have one more; a little more of this, a little more of that. See, don't you think I am nice and beautiful? Don't you think that you can buy so many things if you have a big pocketful of money?" All kinds of temptations come.

The first lesson is to know that everything is here to test you; don't be deceived by it. Pass the test. You don't need to hate the test or the examiner. Don't hate the examiner; love him. Don't try to bribe him. If you bribe him, you deceive yourself. Don't hate the world, but know it well and say, "This is just trying to pull me down."

Everything is tempting and testing you. You must be careful. Be vigilant. That's why the scriptures talk about the dark side of life as well as the light. At least we will know what is not good. By knowing the gates to hell, we exercise our discrimination to choose the right path and go toward the supreme good.

22. **Whoever is good and does good escapes from these three gates of darkness and, instead, rises to the supreme goal of life.**

23. **But those who disregard the scriptural teachings and, instead, follow the impulse of their selfish desires do not attain the supreme goal of life, nor true happiness, nor success.**

In the last *sloka*, Sri Krishna suggests that if you are not sure what is bad, the words of the seers are given in the scriptures to guide you.

24. **In order to know what to do and what not to do, let the scripture be your guide. And when you understand the scriptural guidance, you will know how to live [happily] in this world.**

Thus ends the sixteenth discourse of the *Bhagavad Gita*, the science of Yoga, entitled: "The Yoga of the Divine and the Demonic."

Yoga of the Threefold Faith

This chapter is very practical. Here Krishna talks about *shraddha* which is implicit faith and the application of one's will toward that in which one has faith—you believe in something and then apply your will toward that—that's *shraddha*.

1. Arjuna said: O Krishna, how do you regard the devotion of those who disregard the ordinances in scripture (the *shastras*) but nevertheless offer sacrifices with sincere faith? Is such worship motivated by pure, restless or listless qualities (*sattva, rajas* or *tamas*)?

2. The blessed Lord replied: There are three qualities of active belief. Depending upon one's temperament, each person is endowed predominantly with *shraddha* that is either pure (*sattvic*), passionate (*rajasic*) or dull (*tamasic*).

Even in faith we see these three qualities—*sattva, rajas, tamas*—which we learned of in Chapter Fourteen: "The Yoga of the Three Qualities of Nature."

3. The faith of each person, Arjuna, is in accord with his or her own nature. The quality of one's active belief is indeed the very nature of the person. As the person's faith is, so is the person.

Sri Krishna says one's faith is according to one's own nature. But where do we get this inborn disposition? Here we begin to understand reincarnation. Some people, for example, at even 70 or 80 years of age, are still interested in worldly things. They still want to go fishing, play games, make money and go to Florida or Las Vegas. Yet, some very young people thirst for a spiritual life. How is this?

Imagine an old man who has certainly experienced everything. He has probably married several times. He has amassed lots of money and lost lots of money. He's done everything, but he's still not tired of it. He commits the same blunders again and again. Such people don't think of God or religion. Occasionally those with a lot of money might send a big check to the church—to "dispose" of God quickly. Then they think: "I've sent you a check; now I will do what I want." They think they can buy God.

In a spiritual community we often see people who still have youth, strength and many years ahead of them. But they're not enjoying worldly life, nor have they enjoyed it before. If they chose, they could still indulge more than that old man. What brought them to an *ashram*? They must have exhausted all that earlier; they finished all that in their past lives. They are no longer interested in it. They are the *Yogabrasthas*, the ones who practiced Yoga in previous lives and are now simply continuing where they left off. That is their inborn disposition.

Just look at some of their children, who are even younger . . . when they speak there's no doubt what great souls they are. How is it that they spend their youth in an *ashram*? Their karma could have taken them elsewhere. They are just continuing their predisposition.

Now, Krishna clearly says what the people of different faiths do.

4. Those who are pure by nature, worship one form of God or another (the *devas*). The restless-minded worship power and wealth (*yakshas* and *rakshasas*) and others, who are unenlightened, think only of spirits and ghosts (*pretas* and *bhutas*).

All these objects of worship mentioned are spirits, but at different levels. Like human beings with physical form, these are souls but without the physical bodies; they are astral spirits. When souls who have achieved a certain spiritual height while in their physical bodies lose those bodies, they go to a higher level. They are called the *devas* (gods, angelic beings), masters, *siddhas* (highly accomplished yogis) and so on. The *sattvic* people appreciate and worship them. The purpose in worshipping is to get their guidance and help.

According to the Hindu philosophy, Shiva, Vishnu, Subrahmanya, Ganesh and all the other deities actually represent the divine qualities: all auspicious and omnipresent is Vishnu; all powerful and omniscient is Ganesh; and so on. People with *sattvic shraddha* (calm faith) know what is good for them and what is not conducive. Even though they might sometimes slip and fall, they just want to get up and walk again toward the goal. They want something higher, and their worship is based on that spiritual goal.

Rajasic (restless) people worship the *yakshas* and the *rakshasas*. These are the spirits who haven't conquered their passions. They have left their physical bodies and are waiting to get another body. While waiting, they roam around giving a hand to people who work in the same field. They are *beings* but at a very low mental level, who are sometimes approached to help win a race or fight a war or even rob a bank. In fact, in India, there were incidents when someone wanted to commit a murder, took a gun to a particular temple dedicated to a lower level *yaksha*, put the gun there, decorated it with sandalwood and a garland, performed a devotional service, left it overnight, came back the next morning and said, "May God bless me to murder well."

Remember that even such people are seeking the help of a higher power. So there is a sort of *shraddha* in them. They believe in higher powers but use them for wrong purposes. How many people go to the temple, church or synagogue and say, "If you help me pass my exam, I will light so many candles or repeat a prayer so many times?" In India they say, "If you help me pass my exams, I'll break a couple of coconuts and offer some fruits." What does it mean? They are trying to do business with God. It's foolish, but at least they believe in God. That's *rajasic shraddha*.

There's still one more type—*tamasic shraddha* (dull faith). *Tamasic* people don't think about someone higher. They just want to have some fun to while away the time. There's no particular reason for it. "I'll worship because everybody else does it." It's neither *sattvic* nor *rajasic*, just blind, mechanical action. Or sometimes there might be a base purpose behind it—to hurt somebody. It's very dull and based on ignorance, but still there is faith and application of the will, which is *shraddha*.

We should distinguish between these three kinds *of shraddha*. Ask yourself: "In this life, what is my *shraddha* based on? Do I want to learn the *asanas* (Yoga poses) and *pranayama* (Yoga breathing practices) so I can conduct a television series and demonstrate everything? What is my goal? Well, if I am a Hatha teacher I can have a nice *ashram*, and people will come and fall at my feet!"

There's a little *shraddha*, no doubt, but it's based on getting name and fame, not for your own purification and evolution. We see people who come, quickly grab a little philosophy, learn a few techniques and immediately announce, "I am a yogi now. I have a certificate." Instead, those with *sattvic shraddha* will learn for their own growth and development. Then, when people see beautiful things in someone's life, they will come and say, "Since the Yoga retreat you seem to be a changed person. "You are so beautiful, calm, shining. What's happening to you? Would you share that with me?" When people ask you that way, you can say, "I'm still learning myself, but if you see something nice, okay, let's share it." There's nothing wrong in teaching others, but let people come and ask you after seeing your beautiful qualities. Only then is it *sattvic*. *Sattvic* people are always few in number. Be among those few.

The way of the majority, however, is as follows:

> **5. Those who choose extreme or violent austerities, not advised in scripture, are hypocrites motivated by ego, lust and personal attachments.**

> **6. They are fools to torture their innocent bodies so, for in their demonic resolve, they also torture me, because I live in their very bodies.**

In the name of *shraddha* and *tapas*, many people go to the extreme of hurting their own bodies and senses. We see this in many religious traditions. Sri Krishna clearly says that these are not good practices; they are not needed for spiritual growth. They are not *sattvic*. Some will even take pride, saying, "I've lived in the icy cold Himalayan regions for the past fifteen years." Do they think that will give them the gold key to heaven?

The Buddha experienced these extremes in his life. He swung to both sides, then came back to the golden median. Seekers often tend to the extreme, so they are warned against it by this *sloka*.

There is no need to go to these extremes. Sri Krishna says, "They are torturing me, too, because I live in their bodies." God lives in your body; it is God's temple. If you torture it, you inconvenience God. If you fast too much, what can God do? God might say, "What is this? I'll have to quit this place."

The great South Indian saint Thirumular, who is said to have lived for more than 3,000 years, talks about the importance of the body. He clearly says that you can't realize God without it. God has given you the body as a ladder to climb up. The ladder itself is not going upstairs, no doubt. But *you* need to go up, so you have to take care of it. In the same way, the body is your vehicle. With the help of the body you are walking the path. Torturing the body is not a spiritual practice. Don't go to the extremes.

Next, he begins to speak of the three types of food, sacrifice, austerity and gifts. You will find these very useful points for your daily life.

> 7. Those with one of these three differing qualities of faith also prefer three different types of food, perform their duties and take on disciplines in three different ways. They each give charity in their own way. Listen, and I will distinguish one from the other.

First the three kinds of foods:

> 8. Those of tranquil temperament (*sattvic*) prefer foods that increase vitality, longevity and strength; foods that enhance physical health and make the mind pure and cheerful; foods with substance and natural flavor; foods that are fresh, with natural oils and agreeable to the body.

Krishna gives the nature of *sattvic* foods. They should enhance your vitality and bring energy, vigor, health, good cheer and joy. At the same time, they should be juicy and should have a little oil in them, like sesame and sunflower seeds. They should be substantial and agreeable. What a nice list he has given. And these foods should not only be healthy and energizing; just even seeing the plate of food should cheer you. The food shouldn't just be thrown on the plate in a big mess.

Of course, we should also know what foods are *sattvic*, according to the climate in which we live. In cold countries, the food should be warmth giving; and in warm countries, cooling. In India, for example, the North Indians eat mainly wheat, and the South Indians, rice. Wheat grows more in the colder north and gives more warmth to the body. Rice, which is cooling, grows more in South India, which is very warm. We should eat according to our climate.

Don't simply copy India. Just because they eat something doesn't mean that by your eating the same thing you can get liberation quickly. Think what is suitable for your climate; that's very important. Actually, nature itself provides the right foods. In warm climates, you get a lot of melons. Do you get watermelon in the New England winter? No. God knows we don't need watermelon there at that time. Nature provides. Mother Nature knows what the children need. There is a philosophy that asks you to eat just what grows in your area and in the particular season. It's like telling the baby, "Drink what is developed in your mother's breast." When the baby is growing in the womb, God is already preparing its food. The food *grows* in the same field where the baby grows.

Now, what are the *rajasic* foods?

9. Those of a restless, compulsive temperament (*rajasic*) prefer foods that are very spicy or very sour, piping hot, bitter-dry or quite salty. Such foods give rise to discomfort, pain and disease and, therefore, dismay.

I never tell a student, "You must eat this and must not eat that." It all depends on what you want to develop in your life. If you want to be a *sattvic* person, be *sattvic* in all your habits.

Just because Yoga comes from India doesn't mean you should copy everything done in India. It's not necessary to eat extremely spicy, hot Indian food. Even taking it once in a while for a change is not that good. It affects you afterward for one or two days. The day after eating very hot food, you feel the whole alimentary canal burning.

Of course, some spices are medicinal when used in the proper way. South Indian food, with which I am particularly familiar, is something of a remedy itself. When I was little, if I had a cold, my mother would make me a peppery soup called *rasam*. Black pepper controls a cold. Or, if there were stomach problems and worms were suspected, the mothers would add a little more turmeric, because turmeric is a good antiseptic. If there was any inflammation, they would add something sour. All these remedies come from the food itself, You can treat food as medicine. Intelligent mothers know what to add—more or less for different conditions. But medicine should be taken only when there is a need for it. We shouldn't eat it just because the tongue likes it. The stomach and the entire system should be calling for it.

How do you know when food is *rajasic?* If your tongue tingles and burns, or the eyes get bloodshot and teary, or the nose runs and the stomach burns, know you are eating *rajasic* food.

10. Those of a dull and lazy temperament (*tamasic*) choose foods that are stale and tasteless, overcooked or left overnight, spoiled, rotting or even putrid. Such foods have lost their vitality and nutrition.

You know and agree about stale food. The problem with tasteless and stinking food is also obvious. But food cooked and kept overnight seems to be quite common in the United States. You may think that the Indians probably didn't have refrigeration in the old days so they couldn't keep anything overnight; but since we now have ultramodern refrigeration, why not?

The first time I came to America in 1966, a couple invited me to their country home for the weekend. Sunday afternoon, when we were preparing to return, I found the wife packing a big potful of cooked rice and vegetables.

"What is this?" I asked. "Why did you cook so much? Did you expect more people and nobody came, so you're taking it back?"

"No, this is what we do every weekend. We come here and cook for the whole week, take it back home and keep it in the refrigerator. We take a little each night, warm it up and eat it."

It was a surprise and a shock to me, because I had never experienced that before. "We do this because during the week we don't have time to cook." The mothers work, the fathers work. I won't say eating such food is totally bad. It may look all right. But no matter how you preserve it, it loses some of its freshness and vitality. It may not look spoiled, but it's still old food.

Indian mothers understand this point, so they know how much to cook for a given number of people. Most Americans don't seem to know. I have seen people leaving enough for many when they cook for a few.

There are too many leftovers here. If Americans would only save the food they waste on one given day, they could feed a small country for a whole month. Can you even imagine how much food is just thrown out?

It's a shame. So many people don't even respect food. Just because we have plenty doesn't mean we should be disrespectful toward it. Food is an expression of God. If an Indian lady cooks for fifteen people, there may be food for two or three people left over. Even for that she'll find a use. She'll give it to some poor people, or to the animals. Indian dogs are treated as household members and are given leftovers for their meals. The wives never save leftovers.

In the next *sloka*, we see three types of worship or sacrifice (*yajna*).

11. Any devoted action offered up without desire for reward, but with the entire mind focused on the action for its own sake, is in the true spirit of scripture and is a pure (*sattvic*) sacrifice.

That means *sattvic* worship is offered simply for the joy of it, like a mother's joy in taking care of her child. She doesn't do it for any other reason. There is no reward expected in return. That's a *sattvic yajna*. And in such sacrifice, everything is seen in a higher light. Even if any suffering comes, it won't be experienced as suffering. The *sattvic* person rises above the suffering and sees the beauty in it.

For example, in the *Mahabharata,* the noble Pandava family was forced into exile in the forests. At one point, the Pandavas' wife, Draupadi, said to Yudhisthira, the eldest Pandava brother, "We are all virtuous people who haven't done anything wrong. Why should we suffer like this?"

He didn't answer her directly. He just said, "Look, my beloved, how majestic are the Himalayas, how beautiful the trees. How nice it is to be in the midst of all these beautiful plants and animals in this indescribable nature. Do you think we would have come here ourselves if we weren't chased out of our kingdom by our cousins? They thought they were pushing us into the jungle. They didn't realize the reward we'd get. Don't think of this as punishment. Just look where we are!"

He wasn't thinking: "I should not think negatively; I should appreciate this." Because of his *sattvic* nature, he didn't experience it as suffering.

"Ah, how pleasant to be here. I can't help but feel grateful to the people who sent me here." A *sattvic* person will accept life like that and sacrifice everything for a greater cause.

12. However, Arjuna, any offering made with expectation of a reward for doing so, or for show, is motivated by a restless and desirous (*rajasic*) mental tendency.

Something done for name or fame, or for something in return, is *rajasic*. For example, if you think to yourself, "I will do this service for the *ashram* so that it will support me," it's a business, not a true sacrifice.

13. A sacrifice offered without appropriate prayers (mantras) and gifts, without active belief (*shraddha*) and without sharing food afterward is not in the spirit of scripture and is based on ignorance of the truth (*tamas*).

Remember that we are reading a Hindu scripture. We have to understand the terms used. According to Hindu ritual, there are certain mantras (sacred sound formulas) to be chanted during the ritual sacrifice. And to fulfill the rites you should offer food, then feed many people with the *prasad* and give gifts to those who helped you perform it.

But *tamasic* people will perform the ritual without any of this. If you ask them why they are doing it, they will say, "I don't know; my father used to do it and my grandfather before him." If you search in your own religion, probably you'll find things like that. People often do not even know why they perform such rites. "Our forefathers did it" is all they know. That is *tamasic*—neither done for the joy of doing it, nor for something in return—just mechanical, like a machine.

Now, the threefold austerities, or disciplines, of the body, of speech and of the mind. In each, there are *sattvic, rajasic* and *tamasic* approaches. First, Sri Krishna speaks of physical disciplines:

14. These are the physical disciplines (*tapas*): serving God, the twice-born, spiritual teachers and the wise; staying pure, virtuous, continent and practicing non-injury (*ahimsa*).

"Serving God" could refer to going to temple or church and praying. Or, it could mean your Yoga practices—sitting for meditation or performing your *asanas* and *pranayama*. These are all physical austerities. Then, there's "serving of the twice-born," which means people who have taken a second birth, as it were, in spiritual wisdom. Among Hindus, these are normally *brahmins*, the priests and wise teachers who are called the twice-born because, traditionally, their lives are dedicated to spiritual knowledge.

But it shouldn't be understood just by caste or birth. Who, after all, is a true *brahmin*? The one involved in seeking *Brahman jnana*—knowledge of God. In that sense, all sincere seekers of God or truth are *brahmins*. They are dead to the life they were leading before and are reborn in this spiritual search. That's why you show respect to whomever you see who may be a little more spiritually evolved than yourself, you can bow down or prostrate before them just as when you kneel and bow in a church to show your humility.

"Serving your teachers" means service to the Guru, and that was discussed earlier in the *Gita*. Purity means keeping yourself physically pure. Keep yourself clean and neat in every way—body, dress, room, hair, everything. One of the biblical proverbs says, "Cleanliness is next to godliness." But I like to say, "Cleanliness is godliness," because when you are pure, you will *know* you are God. So keep yourself completely clean and pure.

And, finally, virtuousness, continence and non-injury. Here, Krishna gives some of the *yamas*, or abstinences, of Raja Yoga.

Non-injury means causing as little pain to others as possible. But you must consider all the repercussions of your actions. Occasionally violence is righteous; even killing isn't always a sin. Suppose you are a good marksman and, all of a sudden, you see a crazy man with a machine gun on the road shooting everybody at random. What would you do? Tell him that non-injury is the first moral precept? No. Simply raise your pistol and say, "Drop that gun or I'll kill you." If he drops it, fine. If he points the gun toward you, try to shoot him in the wrist to handicap him. If even that fails, you must kill him. In this way you have saved many other people's lives, your own life, and probably you saved him from committing further sins. In rare instances, even *himsa* (violence) is acceptable.

In the olden days, wars were like that. The war in the *Mahabharata* is an example. Krishna, as a person, went up and down between the two groups of cousins many times trying to dissuade the evil Kauravas from fighting.

"What you are doing is unrighteous," he advised them. "Give the Pandavas their share of the kingdom. If you won't do that, at least give them a small village and let them live somewhere."

But Duryodhana said, "No, not even an inch."

The Pandavas had abided by the agreement and had gone into the jungle for fourteen years. They had so much patience. But everything failed. Krishna simply pleaded with Duryodhana. Finally, Duryodhana admitted, "We want war; we want to destroy these people. Let these cowards come. Why are they sending you here again and again?"

So Sri Krishna went back and said, "I tried my best. But war is inevitable. We have to do it. Come on, fight and dispose of them all." He sanctioned it himself. He permitted the destruction. To uphold righteousness, even violence and war are sanctioned.

But I'm not referring to our present-day wars. Modern warfare is not war at all. It's inhuman. There's no righteousness, no sense to it, no bravery by the decision-makers. They sit safely somewhere under a concrete cave, press a button and kill a few million innocent people somewhere thousands of miles away. Is that righteousness? Where is the bravery? It's a coward's act.

In those days, wars were totally different. You saw your enemies face-to-face and fought with them. If they came with swords, you took a sword. If they came with guns, you took a gun. If they lost their weapons and came bare-handed, you also fought with bare hands. If they were too tired, you would ask if they were willing to admit defeat. If they said no, then you asked them to go back, get refreshed and return the next day.

Sri Rama did that. In the war between Rama and Ravana, as told in the *Ramayana*, it took many days for Rama to destroy all of Ravana's troops. He could have taken advantage of that opportunity to destroy Ravana also. Ravana was standing bare-handed, his chariots broken, his horses killed, his elephants gone. He was all alone. Rama could have easily disposed of him at that time. With one arrow, Rama could have finished the war.

But when Ravana lost his chariot, Rama got down from his own chariot. When Ravana took a sword, Rama put down his bow and took a sword. When Ravana lost that also, Rama said, "What are you going to do now? Do you still want to fight or will you accept your defeat and send Sita back to me?" (Ravana had kidnapped Sita, Rama's wife.)

"No, I can't do that."

"Then I'm sorry. You are too weak to fight anymore today. Go back, rest and come tomorrow."

That's a righteous war. You don't hate the enemy, you try to teach with love. We don't see such wars nowadays.

Now, austerity of speech:

> **15. These are the disciplines of speech: speaking truthfully, pleasantly and kindly with words that do not excite others, and reading scripture (*svadhyaya*).**

Speech that causes no excitement is included because excitement is a type of mental disturbance. It may *seem* pleasant, but it is not really beneficial. Words causing excitement often hurt others. When you are excited, you lose your balance and control, just the same as when you are depressed.

Next is the truth, which is quite difficult to define, because the effects of our words are as important as the content. Sometimes, by speaking the literal truth we might hurt somebody. We shouldn't hurt anybody and, at the same time, we don't want to say something untrue just to avoid hurting somebody. Still, a truth that brings harm is worse than an untruth that brings some good. The much-respected South Indian saint Thiruvalluvar said that even a lie will be accepted as truth if it brings benefits to everybody concerned, without having any undesirable effects on anybody. Here is a story to show you what he means.

Once there was a Swami living in a small hermitage in a dense forest. He had a hut by the riverside and was doing his practices by himself in this secluded spot. One afternoon he saw a beautiful girl bedecked with jewels crying out and running toward him.

"Swami, please help me. A horrible fellow is chasing me. He wants to steal my jewels. Please let me hide somewhere." She didn't even wait for his answer. She ran into his hut and hid in a corner. Within a few minutes a wild, demonic-looking man with a dagger in his hand arrived on the scene shouting.

"Hey, did you see a girl here?"

The Swami is a yogi. He's supposed to be *sattvic* and follow all the precepts. He should always tell the truth, shouldn't he? Here's what he said:

"What? You are looking for a girl? What did she look like?"

"She was very beautiful and wearing a lot of jewels."

"My son, don't you know this is a hermitage and I'm a hermit? This is no place for girls. Can't you see that?"

"So you didn't see her?"

"Well, that's what I'm asking you. What would she do here?"

"All right." And the criminal ran off.

The Swami didn't literally say, "She is not here." He put it in a different way. But even if he had said, "I did not see her," there would be nothing wrong in it. It was a lie, but it would have saved three lives: her life, his life and the robber's life too. If he had told the truth literally, and even if the girl had freely surrendered her jewels, there would have been two witnesses to the crime. A smart thief won't leave any witnesses. He would have disposed of both the girl and the Swami; then he would have run off with the jewels. But certainly the police, in time, would have caught him. The judge would have sentenced him to death for killing two people. That means all three would have lost their lives because a Swami spoke the truth.

The literal truth is not always the best. Speech should be applied properly. When the Swami said, "I haven't seen anybody," nobody was hurt by that. Everyone was saved. If you lie, it should not adversely affect anybody. Otherwise, it is just an excuse to lie.

Now, Sri Krishna speaks of disciplining the mind:

> **16. These are the mental disciplines: tranquility, gentleness, good-heartedness, silence, self-control and purity of thought.**

Next, he further divides the austerities according to the *gunas*.

> **17. When these three disciplines are practiced with zeal and sincerity and without looking for some personal gain, then this is pure *tapas*.**

> **18. Disciplines taken on with the object of gaining respect, honors or admiration are performed for show and motivated by compulsive desires (*rajas*). Such disciplines are not dependable and in time fall away.**

> **19. Sometimes, austerities are practiced in order to control, hurt or destroy someone else; or out of foolish obstinacy; or out of the mistaken belief that self-torture is somehow spiritually beneficial. Such disciplines are based on delusion and ignorance.**

Now, Sri Krishna discusses the three kinds of gift-giving.

> **20. When you give something to someone simply because you feel it is right to give it, and there is no thought of receiving anything in return, and it is given at the right moment, at the right place and to the right person, then it is pure giving.**

> **21. If a gift is given reluctantly, or in hopes of receiving a favor, or anything else in return, that giving is motivated primarily by the desires of a restless mind.**

> **22. If a gift is given rudely or without affection to an inappropriate person at the wrong place and wrong time, that is giving from a state of dullness.**

Here you see that a gift is not always a gift. A *sattvic* gift is one where you have carefully considered the person who will receive it, the time, the place and everything else about it. You know that the person can use the gift, and you give it as a joy without any expectation of something in return.

So-called business gifts are *rajasic,* which is what we often see. That's why Sri Krishna recommends giving to someone who isn't able to return anything to you. Then, there isn't even any thinking about getting something back. And such a person is the most deserving recipient. If someone already has something and you give her something more, it may be a good act. But, of course, the most deserving person to receive your gift is the one who doesn't have anything.

23. The three words that represent the Absolute (*Brahman*) are: *Om Tat Sat*. Out of this (*mantra*) arose the spiritual wisdom (*Brahmanas*) the scriptures (*Vedas*) and self-sacrifice (*yajna*).

Om Tat Sat Om, that is the Truth. *Tat* means *that. Sat* means *truth: Om*— that's the Truth. The first manifestation of the absolute truth takes form as the unspoken sound, *Om.* That's why *Om* is sometimes called *pranava,* the one that hums. The true *Om* is the hum: "mmm." When people repeat their mantras, they should stress the mmmm, the humming part of the mantra. That hum is the very first sound, or first word, which is God.

The *Bible* says: "In the beginning was the Word. The Word was with God and the Word was God." And it still is God. Don't worry about the grammar. The spirit of scriptural wisdom is more important than taking every letter literally. The word itself is God. The word and God are not two different things. Name and the one denoted by the name are not two different things at all. The name itself becomes the form. If you keep repeating the name, it becomes solidified and creates a form.

Sprinkle a few sand particles on a thin piece of glass; put a speaker below, then continually repeat a sound. Sound creates patterns. So it is with everything. All the forms are created by names, by sound. If you look at a person and constantly call him or her a monkey, in one sense, that person will become one. You can make a monkey out of that person.

As we think and speak, so we become. We take on the qualities of what we talk about. That's why if we keep talking about others' problems, we will be filled with problems. Sometimes, we don't see the best in others. Instead, we constantly think terrible things about them. Too seldom do we praise people. But what happens? The more we think and talk of undesirable things, the more *we* become that. At least for our own safety, we should not constantly be speaking ill of others. Everybody has a little weakness. But if we keep talking about it, we become that ultimately.

Chapter Seventeen

It all goes back to sound vibrations, which are all variations of the ultimate sound that creates everything. That hum is the truth behind everything. Modern science also is coming to a similar conclusion: everything is sound. The atoms are actually humming. God named the first man Adam. That humming became Adam. The scientists are humming *atom*. And underneath the atom or Adam is the humming, the *Om*. Is it a coincidence that even our electricity is measured in ohms today? They use an ohm meter.

Who lives in the h*Om*e? *Om*. Who's around the *Om*? God. And that's the truth. All trinities are products of that *Om*. The basic sound expresses itself as a trinity: *Sat-Chid-Ananda, Om Tat Sat*. The three-fold designation of the Absolute is saying that the truth, *Om*, takes expression so we can recognize it and know of it. There's existence, which is truth (*Sat*) and realization of truth is knowledge (*Chit*). Then by recognizing it, you enjoy its benefits, which is bliss (*Ananda*): *Sat-Chid-Ananda*. The very basis, Existence, is the Father (*Sat*). The expression of the Father, Knowledge, is the Son (*Chit*). And then through the Son, you get the Holy Spirit. Sometimes it's called the Holy Ghost, which is joyful (*Ananda*). All of this is another three-fold designation of *Brahman*.

The *sloka* continues: Out of that (mantra) arose the old *Brahmanas*, the *Vedas* and *yajnas*. *Yajnas* are sacrifices; *Vedas* are the scriptures; and the *Brahmanas* are the spiritual aspect of the *Upanishads*. The *jnana*, or wisdom portion of the scriptures, that speaks of absolute spirit; the portion that speaks about ritual; and even the very act of ritual devotion, which are the *yajnas*—all three parts of this trinity, come out of the hum, the *Om*, which is the original sound.

24. Students of scripture repeat the word *Om* when undertaking spiritual disciplines, making devotional offerings, and giving charity (*danam*).

25. Students of scripture who seek enlightenment (*moksha*) also repeat the word *tat* to ensure that the undertaking of spiritual disciplines, devotional offerings and giving charity will have no taint of personal reward-seeking.

26. *Sat* means reality (that which is) and indicates goodness. Therefore, its use, Arjuna, blesses an undertaking with auspiciousness.

27. *Sat* also describes steady and continuous self-sacrifice, self-discipline, and selfless giving. *Sat* is also anything you do as part of these three, which in fact is serving God.

28. However, any sacrifice offered, gift given, duty performed or spiritual discipline taken on—without *shraddha*—is not worthwhile, because it is *asat*, not truth.

Thus ends the seventeenth discourse of the *Bhagavad Gita,* the science of Yoga, entitled: "Yoga of the Three-fold Faith."

Chapter Eighteen
_____

Yoga of Freedom through Renunciation

All are going to be enlightened by renunciation. In this chapter
Sri Krishna again divides his subject of renunciation into the three *gunas:*
sattva, rajas and *tamas.* The eighteenth chapter is also a synopsis of the
entire *Gita.* He gives us everything in a nutshell.

The chapter begins with Arjuna questioning Sri Krishna about the
meaning of renunciation.

> 1. Arjuna said: O Krishna, please tell me the essence of
> renunciation (*sannyas*) and non-attachment (*tyaga*).

> 2. The blessed Lord said: Renouncing all personally motivated
> actions is renunciation and letting go of the desire for the fruits of
> your actions is non-attachment.

> 3. Some wise people believe that *all* actions should be renounced as
> seeds of evil, while others believe that certain actions should not be
> renounced—self-sacrifice, selfless giving and self-discipline.

> 4. Listen, Arjuna, and I will now teach you the essence of non-
> attachment. Actually, there are three levels of non-attachment.

> 5. Self-sacrifice, selfless giving and self-discipline, in fact, should
> not be renounced. Instead, they should certainly be continued
> because such actions purify the mind and make you wise.

Under the guise of renunciation, Sri Krishna explains, we shouldn't
renounce every action. In fact, we should perform certain actions that
will purify our minds. This is very important because the minute we hear
that renunciation leads to liberation, immediately we want to drop all the
uncomfortable duties. Anything we don't like, we quickly "renounce." We
might renounce eating salad and plain bread, but not ice cream. We tend
to choose what we want to renounce.

But here he says there are certain things that should not be renounced by
a spiritual seeker—*yajna, danam* and *tapas. Yajna,* as you know, is sacrifice;

danam is gift-giving; and *tapas* is austerity, self-discipline. These three ought to be performed by people who want to be wise. In other words, intelligent people will not renounce these acts.

Sri Krishna warns that even these obligatory actions are not to be performed for their fruits, but simply as part of your duty.

> 6. However, it is essential, Arjuna, that these actions too be performed without attachment to the fruits.

> 7. Actually, it is wrong to renounce any duty that is appropriate for you to do. Such [so-called] renunciation comes from ignorance of reality (**tamas**).

It's *tamasic*, because, in this case, you don't know why you are ignoring your duty, and you're too lazy to find out; you just renounce without any discernment. That so-called "renunciation" won't bring many results.

> 8. Abandoning a duty because it is [or may be] difficult or painful is *rajasic* detachment and does not bring about merit.

Sometimes we do abandon or drop our duties. If you are a *tamasic* person you won't even know why you let it go. But if you are a *rajasic* person you know it's too painful or too difficult for you. At least you know why, but your reasoning isn't sound. It's escapist mentality.

Many times we want to run away from certain places or actions, so we bring in some nice philosophy: "I'm a renunciate, so I'm renouncing this." We're not renouncing with understanding, but out of fear. That escapism will bind us. So here, Krishna indirectly points out that Arjuna's renunciation of his part in the war is *rajasic*. Arjuna just wants an excuse not to fight. He feels sad about killing his own kith and kin. But that's not the proper reason to renounce.

> 9. Pure (*sattvic*) non-attachment is carrying out your responsibilities simply because it is right that you do so—while at the same time renouncing attachment to the fruits of your efforts.

> 10. After you renounce all personal attachments, you will be filled with purity and clearly discern the nature of dispassion (*tyaga*).

[Then] all remaining doubts fall away, and you feel neither aversion nor attraction toward unpleasant or pleasant work.

Sattvic tyaga (pure non-attachment) means your action is done merely because it ought to be done, letting go of attachment and also the fruits of the act. Such a person performs work as a duty. Sometimes we do Karma Yoga, selfless service and remind ourselves: "I'm not interested in the fruit." But that disinterest sometimes carries over even into the action itself: "I'm not interested in the fruit, so I'm not interested in doing it well either; it's just Karma Yoga." But the *sattvic* renunciate, the true Karma Yogi, is the one who performs his or her duty as perfectly as possible and, at the same time, offers the fruits to God, humanity, family or whomever.

It's like giving something to your beloved. You choose the best. If you prepare a room for your special friend, you take care of every minute detail, seeing that it's absolutely clean and beautifully decorated, you enjoy doing it, but not for your own personal sake. Even there, *rajas* could easily sneak in. You might do it for show or out of pride: "See what a beautiful room I am giving you?" To others it might appear that you're really interested in your guest and that's why you're doing everything so nicely. But your own mind will know the motive. As a seeker you must be true to yourself. It's not always possible for others to know and point out your motives.

11. As long as you have a physical body, you cannot entirely renounce *all* actions. But you can let go of the attachment to the fruits of your actions, and that, after all, is true detachment.

12. Those who do not let go [of] attachment after physical death will experience three types of consequences of their actions (karma): some pleasant, some unpleasant and some mixed. But those who do let go of the desire for the fruits, will transcend their karma.

13. Now, Arjuna, I will teach you the five constituents that, according to *Samkhya* Yoga, make every action happen.

14. The seat of action, which is the body; the ego, which is the agent of action; the sense organs; the actual functioning of the body

and mind that perform actions; and the various aspects of God (the *devas*) that correspond with different parts of the body.

15. Whatever a person does—whether right or wrong; whether thought, word or deed—these are the five elements that bring about each action.

16. This is the way it is. But people whose minds are not trained imagine themselves (who are agents of action) to be the doers; or they think that the doer is the true Self, who is absolutely independent (*kevalam*). Their discernment is perverted, and they don't see.

17. When you are free of the ego sense of separateness (*ahamkara*), your discerning intelligence (*buddhi*) is no longer tainted. Though it may appear that you slay your enemies, in fact you are not the doer and you are not bound by those actions (karma).

18. There are three incitements to action: knowledge, what is to be known and the knower. There are three components of an action: the means (the body part that performs the action), the doing of the action and the agent of the action (the individual).

The seed of all that has manifested is in this trinity: the knowledge, the knowable and the Knower. Unfortunately, we don't usually see these separately. For example: I as the seer, you as the seen and my seeing you as the action. Seer, seen, and seeing. These three—subject, object and the interaction between them—always come up together. We don't usually distinguish one aspect from the next.

If we could separate them, we would always see: I am the subject and what I see becomes the object. It becomes the object because I see it so. An awareness of this will create a new outlook on the world. The object becomes a particular object because we see it so. I can see this person as a woman. I can see this person as just a human being. I can see this person as a brilliant, intelligent person. I can see this person as holy spirit. I can see this person as tall, thin, fat, white or black. All are one and the same person. But is she all of that, or none of that or some of that? It depends upon how we see.

That means the entire visible world, as you know it, is nothing but your projection, how you see it. The world is the seer's creation. You see it, so it is so. But if you can see it differently, it will be different. (An atom, for example, can be seen as a particle or a wave; it depends on the viewer.) The difference lies in your seeing. That's probably the reason why the same person is a wonderful, loving friend to one person, but to another seems quite terrible. How can she be both devil and angel? It's your subjective projection.

A movie theater is a beautiful analogy because it has three main things: first is the silver screen—completely blank. And at the other end of the theater, just a brilliant light inside the projector. The theater needs a blank screen and a brilliant, clear light. And, in between, the roll of film. In all movie theaters, wherever you go, the screen is the same, the light is the same; they're constant. But they present different shows by changing the rolls of film. And they show it in a dark place.

The darkness is ignorance. In our lives we may also see such filmmaking. The pure Self inside is the clear light, the projector's bulb, the illumination. The world outside is just a blank screen. But in that world, you see many dramas, many things: heroes, heroines, villains and all the different roles. Where do they come from? The roll of film built into your projector. That roll of film is your mind.

When you got it originally, that roll of film didn't have anything on it. It came to you blank with unexposed or unspoiled film. Even before you bought the film, how was it made? When I was younger they would use pure mica sheets. Then they would coat that plain glass-like sheet with some chemicals, such as silver nitrate and other things. The composition varied. According to the different chemical compositions, the sensitivity of the film increased or decreased. The moment the pure, plain plastic sheet is coated with the sensitive chemical composition, it becomes a sensitive film.

That sensitivity is measured in ASA. Is it a coincidence that *asa* in Sanskrit means desire? Until that coating of sensitivity, the film was innocent, crystal clear and pure. And the moment it becomes sensitive to light, it must stay in the dark or it will become exposed. That is why unexposed film is put on rolls and then in cans in darkness. From then on, it is kept in the dark until it is exposed. Even after exposure, it is developed in a darkroom and later projected in a dark room. It's all darkroom business.

Our minds are like that. Originally, the mind was crystal clear, like a pure mica sheet, very innocent. No desire there at all. Then somehow the mind became coated with sensitivity. We sometimes say, "Beware of that fellow, he's so sensitive," which means egoistic. That beautifully untouched film becomes coated with a little ego-chemical. How sensitive to light the mind becomes depends on the thickness of ego. Some minds even hate the light. They want to be in darkness. They are happy in their ignorance.

But we don't just stay there. We want to take pictures. And we have a highly refined camera with a double lens for three dimensions: our eyes. We even have a camera with a built-in, automatically opening aperture: the iris. Our lens is also exceptional: wide-angle, normal or telephoto. It can become anything, because God created *this* camera. It's different, doesn't need any adjustments, and not even a battery. There's a shutter too. Open that shutter and immediately the images pass through.

And where do those images go? Straight onto the egoistic film of the mind, at which point you carefully take it home and develop it. First you see it: "Ahh, what a pretty thing." You just took a picture of it. You go home thinking, "How can I get it? It's only $150. I have $100 in the bank. Well, I can borrow another $50 from a friend." Now, you're developing the picture. Once you decide to buy it, you've fixed it. That's the developing bath and fixing bath in the darkroom of ignorance.

Thinking, "Yes, by getting this I'll be happy," is the ignorance. Once you fix it, you print it and project it. So, whatever is printed and fixed becomes your roll of film. You have millions of photographs on that roll, which keeps revolving. The clear light of your pure Self is inside giving off light. Without that light, the mind can't do anything. Because it is in the presence of that light, it projects onto the clear screen. And that's why what you see is nothing but your projection. If you erase all the images, if you take the roll of film away, you will see only a pure world.

Actually there is nothing to distinguish you as separate from the world.

So, that is why we say, that if in the early stages you still want to take pictures, take nice pictures. Listen to the Chinese monkeys: Hear no evil on your tape recorder; see no evil with your camera. You have a tape recorder, a camera and a playback machine. You have everything. If you still want to use your camera, then use it. But speak no evil, hear no evil, see no evil. Then the world outside will seem better to you.

Most enmities are created by speaking. If you are silent, you avoid many quarrels. That's why the proverb: *Silence is golden.* People who properly observe silence are always happy. They don't expose their foolishness. It saves you and others too. Everything is recorded on this magnetized audio-visual tape with playback. Everything that we do should keep this film clean.

The *Bible* says, "Blessed are the pure in heart. They shall see God." They see nothing but God because the film roll in the heart has been purified. God shines through and all they see is light everywhere. To see God everywhere, let God shine through your crystal-clear mind. Until then, saying, "Everything is God," is just theory, not real experience.

These *slokas* are talking about the basic three-part principle: the seer, the seen and seeing; or the knower, the knowable and knowledge. On the outside are the *indriyas* or the senses, which are two-fold: the inner, subtle senses that bring in all the ideas, and then the active senses that turn the ideas into action. First you get the idea and then you put it into action. That's why we ask, "Where did you get that idea?" The idea comes before the action. Even to get an idea, there's an I, an ego. First comes thought—the idea; then speech and doing—action. Speaking also is action. But thought is the basis.

19. There are three types of knowledge, actions and agents. I will describe each for you according to its predominant *guna*, as presented in the science of *Samkhya* Yoga.

20. There is one eternal reality that pervades everything and everyone. In the midst of the many, it is the indivisible oneness. In all (so-called) separate beings, it is never separated or divided. Perception of this reality is pure, or *sattvic*, knowledge.

Chapter Eighteen

Sattvic knowing means the mind has become more tranquil. Only when this happens will you perceive the essence in everything. Whenever the mind is not *sattvic*—tranquil, peaceful and balanced—it is impossible to see the essence behind everything. That's why *rajas* and *tamas* should be overcome. You literally destroy the *rajasic* and *tamasic* qualities and construct *sattva*. Then, at a certain level, even *sattva* should be transcended. That will happen later. Right now, just change *tamas* to *rajas*, and *rajas* to *sattva*.

Don't even hurry to reach the *sattvic* state of tranquility. Just get rid of *tamas,* the dull, sleepy, always-take-it-easy attitude. Don't fall into that. Get up! Get dressed, ready to go. Overcome *tamas* with *rajas.*

I admire the great Sri Swami Vivekananda. He was the foremost disciple of Sri Ramakrishna Paramahamsa and himself an inspirational sage who was among the very first to bring Eastern wisdom to North America. He used to say, "Forget about all your philosophy, all your scripture studies, all your temples. Close everything and go to the field, play some football and volleyball. You so-called religious people in the name of scripture, temple and dogma, you are all dull-headed and sleeping. You need *rajas* now. Don't mistake *tamas* to be *sattvic.*"

I think that sounds like a good idea. We shouldn't fool ourselves thinking we are all *sattvic,* while really we are just sleeping. It's better to get up, go into the field, do some digging, drive a bulldozer, cut some trees, clear some land. Then you will feel active, warmed up. So let's build up a little *rajas.* I'm for action. I don't even like sitting and talking. I prefer to be somewhere in the fields doing some work. When you are moderately *rajasic* then you are ready to experience *sattva.*

21. However, perceiving everything and all the various creatures as distinctly separate and different, one from the other, is *rajasic* knowledge [based on a restless mind].

Rajas creates division, no doubt. But we can't rise to the *sattvic* stage without passing through *rajas.* We must pass through *rajas* because the mind must first be warmed up by *rajas.* Every machine takes a little time to warm up. Only then does it give real energy. Even a car. In cold weather, we can't immediately put it in gear and go. The engine will stall because it hasn't been warmed up. That warming up is *rajas*. Before it was inert, which is the *tamasic* state. So we warm it up. Then after it begins to run well, we can put it in overdrive, *sattva*, and with less fuel it will go faster. So it is all right to develop a little *rajas*.

You will know you are too *rajasic* if you get into trouble. It's very simple. The minute you see you are in trouble, then you are a little too *rajasic*, and you're using it the wrong way.

In the next *sloka* he talks about *tamas* also:

> 22. There is also perception that clings to a view that sees one small part of the whole and mistakes it for all there is. This is *tamasic* knowledge, which is not true, not reasonable and myopic.

Tamasic knowledge isn't reasonable because you don't even have the energy to think rationally. It's not that you can't think well; it's that you choose not to: "Oh, forget about it. Nothing matters. Why worry about anything?" That's *tamas*.

There's a Tamil story: A sleepy fellow was hungry and said so. A friend said, "There's a banana; why don't you take it?"

"You just peel it and put it in my mouth."

He was so lazy he wouldn't even reach out for the one easiest fruit, the banana. He wanted somebody to peel it for him and then put it in his mouth. Some people are that *tamasic*. How can they be rational then? They don't even have the energy. And without a rational mind, they can't recognize the truth.

Even to practice Yoga, some *rajas* is needed. "I must do my *asanas* and meditations daily. I have to do my job well." Yes, there's a reason for that "I" feeling of *rajas*: "I have to stick to one place. Come what may, I'll face it!" All that needs *rajas*. Don't think *rajas* is so bad. We do need *rajas*. The key is to utilize it the right way. *Rajasic* energy is strength, even a stubbornness. Be stubborn about your practices. "Unless I do a half-hour meditation I can't go out!" Let's develop that positive kind of *rajas*. Everything has its positive aspect.

23. If you do what is right to do, and you do it without attachment to the fruits, without thought of a reward for yourself, and without judging if it is pleasant or unpleasant, that is pure, *sattvic* action.

24. However, anything done to fulfill the craving of personal desire, or to satisfy the selfish ego or carried out with so much effort that is straining is *rajasic* action of a restless mind.

25. Anything undertaken blindly, that is, without considering the consequences—such as waste or injury—or without even pausing to consider one's ability to succeed, that action is dark with ignorance and is *tamasic*.

26. When the agent of an action (the individual) has let go of attachment to the fruits and [thus] is free of the egoistic feeling of separateness, yet is still full of enthusiasm and fully committed, then that agent is not affected by [so-called] success or failure.

27. The *rajasic* agent (individual) acts primarily out of personal desire, or in order to get the fruits of his or her actions, or out of greed, cruelty or for other impure purposes. That agent of action is easily carried away by excitement or dismay about the results of his actions.

28. The *tamasic* agent does things stubbornly, yet without steadiness. His or her actions, which are vulgar, deceitful, malicious and dishonest, arise from a mind that is lazy, procrastinating and easily dejected (*tamasic*).

29. Listen now, Arjuna, and I will fully teach you the three degrees of understanding and three types of will, according to each one's predominant *guna*.

30. These are the signs of clear understanding (*buddhi sattva*): knowing when and when not to act; knowing what is right and what is wrong to do; knowing the causes of fear (*bhaya*) and fearlessness (*abhaya*); and knowing also the paths of bondage and freedom (*moksha*).

Out of the *sattvic* quality of the mind, the discriminative faculty arises. That means clear, rational thinking and clear understanding of what is and what is not to be done. With the *sattvic* quality you clearly see what binds you and what liberates you.

31. *Rajasic* understanding does not easily distinguish the virtuous way (*dharma*) from the evil way (*adharma*), and therefore, Arjuna, often errs deciding what and what not to do.

Understanding itself is divided into *sattva, rajas* and *tamas*. Everything, even knowledge, has these three qualities. In the same way, the intellectual part of the mind, the discriminative faculty, also has three qualities. *Rajasic* understanding misconstrues right and wrong. But the *tamasic* intellect, enveloped in ignorance, imagines wrong to be right; it perceives everything backward. That's also a type of intelligence, but it's perverted. What's wrong for everybody else is just right for that person. He or she will say, "Let's argue. That's my way." That's *tamasic* intelligence.

32. *Tamasic* understanding is enveloped in a curtain of darkness (ignorance of reality). Because it perceives all and everything through this distorted lens, Arjuna, it utterly reverses right action with wrong action.

33. Yoga meditations make the mind pure, steady and strong. With that *sattvic* will (firmness of mind) one can control and regulate the life force (*prana*), the senses and the functioning of the mind.

34. But if the will is strong, out of personal desires for wealth, sense pleasures (*kama*) and respectability, then, Arjuna, this is *rajasic* will.

35. These are the signs of a *tamasic* will (steeped in ignorance): obstinately clinging to the habit of oversleeping; also fear, grief, depression and conceit.

36. These are the three kinds of pleasure (*sukha*), one of which, Arjuna, will surely lead a person to the end of all sorrow by the way of steady and continuous effort.

37. Pleasure that at first seems like poison, but in the end is nectar, is pure (*sattvic*) joy arising in the clear mind of Self-realization.

It's good for us to know that a *sattvic* joy will probably begin with a little bitterness. There is a Tamil proverb, "Advice of the wise is like a ripe gooseberry." When you begin to chew, it's very bitter. You'll feel like spitting it out immediately. But if you are patient and keep on chewing until saliva mixes with it, you begin to get a sweet taste. Then, the more you chew the more sugary it becomes. So the joy that comes after having "chewed" enough is what we call *sattvic;* it lasts long.

This applies to any practice. For example, swimming. Before you know how to swim, you may not even want to go near the water. Somebody might have to drag you or push you into the water. The minute you get in, you cry and shout, you want to jump out again. But little by little, you learn to like it. Then a time comes when you don't even want to come out of the water. That's *sattvic* happiness. It takes some time to bring its result, but once obtained, it is lasting.

38. The pleasure that arises when the senses contact the sense objects seems at first to be nectar, but in the end is bitter as poison. This is *rajasic* pleasure of a desirous mind.

Sensual pleasures are pleasant in the beginning, like scratching an itch. Just a little scratching feels nice. Then you feel like scratching more and more. After some time, you can't take your fingers away, because the moment you do it burns. But can you keep on scratching? If you do, it bleeds. Either way, it's terrible.

It is better not even to start such "happiness," because once you start, it's both hard to stop and hard to continue. That's why Sri Krishna says it is poisonous.

One should be very careful about these points in spiritual life. Remember, *sattvic* happiness seems like poison at first but ends up with joy. *Rajasic* happiness is joyous in the beginning but ends up as poison. This is nicely illustrated in a mythological story.

Once the *devas* and *asuras* (gods and demons) started a cooperative business. They learned that if they churned the ocean of milk, they would get nectar to drink. Both groups were interested in the nectar, so they started churning the ocean together. Soon after they began to churn, very nice things came out of the ocean of milk: the Goddesses Sarasvati and Lakshmi and a white horse came first.

The esoteric meaning of the ocean of milk is the universe itself, probably the Milky Way. Sarasvati, Lakshmi and the horse represent education, wealth and good transportation facilities. It's true, if you really delve deeply into material nature and "churn" it, or explore it, you can gain knowledge and wealth and get scientific truths. You'll be able to handle matter and its forces well, which seems very nice at first. You could say it brings happiness. But the *Gita* categorizes that as *rajasic* happiness because it will end in a poisonous way, as the story explains.

As the *devas* and *asuras* kept on churning, a deadly poison came next. It began with nectar and ended with poison. In a way, we are seeing this nowadays as the result of all our explorations, developments and inventions. They seem to be bringing more suffering than joy. Of course, neither the *devas* nor the *asuras* wanted the poison, but it started chasing them. They ran and ran and finally took refuge at the feet of Lord Shiva.

And he, being the merciful Supreme God, said, "Okay, don't worry, I'll take care of it." He just took the poison and swallowed it, because for him there is no nectar or poison; everything is equal.

Here we see that even though we go and churn for the sake of *rajasic* happiness and must face the bitterness of it, we can still save ourselves if we take refuge in God. Life's experiences ultimately take us to the goal, no doubt. But not everybody needs to undergo all the same experiences. Sensible people will not always wait for a bitter experience to teach them. They will learn from the scriptures and from others' experiences.

39. Pleasure that is delusive in the beginning and also at the end, arises in a dull and listless mind (*tamas*). Its signs are oversleeping, laziness and using intoxicants.

Some people say, "I don't want to face anything in life." How many people with shallow lives ultimately end up using sleeping pills? They can't face life. They think they could be happier by swallowing a tranquilizer, drugging themselves or getting drunk. It is not our aim to be happy at any cost. It should come in a *sattvic* way. Only such happiness will last. Other kinds of happiness will end in unhappiness.

40. There is no one on earth or among the gods of heaven (*devas*) who is beyond the three qualities of nature.

Unfortunately, the fortieth *sloka* says there's no one on earth or even in heaven, including the gods, who is free from these three *gunas*.

At first that sounds a little discouraging. But it doesn't have to be. The three *gunas* are always there; we can't avoid them. In fact, the moment we rise above the three *gunas*, we become totally unfit for anything in this world and we might as well leave. Our job is over; the main switch is off; no impetus remains.

But this will happen automatically when our part of the job is finished. Automatically, the switch goes off. Until then, we are in the world and thus affected by the three *gunas*. So let's not try to avoid them and jump out.

Let's just stay in the world and get fried well, even though it's hot work, very *rajasic*. At first, we simply make a lot of noise, jump all around and create a lot of bubbles—that's the three *gunas* tossing our minds. But once we have been completely seasoned and cooked by nature, then we step out of the frying pan to make room for other fritters.

Those well-seasoned ones are the gods, the angels. Don't think gods are superior to human beings. In a way, they are even inferior. They are only experiencing one type of karma, the tasty fruits they deserve because of nice things that they did earlier. They are simply getting their reward. They don't have human freedom. Only at the human level is there freedom to understand the truth. Only humans have the capacity to discriminate.

The gods are in the heavens. In hell and in heaven you can't discriminate. You simply purge your bad or good karma. Some are in a sort of hell to purge bad karma. Some are in a heaven to purge good karma. But to create new karma or to rise beyond all karma, you have to come back here as a human being, get caught up again in the three *gunas* and learn all the lessons. Once you learn the lessons, then automatically you are freed. It's not that you get out simply by your own effort. It just happens, like a fully matured fruit that drops out of the tree. So, in time we will all drop out, naturally. Don't try to jump out of the tree prematurely. Don't jump out of the frying pan half-fried; you won't be so tasty. This beautiful *sloka* is saying that no one is excluded.

41. Indeed, Arjuna, the qualities in one's own nature determine the appropriate role and duties for each person—whether scholar or priest (*brahmin*), leader or warrior (*kshatriya*); tradesperson (*vaisya*), or laborer (*sudra*).

Now we come to the four-fold castes and their duties: Hindu tradition divides people into four groups or castes: *brahmins, kshatriyas, vaisyas* and *sudras. Brahmins* are the priests and teachers; *kshatriyas,* the rulers and warriors; *vaisyas* are the business people; and *sudras,* the working class. Unfortunately these four castes gradually came down to the level where a *brahmin's* child is called a *brahmin;* a *vaisya's* child, a *vaisya,* and so on. But these four categories are supposed to be based on people's temperaments.

What are the qualities or temperament of a *brahmin?* These are intelligent people who use that intelligence in the pursuit of the supreme knowledge.

42. By nature the priest or teacher (*brahmin*) is inclined toward serenity, self-control, self-discipline, purity and forgiveness, as well as virtuous behavior, learning, Self-realization and faith in the eternal.

These are qualities of *brahmins.* Not that they cultivate them as *brahmins.* They must have developed these qualities before, probably as *kshatriyas* or *vaisyas.* They no longer need to force themselves to do spiritual practices or to be morally perfect or to control their senses; it comes naturally to them. We see this even among some spiritual seekers. For some people, it's easy to control the tongue. For some it's very easy to get up at four or five o'clock in the morning for meditation. They don't even think about it. These qualities are inborn. You don't need to teach swimming to a duckling; it's just born with that knowledge.

43. The leader or warrior (*kshatriya*) is naturally inclined to courage, vigor, firmness of mind, resourcefulness, generosity, leadership and the resolve not to flee, but to persevere in the midst of battle.

While the *brahmins* are embodiments of divinity, the *kshatriyas* are embodiments of *dharma*, truth and virtue. Traditionally, the kings or rulers are *kshatriyas* because their duty is to protect the nation, to maintain law and order and to save the wise and righteous people from the wicked. Arjuna is a *kshatriya*, but because of his emotional feelings, his sentiments, he wants to reject his duty and become something of a *brahmin*. It's not that he evolved to that category. But he wants to reject his duty by force.

The duty of *kshatriyas* can be compared to that of farmers. Farmers cultivate the land; they have to keep pests from their crops. They may choose not to use poisonous chemicals, but somehow they must protect the crops from pests and weeds. So they spray some ash on their fields and pull out the weeds. In the same way, the *kshatriyas* should weed out the pests in their country and see that the right types of plants are growing there.

44. The tradesperson (*vaisya*) is naturally inclined toward farming, dairying, and other business trades. And working people by nature are inclined toward service.

Vaisyas are the business people and *sudras* the servants and workers. Probably, the *sudras* have neither the intelligence to seek the higher goals, nor the strength to protect the *dharma*, nor even the intelligence to do business. They are good at performing duties that are given to them. But we should never think that one type is higher or lower than another. All are equally necessary to maintain an orderly society. And know for sure, the same people could be *sudras* at one time and *brahmins* at another. But if the major part of their lives shows a particular quality, then it is said that they are from this or that category.

That's how the caste system came into being. The duty of the *vaisya* was to create and distribute the material wealth to the society. Of course in those days, traditional means were through agriculture, cattle-rearing and trade. Now, we have so many other businesses also: mining, crafts, all the thousands of different industries.

Even lawyers and doctors could be treated as *vaisyas* if they use their knowledge primarily for the purpose of trading it for something in return.

Whenever you give something to get something in return, a give and take, that's business. In that respect, you are a *vaisya*.

Those who can do only physical labor and are incapable of setting up callings of their own are *sudras*. Those employed as paid lower subordinates to others are *sudras*. They depend on others for their livelihood. Clerks who just do whatever they're asked to do and get the pay can be categorized as *sudras*—at least at that time.

But you can't classify everybody who gets paid as a *sudra*. A schoolteacher with the right mental attitude is a *brahmin*. A government officer is a *kshatriya*. People who sell their labor and independence and those who take bribes and tips are all *sudras*. Whoever's principle interest in life is centered in the body and has no higher outlook in life is also a *sudra*.

You see these four types of people in all societies, not just in India or the East. Only there they were recognized and classified this way. We also have *brahmins, kshatriyas, vaisyas* and *sudras* in America. All over the globe you see these types. You may even see all of them in one family. Among four brothers, one may be a *brahmin* by temperament and another a *sudra*.

One's temperament is not simply inherited. If it were, then a lawyer's child should always be a lawyer; a judge's child, a judge; a doctor's child, a doctor. It's not by birth, but by qualification. Although the skillful attainments of the four categories vary, there is no difference in the virtues of their respective duties. The duties of the one are as sacred and conducive to enlightenment as that of the others. A *sudra* may be as qualified for the practice of Yoga as another. Temperamentally that person is a *sudra*, but if he or she is interested in spiritual growth, that person shouldn't be rejected.

That, unfortunately, is what happened in India. A *brahmin* won't teach a *sudra*, even if he or she wants to learn. ("Oh, you are the child of a *sudra*: I won't even touch you.") It was this mistaken understanding that degenerated and nullified the value of the caste system.

Scriptures present these castes as originating from four parts of Brahma, the Creator. From his head, Brahma created the *brahmins*. From his shoulders, the *kshatriyas;* the *vaisyas* from his thighs and the *sudras* from his feet. How could God, in a masculine form, as Brahma, create people from his head, shoulders, thighs and feet? It's not to be taken literally. The head represents the intelligence; the shoulders, strength; the thighs, movement and therefore business; and the feet support and carry all the other three. If you think a *sudra* is undesirable, imagine chopping off your feet. How will you move? Even the *brahmin* needs feet to go to the dining table.

There's no superiority or inferiority. In fact, in many traditions you see ordinary, unlettered people, not at all intellectual, who become great saints—Jesus' apostles, for example. He selected those fishermen who, for the most part, were simple, unlettered people. In the East we also see very ordinary people rising up to become great saints.

According to their *varna*, or caste, people take to different yogic paths. A *sudra*, for example, whose temperament is to serve, takes more to Karma Yoga. Whereas a *vaisya* would tend toward the business of offering and accepting and would follow Bhakti Yoga. A *kshatriya* would be more likely to follow Raja Yoga, the path that needs more will power. And a *brahmin* will be practicing Jnana Yoga.

Whichever is your Yoga, you can still reach the goal. Just choose one path according to your temperament. If you sit and read scriptures, you should not look down on those who do Karma Yoga. "Look there, they are always in the garden; they don't come and teach classes. They don't meditate for half an hour like me." Sometimes, feelings like that might arise. Those who sit and meditate might think they are the great yogis while those constantly working in the kitchen or garden are "just" *karma yogis*. But those in the kitchen or garden might be *better* yogis. Temperamentally that service suits them.

There can be Yoga behind all their actions. When someone pulls up a weed, he's pulling out some of his own undesirable *samskaras*, or habits of mind. When he throws a rock out, he's taking a rock out of his heart that was weighing him down. He is also farming within. When such karma or action is performed with that kind of feeling, it is Karma Yoga. Probably that person will be way ahead, patiently waiting for you scripture readers to reach heaven. Jnana Yogis, with all their grammar and Sanskrit and other holy books, are still learning all these *slokas* by heart, while the Karma Yogis are happily waiting for them in heaven.

In our Integral Yoga, when you feel like working, you become a Karma Yogi. When you feel like meditating, you become a Raja Yogi. In truth, each individual is a mixture of all these. That's why we recommend Integral Yoga. You are not always one or the other. If you are an Integral Yogi, whatever you are doing at that time is your Yoga. When you work, "Yes, I'm a Karma Yogi now." If you are sitting and meditating, "I'm a Raja Yogi." If you sing and chant and pray and do *puja*, "Oh, now I'm a Bhakti Yogi." Make every action into Yoga. As my master, Swami Sivanandaji, used to say, the head, heart and the hand should develop simultaneously. So you are a *brahmin, kshatriya,* a *vaisya* and a *sudra.* You have head, shoulders, thighs and feet.

45. You can attain perfection by devoting yourself to the work that comes most naturally. I will explain how.

46. When you do the work that by your nature is your calling, you are worshipping the Creator of all beings who is omnipresent, and thus you attain perfection.

A sensible person will attain perfection in his or her own *dharma,* and make that duty a form of worship. Whatever you do should be done as a form of worship. That's the sensible way to live. The famous *Vyadha Gita* is a beautiful example of this. Vyadhan was born into a butcher's family, so he just accepted it. "Well, probably the cosmic law made me take birth in a butcher's family," he thought. "So I am a butcher. The world needs this job also. Though I am a vegetarian, many people do eat meat. So I am doing my *dharma,* my specific duty. I'm not attached to this, nor am I rejecting it." That way his mind stayed calm and clean.

A truly *sattvic* person will not reject or reach for anything under the force of his or her own egoism. Instead, you accept whatever comes and perform that duty well. Providence brought Vyadhan into a butcher's family. So he became a butcher, but still his mind was peaceful. It was not that he was disturbed at first until he decided, "Yes, this is my *svadharma,* my appointed duty; I have to do it." No, it was his nature. He naturally accepted it, so his mind stayed calm and clean.

Next is a very important and famous *sloka*.

> **47. It is better to do your own *dharma* imperfectly than to excel at another's *dharma*. If you accept the duties of your own nature, you are free from sin.**

We see this in Vyadhan's case. In ancient India and in many other lands, your *dharma* was to carry on your father's work. But in present society, it's not so clear. How does one know one's own *dharma?* That's the problem now. (I could easily have avoided this *sloka* and gone to the next one, but somehow I know that's not *my dharma*.) This one really needs a lot of understanding.

Your *dharma*, as was said in discussing the caste system, is determined by your temperament, not just your family line. Even before birth, according to your temperament, you come into a particular womb. It's not that you consciously choose your parents with your limited mind.

It's all determined according to your previous actions and the *samskaras*, or mental impressions, that you acquired earlier. The cosmic law decides, "Okay, you have received all the necessary lessons from the previous class (life experience). For further promotion, go and study in that classroom."

If we each were literally to choose the wombs for the next experience, everybody would choose to be the baby of the First Lady or Queen Elizabeth. Why should we go into a poor woman somewhere in a corner who won't even have a piece of bread for us? Certainly we would all choose rich families. So it's not that we choose consciously. Without our even knowing, because we did so many things before, that karma selects our next birth. If we really wanted a certain birth, we should have been thinking along those lines earlier when we started sowing, not when we're reaping. We sowed earlier; now we simply have to face it.

It was in this way that Vyadhan accepted it when he was born into a butcher's family. "Yes, I must have done some karma that pushed me into a butcher's family. But it doesn't matter. At least now let me be enlightened and accept it." Traditionally, the enlightened person just performs the duty allotted by his or her birth without choosing, rejecting or even accepting intellectually. It's not even an intellectual acceptance. The enlightened person just goes to it like a duck goes to water.

Even in these times, it's usually the same. When you want to change your present life or work, usually the ego has entered: "I don't like this anymore. That person seems to have a better job." You compare: "That's a decent, white-collar job. This is just a dirty job. I want to do what he's doing."

You can do that, but what will you gain? You have certain innate tendencies. Respect them. A certain preparation has brought you to this situation. If you change, you lose all that. Carpenters' children often can easily become carpenters. They need not laboriously, or even consciously, learn these skills one by one. Poets' children often becomes poets automatically. It's not that they consciously learn how to write poetry. But if the children come to feel that carpentry is no good and poetry would be really nice, then they have to begin anew. They lose what they had already. They leave a nice, well-built home and go out to build a new one. And, probably, very soon they will want still another home, because it's all based on egoistic choice, not nature's choice.

But if you are transformed into something different without your even knowing, then that's part of nature. In this case, you didn't personally choose to reject this and accept that, but rather the outcome of this is that; you were a bitter fruit yesterday, but today you are sweet. Nature pushes you up. It so happens that you are a carpenter. But without your even thinking or consciously changing, you move to a Yoga community and start using your carpentry as Karma Yoga. Then slowly you go some steps further in meditation, and maybe you begin sharing what you are learning as a Yoga teacher, and so on. You never rejected the carpenter's life. Other activities began to take precedence just naturally, little by little.

Sometimes you might try to avoid your nature and do something else temporarily. But if it is your *dharma* to do something, eventually you will be drawn back to that because the inborn trait is there. At one point,

Chapter Eighteen

Krishna says to Arjuna, "Consciously you are rejecting your *kshatriya dharma* (the destiny of a warrior-ruler). But I know this is just temporary. Now you want to go into the jungle to meditate and take on austerities, but I'm positive you wouldn't stay there. You'll be back here fighting, so why waste time? Do it now."

Many people move into an *ashram* and think, "Now that I'm here, I'm just going to sit and meditate for fifteen hours a day and probably just eat fruit and nuts." But if you are a carpenter, within a couple of months you will be doing some carpentry work. If you are a gardener, within a couple of months you will be doing some work in the garden. If you are a mason, you will be doing some cement work. When you see these things that need to be done, you are prompted to do them. Something inside tells you, "I can do it. It needs to be done. I should do it." If you are an accountant, you will just start doing the books and probably end up as the *ashram* accountant.

But this accounting is different from the accounting you did before. The *dharma* is the same but it is elevated to a higher level. You are not doing it as karma (selfish action), but as Karma Yoga (selfless action). You were working as a carpenter, lawyer or mason. Now your work has become worship itself. This means that you needn't change the work, just the attitude. Have a worshipful attitude as you do your own work. Learn to grow from where you are. Don't simply drop your old life and begin something new. The world needs every action, every function. One is not superior to the other.

> **48. If you perform the duties of your own nature imperfectly, that is no reason to abandon those duties and begin something else. For all your undertakings, at the outset, are enveloped by evil, as smoke surrounds fire.**

He says that whatever you undertake is enveloped by evil. Why? Because it's your *personal* undertaking. You chose to do it instead of letting it come along naturally. Let nature move you along into different classes. You don't have to leave one class on your own and go sit in another. Grow gradually. Natural growth is best. You may not even be able to see your own growth.

I've seen this in my own experience. I never consciously chose to reject another way of living and become a Swami. People ask, "Why did you renounce everything and become a spiritual seeker and a Swami?" I didn't. Even now I wonder at what point I was put into this. It just flowed from one stage to another. I was just guided. It wasn't that I consciously chose something and rejected something else. Just trust nature's hand. Let the Mother shape you. Allow Her hand to work. She'll take care of you.

Sometimes, of course, it's difficult to know when you are following nature's path and when the egoistic mind is telling you to do something. That problem arises when you allow the mind to play. In blunt language, I'm saying: down with your intellect. It's a little difficult to say such things in this technical, cultured society. But this is how I feel. Allow the unseen hand to work on you. Then, without your even knowing, you will be transformed. If something isn't good for you, you won't have to reject it. Something will happen, you will be taken and put somewhere else, away from it. Your conscious rejection isn't necessary, because there is a Cosmic Intelligence that will direct you to your *svadharma*, your best service. The Cosmic Intelligence takes care of everything. It puts you in certain places; and, when you finish there, puts you somewhere else.

It's a little hard to accept and follow, or even to understand, because we always want to use our intelligence to decide what is right and what is wrong. But, in truth, it is impossible for us to know what is really right from wrong. One person's poison is another person's nectar.

49. When the discerning mind (*buddhi*) is no longer attached to the fruits and the egoistic self (*jivatma*) no longer predominates because personal desire is gone, by this renunciation you rise to a supreme state of perfection which is freedom from [the effects of] all actions.

You can't attain freedom from action by conscious thinking or by applying your ego. Only by your total detachment from thinking and ego is that freedom known. "But what should I do then?" you may wonder. "I can't seem to make myself be that way. Somehow, my intelligence won't allow me to accept this." As long as you have such feelings, then use your own intelligence to decide what's good and bad for you. But if it fails, don't be surprised and disappointed. Accept that and say, "Probably the Higher Intelligence wanted it another way."

Yes, you have full freedom to do what you want. But when things don't turn out the way you hoped, at least remember that is because some higher force wanted it to be different. That way you will be happy. You can make anything you want, but when it comes out of the factory, the final inspector should okay it. It takes hundreds of people to manufacture a car, but the final inspector must say it's okay before it goes to the showroom. The same way, the supreme supervisor should okay your actions.

Sometimes God okays what you set out to do. You may not realize that and think, "See, I wanted it and I did it." You don't see God's seal of approval there. God doesn't come and interfere. God says, "You want the credit for yourself? Okay, keep it." But if it doesn't go the way you wanted, instead of getting disheartened or blaming others, think, "Probably God didn't okay it." That way you can retain your peace and avoid creating enemies around you.

Intelligence and free will are fine, but that free will isn't totally free. It's free within limitations. Beyond that limitation, it is subject to that Higher Will, a Cosmic Intelligence. Your so-called free will is part of that cosmic will. It's like the ocean and the wave. You can jump up high as a wave and say, "I'm a big wave." But where are you really? You are still within the ocean. You might really jump and roll. But afterward, you go down into the sea again. An ocean wave probably lasts no more than a minute or two, while this ego wave of human birth lasts for 60 or 70 years. Still, it is just a wave of that mighty ocean.

> **50. Now in a few words, Arjuna, I will tell you how one who attains the perfection of freedom from actions also realizes the oneness of the Absolute (*Brahman*), who is the consummation of wisdom.**
>
> **51. That person becomes one with *Brahman*, who has pure understanding, *sattva*, and firm control of his or her senses and passions; who turns from the clamor of sense objects; and renounces likes and dislikes.**

Endowed with pure understanding means that your understanding is not prejudiced. You understand from the zero, or neutral point, not from positive or negative. Purity means neutrality. You can never have a pure mind swinging either to positive or negative, because those are already prejudiced views. If you like or dislike people, you are projecting your own colored feelings onto them. Then you can't judge them accurately. That's why real judges must always be at the zero point on a balance scale. Then, they can weigh a case well and pass correct judgment. If judges are already leaning to one side, they will err in judgment.

"Turning from the clamor of the sense objects and renouncing likes and dislikes" means turning away from anything that would disturb you. More or less closing your senses to it. That's not the same as running from it.

You choose your own way to keep your mind steady. That's your Yoga; that's your religion. Could there be anything simpler than this? That's my teaching summed up. I don't say, "I'll teach you this in three minutes or in a ten-day course." If you ask me the traditional ways, I may give you a few ideas: "Moses did this, Jesus did that, Shankara did that." And some examples: "Some people meditate on the light; some on an image; some on a mantra." I would give you a few choices. If you like any one of these, do it. If not, choose your own. But don't forget the purposes of all these things: It's to keep the mind steady, peaceful and happy.

Peace, joy, bliss—whatever happens, don't think it's impossible to live like that; it is possible! What else do you need but that constant joy? And in that joy you may feel, "All right, I seem to have this talent; this is my *svadharma* (my duty), I feel like doing it. So I will." In that peace of mind, whatever you do becomes Yoga, whether it is gardening, carpentry, accounting, painting or candle making. Whatever you do is a joy for you. You don't even need to pick and choose.

Keep the goal in mind. Use any means. But always ask: "Is this going to take me toward that goal?" If at any point, you see that it won't, that it will disturb your peace, then immediately say, "No, it's not for me." Sometimes due to habit, the mind wants to do something disturbing that it used to do before. Then if you try to cultivate something new, the mind dislikes it and makes you think you're disturbing your peace. For example, rising at 4 or 5 a.m. for meditation. In the beginning some practices might be bitter, but keep on chewing and they will become sweet. So build up that peace on a strong foundation. Don't settle just for momentary peace or joy, which create bitter poisons later.

52. Instead, you live in [a sense of] solitude, eat sparingly and control your thoughts, words and actions. You continually engage in yogic meditation (Dhyana Yoga) and take refuge in non-attachment (*vairagya*).

Don't take "live in solitude" literally and demand a separate cabin in the jungle. Living in solitude means that even in the midst of a hundred people, you feel you are alone. If some useful vibrations come, accept them. Otherwise, feel you are by yourself. As a sincere seeker, you will not worry much about what is happening around you. You are just engrossed in your meditation. When you eat, you meditate on eating. You don't sit there gossiping and bringing the whole world inside your mind by the time you finish your apple or orange. You meditate on what you are doing. That's the quality of a spiritual seeker. Unless it's warranted, you don't even need to talk simply for the sake of talking. Don't think you have to always smile or talk to others, or they will wonder about you. Are you more interested in others' opinions more than in your own growth?

Speak sparingly. A word is a bird. Once let out, you can't whistle it back. Measure your words. Think that every word is a dollar and once it goes out, it won't return. Think two or three times before speaking. Let people know that you really mean what you say when you speak. People often say, "I don't know, do you know what I mean?" Such talking creates confusion. If you think well before you utter a word, then you can convey so much with fewer words. With less energy, you perform a better job.

"Eating sparingly" means neither starving nor feasting. Eat according to the body's needs. "Control of thoughts, words and actions" and "continuously in meditation and concentration" means that you concentrate and meditate even while you do things, which is meditation in action.

It's quite a long list. But if even one of these qualities is developed, all the rest will automatically follow.

53. Because you are free of the ego sense of separateness (*ahamkara*), you no longer suffer possessive attitudes of my and

mine. Thus, you overcome aggressiveness, arrogance, personal desires and anger. You are peacefully prepared to experience oneness with the Absolute.

You don't have to take on such a big list. Just pick one: that's enough. For example, feeling that nothing is "mine." Completely free yourself from selfishness. I'll say it again and again. You might even think this Swami doesn't know anything else. I don't need to know anything else. I just know that selflessness is the key to spiritual life. All these other things—egoism, violence, arrogance, desire, etc.—are just the outcome of selfishness or personal desire. Remember these *slokas* in Chapter Two: From brooding on sense objects, attachment to them arises. Out of that attachment personal desire is born. And from desire, anger appears (2:62). Anger confuses the thinking process, which in turn disturbs memory. When memory fails, reasoning is ruined. And when reason is gone, the person is lost (2:63).

The minute you desire something, or even think of it with a little lust pushing you on, immediately all the rest follows. You become attached to the object of your desires. Attachment makes you want to somehow possess it. And if you don't get it, you feel disappointed or if somebody interferes, you get angry and deluded. So the main trait to develop—at any cost—is selflessness.

54. When you realize oneness with the Absolute, you are always serene and no longer subject to sorrow or the anxiety of personal desires. You feel the same regard for all creatures and rise to a state of supreme devotion to God.

55. By such devotion, you will know me truly—what and who I am. When you know that, you immediately enter into my infinite being.

56. Because you take refuge in me, all your actions—whatever they may be—are serving me. Thus, you are graced to realize the imperishable state of immortality.

57. Mentally offer every action to me; have me as your foremost goal, and diligently practice Buddhi Yoga—discerning the real from the unreal. This way you will keep your mind always fixed on me.

Chapter Eighteen

Now Krishna asks a beautiful question. "How are you going to conduct yourself in life with all these problems?" Then he shows the way: "At least mentally dedicate all your actions to me; by setting your sights on me as the highest goal and practicing Buddhi Yoga, discernment, you can keep your mind on me constantly."

It's the same teaching, but with a promise: "Don't worry about anything, or even this philosophy. The simplest thing is just to think of me. Do everything in my name. Don't lose sight of me, of God."

It's easy to say. And it really becomes quite easy once you realize the danger of not doing this. There were two great saints. One, the sage Nandinar, a person from the untouchable community who lived close to prehistoric time, would sing about experiencing God: "Oh, Lord, it's very difficult to reach you." But early in the 20th century, in the 1940s, there lived a sage, Sri Ramana Maharshi. He used to sing Nandinar's song, but with the opposite meaning: "Oh Lord," Sri Ramana sang, "it's very easy to reach you."

How can it be very difficult and very easy? Experiencing God is easy only for the person who really gets sick of the other side, trying everything else. "Enough, I've had enough!" Like the first hippies. They seemed to feel: "I've had enough of this nonsense—school, college, church, synagogue, suits and dresses, polished words. I'm sick and tired of this whole thing. Let me go to Vermont, put up a teepee and just live there."

Why did so many thousands and thousands from everywhere just drop everything and leave? Why? Didn't they have enough education, or enough money for food and clothes or a house to live in? Most of the people who dropped out were well-off and well-educated—graduates, university people, even professors.

There lies the secret. They got sick of it all. In fact, that's what has to happen. Until and unless you feel sick of this whole thing, you won't really turn totally the other way. But, sometimes, even after people turn from worldly things, you see them going back to them again. That means temporarily they were disgusted, but they didn't really fall sick. It was only superficial. They didn't get burned enough.

But the turning is very easy for people who *have* really been burned. "Nonsense," they say. "Forget it! I don't want anything! I'm happy just as I am." You already know that to give up is easy; to gather is difficult. So just let go; it is easy. Clinging and holding on—how difficult it is. That's why renunciation is very easy—if you renounce after fully knowing the temporary pleasures of the other things. But if you have not yet been thoroughly baked, then after some time you will go back again.

I sympathize with those people, and I have complete faith in them. I always say, "It's all right. Go. You didn't come well-baked. Go, get baked, get roasted again. Because if you are half-baked, you won't be tasty. Go on back." It is easy to know God, but only after you know the other side well enough. That's why you have to see the fleeting pleasures of the world. Understand it well; then it's very easy to turn toward permanent happiness.

Then everything is beautiful, you will say, "I'm free, I'm relieved. I'm so happy. I'm super now." Even if people offer you some of the nice things you once wanted, you will just say, "Forget it." If you still want to enjoy them, maybe you will, but just for fun—it's not that you want it. If something naturally comes, "Well, all right. I'll try a little just to make you happy." You aren't really that interested. It's total freedom, you neither like nor dislike anything.

Of course, in the beginning there will be some dislike of those things; it's necessary. After some time, when you are rooted in this condition, even the dislike falls away. Then you rise completely beyond likes and dislikes. That's real equanimity. At that point, it is easy to fulfill this commandment: "Offer up every action to me; have me as your highest goal."

> **58. By continually fixing your mind on me, you open to my grace and thereby overcome all obstacles. But if you will not hear me because of your ego, then you perish.**

It's not that Sri Krishna is cursing such a person. He is just telling us the danger of projecting our egos. If you trust in that higher will, all the obstacles will just disappear. But even as I say this, someone might answer, "Well, I do believe in that higher will, but sometimes I still face obstacles. They haven't disappeared. I face suffering. What can I do?"

If someone speaks this way, then I have to ask, "Are you really trusting in that higher will? Do you have trust only when everything goes the way you think it should?" It's one thing to say you trust in God when you get a million dollars profit. But if you lose ten dollars, "My goodness, how can God rob me this way?" If you really trust God, you will say, "Fine. Probably God wanted to take it away." You must trust in both the profit and the loss.

In fact, you have to prove that you are really trusting God. God will test you. God tests seekers at first and doesn't just give you everything in the beginning. God wants to make sure your faith is total.

We should trust that there is a Cosmic Intelligence who takes care of everything. Every minute, every second, God knows what is happening in your stomach. God knows how much air goes into your lungs, how many more days you have to survive. You may call it "He" or "She" or "It;" it doesn't matter, but it's the Cosmic Intelligence. And it's part of that Intelligence that works in you.

Normally, in our egoistic way, we just work with a little part of that greater Intelligence. With that we are able to discover audio waves, radio waves, nuclear energy and so many things. We have discovered all this with the tiny intelligence we have. Yet, compared to the Cosmic Intelligence, all our intelligence is nothing.

And with this tiny intelligence we still become so egoistic. But if we want to feel God's grace, we must face the tests. That's why if we read about the lives of sages and saints, they all underwent many troubles. It happens all over the globe, not just in the West or East.

59. If, because of egoism, you still insist: "I will not fight [the battle]," that is an empty vow. Your own nature will compel you.

He tells Arjuna that if he decides not to fight due to egoism, his decision won't last long. Ultimately, his nature will prompt him to fight because he is a *kshatriya*. Because of that inborn trait, he need not *consciously* decide to fight for righteousness. For example, the inborn fear of death makes you take care of your body even while you sleep. If a mosquito bites you at night, without your even knowing, you will slap it. You won't even wake up. That is the inborn trait of protecting the life of your body. It's not even done consciously. Sri Krishna is saying that even without Arjuna's knowing, he will suddenly get up and start fighting. He has consciously rejected his duty, but it won't last long.

60. Arjuna, you are bound by your karma (past actions), which arose from your own nature. Therefore, you must do that which, out of delusion, you still may not wish to do.

61. God is present in the hearts of all beings, Arjuna. And by the power of God's illusion (*maya*), God circles all about as if on a wheel.

Here is yet another way of saying that it is the same spirit functioning through all beings.

62. With all your heart, take refuge in God. Then you will feel God's grace and know profound peace, which is God's abode, forever.

63. Now I have given you the most precious and profound knowledge, the secret of secrets. Reflect on it fully; then do as you wish.

This is a very important instruction: "Arjuna, I have given you the most profound knowledge, most sacred and secret, because you are dear to me. But you need not accept it just because I give it to you. No. Reflect on it fully. If you are convinced, act. If not, reflect more. Make it your own. Become totally convinced. It's not that I'm just firing a cannon at you—either do it or die. No, I'm just presenting the facts. Take them, chew them well, get the taste, then either swallow it or spit it out."

If there is no freedom in religious or spiritual practice, where can you find freedom? The whole purpose of the spiritual path is to find freedom, of course. It should liberate you from all bondage. But if the person who gives you spiritual knowledge is himself or herself going to bind you—"Do as I say whether you like it or not!"—then you are not free. You come for freedom, but go away bound. So here Sri Krishna clearly says, "Reflect on what I have said. Don't reject it immediately. You have heard, now contemplate and meditate on it. If you are convinced, apply it in your life." What a beautiful instruction this is.

People must always be given such freedom. I don't think that it's ever sinful to doubt God's existence. Probably, a person who feels that doubt doesn't have enough conviction yet. No matter what others say, there is no need to accept God blindly. Spiritual practices should never be followed blindly. Go deep; get some experience to be convinced. Just begin where you are and go ahead from there. Even if your approach is wrong, you will go, bump your head and quickly discover, "This is a dead end." Then you will come back soon, totally convinced because of direct experience.

64. Because your devotion is steady and strong, you are my beloved whom I cherish. Now listen carefully. For the sake of your spiritual growth, I am about to tell you my highest teaching for the last time.

How beautifully Krishna speaks: "I am telling you because you are my beloved whom I cherish." Sacred knowledge is not imparted until you are completely receptive and feel total communion with the divine. But how does one become dear to God? We saw the answer in the twelfth chapter: "Who is dear to me?" asks Sri Krishna. "The one who has attained serenity of mind."

The next two *slokas* are the essence of the entire *Bhagavad Gita*.

65. Always think of me; worship me; dedicate every action to me; and surrender yourself to me. In this way, you will certainly come to me. I promise you this because you are my beloved.

Each word indicates one of the paths of Yoga. He says, Fix your mind on me: Raja Yoga; worship me: Bhakti Yoga; dedicate every action to me: Karma Yoga; surrender yourself to me: humility; Come to me: Jnana Yoga. Integrate all these Yogas into your life: Integral Yoga.

Either by one or two, or all of these methods, he says, "You will come to me. I'm not simply saying this lightly. It is a promise. There is no doubt about it. You shall come to me. I am making this promise because you are my beloved." It's a beautiful statement by Sri Krishna.

And the next *sloka* is even better than the previous one. It's called the *sloka* of surrender. If you want to summarize the entire *Gita* in just one *sloka*, this is the one.

66. Renounce all duties (*dharma*), and just come to me for refuge. I will take you beyond sin and guilt, where there is neither grief nor sorrow.

What great assurance he gives! It's not that you consciously reject anything, but you do things according to your nature, which is your *svadharma*, while renouncing the fruits. Even as your body and mind are functioning, you feel that you aren't the one who is acting. Simply feel that things are being done, or "things are happening through me." You are simply a witness. You let things happen through your body and mind. Whatever happens, you observe it—like watching a movie.

This is renunciation of the *dharmas. Dharmas* will still happen. Duties are being performed. Your mind performs the duty through your body, while the real you just sits and watches. You are the one who drives the car. The engine runs; the wheels turn; but you just sit behind the wheel watching the whole thing. *You* are unaffected by the *dharma*, the dutiful action.

You are neither the actor, nor the agent, nor the action itself. The cosmic force functions through your body and mind. Just realize: "It is that force that sustains me and keeps my breath going. I'm not even consciously breathing. Something else is conscious of my breathing."

It's true. You are not conscious of your breathing or your digesting, or even the beating of your heart. Do you tell your heart to beat? Do you tell your lungs, "Come on, breathe in and out?" No. These things just happen. Call it motor nerves or involuntary muscles; it doesn't matter. The doctors may have their own names for it. But behind all the involuntary muscles, there's one super-voluntary power. It's that Cosmic Intelligence that takes care of us. From the moment the sperm fertilizes the egg, the Cosmic Intelligence knows, "Yes, one soul is getting ready for a body. It should have food; I will prepare milk for it."

Have you seen an expectant mother? As soon as she conceives, milk is being prepared in her breasts. Whether she wants it or not, whether she knows or not, milk is being prepared. Who is doing that? Neither the father nor the mother. Sometimes if you break open a rock, you will see a small, frog-like creature living inside the cavity. Who feeds it? Who takes care of it? Give it any name you want, but know that there is one Cosmic Intelligence which knows and cares for everything.

Even your knowing comes through that. Without that Cosmic Intelligence you wouldn't know anything. You couldn't know anything. So just trust it completely. Resign yourself to that intelligence and *you* won't need to do anything. You will be made to do what is necessary. That Intelligence will take you over and perform everything through you. Then your actions are not *your* actions anymore. They are God's actions, and you simply function as an instrument. Then there is nothing that will disturb your mind in this life. Your peace is eternal. That's the real Yoga, the true religion, the supreme peace and joy.

And that is what Sri Krishna is saying: "Just renounce everything, and I will take care of it all. You don't need to worry. Grieve not. I'll liberate you from all wrongdoing." The sins you are still carrying are nothing but your own feeling that you have done something bad. If you really renounce all *dharmas,* which you have been thinking are your own personal duties, and accept that everything is being done by God, how can *you* be a sinner or a saint? You are neither one.

Some years ago a well-known saint was praised for being so great. Then he said, "I don't know about that. But I do remember one day many years ago when I was just some sort of stuff heaped up like cement and mortar, sand, colors and other mixtures. The masons were ready. Then the building supervisor, the Creator, came in. The masons asked, 'Sir, everything is ready. What shall we make today?'"

"He turned to the shopkeeper, 'What is diminished in our stock? What items should we produce today?'"

"The shopkeeper said, 'The stock is nearly complete, but to make the shelves full we need a pig and a saint.'"

"'All right,' said the Creator, 'Make a saint.' And that's why I'm here in this form," said the saint.

Maybe you are still a little doubtful about renouncing everything. "What will happen to my intelligence?" you might ask. But don't think it means you have to lose your intelligence. Keep it. But know that the most intelligent person will put the load on that Higher Intelligence, and just sit quietly enjoying everything. Your intelligence was given to you for that purpose. God just gave you a little intelligence and is waiting to see if you are intelligent enough to use it properly by linking your intelligence with

God. You're still free to keep it separate and say, "It's mine. I'm just going to play with it and do everything myself." But the truly intelligent person will link his or her intelligence with the Higher Intelligence.

With this *sloka* (18:66), Sri Krishna concludes his instructions to Arjuna. In the very beginning, he told Arjuna; "Cast off weakness. Wake up. Be a man. Do your duty! Perform your *dharma*." Now he ends by saying: "Renounce all duties and be in eternal union with me."

Here are his concluding words:

67. **In the presence of someone without self-discipline or devotion, or one who is not serviceful or who speaks of me disrespectfully— concerning these sacred teachings, don't say a word!**

Jesus says the same thing: "Don't cast pearls before swine." Krishna says, sometimes they may even misunderstand you or your words. So give them only to students fit to hear them.

68. **Whoever, through great devotion, teaches my devotees the profound and sacred wisdom (of the *Bhagavad Gita*) will certainly come directly to me.**

69. **No man or woman anywhere serves me more lovingly, nor is anyone on earth more beloved to me.**

70. **Whoever sincerely studies this sacred dialogue is worshipping me with wisdom and devotion.**

71. **Moreover, if a person with active belief just hears or reads these teachings, that person will rise beyond all remaining doubts and, liberated from evil, enter the joyful realms (*lokas*) of those who perform noble deeds.**

Hearing or reading this sacred dialogue doesn't mean merely listening or browsing. It's not hearing with the ear alone; it should go deep into the heart. Hear it with the entire mind, clean and clear. With such hearing there is no need to hear it many times. Once is enough, and you've got it. It's like well-dried wood. One match is enough. If it's soaking wet, you need the whole matchbox. And even then, there's a lot of smoke.

One should have that dryness: no moisture, no attachments. Moisture is attachment. The mind should be completely dried by *tapasya*, austerity.

With that *tapasya,* or dryness, if you come near the sacred teaching even once, it's absorbed immediately.

But now Sri Krishna is slowly coming to the end of the *Gita.* He sees that Arjuna is at least ready to hear. But that doesn't mean we all become Arjuna overnight because we are finishing the book. Still, we all will know, "Yes, there's a possibility. I'm hearing it now. One day or another I am certainly going to get it. I am going to reach that place. Until then, no matter what, I am not going to stop!"

Arise! Awake! Stop not until the goal is reached. Never turn back. Turning back is almost like trying to eat what you have vomited. No sensible person would do that. Sometimes, people are tempted to go back to their old ways. They should just stay a little while and think: "What will I get that's new that I haven't tasted before? Anything? No, the same rotten stuff that once was bitter to me. How can it be tasty now?" The mind has simply forgotten the bitterness. Now it looks a little tasty. That's the trick of the mind. So, let us never look back, but march on and on until we reach the goal.

> **72. Arjuna, have you truly heard and understood? Have you listened with a one-pointed mind? Has the delusion of your ignorance finally been destroyed?**

He asks Arjuna: "Were you concentrating on what I said, or were you thinking of your comfortable bed and ice cream? Has this been heard by you with an attentive mind? Has the delusion of your ignorance been destroyed?" How well Sri Krishna knows the human mind. If *he* doesn't know, who will? He knows its weaknesses, so he wants to be sure Arjuna really heard everything and came out of his delusion.

And here, the beautiful seeker Arjuna says,

> **73. Yes, my delusion has been destroyed. Through your grace, Krishna, my knowledge is returned. I now remember the way, I am free of doubt, and strong and steady [on the path]. From now on, I will act according to your words (*vak*).**

Arjuna gives his word. Probably I don't need to say what happened afterward. All that had to happen, happened. You can read the whole story in the *Mahabharata.*

The *Bhagavad Gita* concludes as Sanjaya, the narrator, speaks these words to the blind king Dhritarashtra, who is listening to find out what is happening on the battlefield.

74. Then Sanjaya said: This amazing dialogue between Sri Krishna and the great-hearted Arjuna is so full of wonders that just hearing it makes my hair stand on end.

75. Because I have been blessed by Vyasa, I have overheard this most sacred Yoga wisdom directly from Krishna, the Lord of Yoga himself, who is teaching this.

76. O my king, whenever I remember this wonderful dialogue between Krishna and Arjuna, I am overcome with bliss.

77. And whenever I recall this breathtaking form of God (as Krishna), I am astonished, and again and again my joy overflows.

What a lucky man! As you may remember, the entire *Gita* dialogue between Krishna and Arjuna happened on the battlefield. There was no time to record anything. And they didn't bother to, because Sri Krishna said it and Arjuna heard it, and that's enough. But Sanjaya was gifted with a special vision. Sitting far away in the palace, he was able to see everything that was happening there on the battlefield. And, thus, he was telling Dhritarashtra, who couldn't go to the battlefield personally and see for himself.

Sanjaya got all the information. The very name Sanjaya means *well-won*. There was nothing for him to win. He was victorious over everything; that is, he had mastered his own body and mind. Sanjaya means the one who has won everything. That's why he had such beautiful perception, the divine vision to see, hear and know what was happening far away. This he passed on to the king.

The *Bhagavad Gita* culminates with a very beautiful *sloka*:

78. Whenever you come upon Krishna, the Lord of Yoga and the great archer, Arjuna, there too you will find prosperity, victory, happiness and sound judgment. Of this I am certain!

He was totally sure of this reality. Wherever there is the Lord of Yoga and the great archer, Arjuna, means: Wherever there is Yoga and a practitioner with a one-pointed mind, then all the fruits and benefits are naturally there.

There is *always* Yoga, no question about it. What is needed are you Arjunas—one-pointed practitioners.

This *sloka* brings to mind a wonderful story in the *Mahabharata* that occurs before the battle and this *Gita* dialogue. Duryodhana, the head of the hundred evil Kaurava brothers, and Arjuna were always competitors, fighting with each other for everything. Once, they were all like brothers studying under Drona, who taught them archery. At that time, Duryodhana became jealous of Arjuna because he felt their teacher was favoring Arjuna. Duryodhana didn't realize that Arjuna was such a gifted student. A teacher naturally shows a little more appreciation for such students. But because of his evil mind, Duryodhana didn't recognize this and he became jealous. So, Drona decided to teach him a lesson.

"You both come with me," said Drona. They went outside the palace. "See there, I've tied a mark," he said, "A clay parrot with a red ring around its neck. It's there at the top of that tree. Duryodhana, come over here. Raise your bow. Ready your arrow, aim there." Duryodhana did all that.

"Look at the parrot. What do you see?"

"I see the parrot."

"Where is the parrot?"

"Sitting on a branch."

"Do you see anything else on the branch?"

"Yes, a few fruits next to it."

"What is the parrot doing?"

"Simply sitting."

"You see all that?"

"Yes."

"You don't have to release the arrow. Take it out."

Duryodhana was puzzled. "Why? I could hit it, sir."

"No, just leave it." He called, "Arjuna, come get ready and aim."

"I'm ready."

"Do you see the branch?"

"No, sir."

"Do you see the parrot?"

"No, sir."

"What do you see?"

"I see only the red strip, sir."

Got the point? That's concentration, a one-pointed mind. He was taught to aim at the neck of the parrot. Once he found the neck, he saw nothing else. Whereas Duryodhana saw the whole branch, the fruits nearby and the body of the parrot. That's why Arjuna is an example among human beings of one who is totally one-pointed. We should have that one-pointedness of mind. And with that one-pointedness, Yoga can bring so many things: prosperity, victory, happiness and sound judgment.

If you complain, "I don't have prosperity; I'm not victorious. I am a wishy-washy person," don't blame Yoga. Know that you are not looking at the red strip. You are not one-pointed. You're looking all about. And this is the very reason meditation is such an important part of our practice. Even Yoga postures and breathing practices are secondary compared to that. The most important thing is concentration, which leads to meditation. Once you reach the level of *dharana* and *dhyana*, concentration and meditation, the next thing is *samadhi*, superconsciousness, which just happens automatically. So there's no point blaming or complaining.

Fortunately, we have Yoga. All we need is a one-pointed mind. If we get that, then prosperity, victory, bliss and peace of mind are ours. Let's go for it!

In the *Bhagavad Gita*, or Song *of God*, which is full of knowledge of the Supreme and Absolute, which is the science of Yoga, this ends the eighteenth and final discourse entitled: "Yoga of Freedom Through Renunciation."

Epilogue

My master Sri Swami Sivanandaji simplified it all. He said, "The essence of Yoga is: Be good, do good."

How simple it is. But if it's said so simply, people might not believe it. "What kind of philosophy is this? It's too simple." To give it weight and bring a little devotion, people want a big book, with lengthy commentaries, which ultimately says: "Be a good person."

Once there were some disciples living in an *ashram*. They really wanted to make their Guru happy through their devotion. One day, while they were all sitting together, their teacher said, "I would like to have a sewing needle."

Immediately, everybody jumped up and ran to the store to buy a needle. Of course, they didn't all have money in their pockets. Only the treasurer had the money. So he bought the needle. Then there was a little quarrel.

"Who is to carry it back to our Guru?"

The treasurer had it, but the others objected. "You are only the custodian of the funds. You just bought it with everybody's money. Somebody else should carry it."

"It's our money, and we all want to do something for our teacher; but how can we all carry this needle to him?"

They sat, meditated on it and came up with an idea. They found a big log of wood, stuck the needle into the log, and, together, carried the log to their Guru.

"Master, we brought a needle for you." They were so tired that they dropped the log in front of him.

"What's all this? I just need a little needle."

"The needle is there, Master."

"All right, thank you."

But when they dropped the log, the needle had fallen out. They searched everywhere, but to no avail. The needle was lost.

So let us all learn a good lesson from their mistake. Let's use the book well and not forget the message it carries.

Remember, don't just carry a big book and lose the essential teaching.

Note to the Reader
about this Sanskrit Transliteration

We have decided not to use one of the standard methods for the transliteration of Sanskrit terms. Instead, we have used a simplified system, meant to make the reading of the text more fluid and enjoyable. The transliteration does remain faithful to the correct pronunciation of the words.

Glossary

Abhaya—fearlessness

Abhyasa—spiritual practice

Abhishekam—during worship, pouring milk or water over an image of God

Acharya Shankara—great religious reformer and teacher of Vedanta

Adharma—unrighteousness

Adhibhuta—earthly realm

Adhidaiva—kingdom of light

Adhiyajna—self-sacrifice

Adhyatman—Supreme Self

Adideva—the original One; primal God

Aditya(s)-gods of light

Agni—fire; god of fire

Ahamkara—ego feeling

Ahimsa—non-injury

Airavata—primordial elephant of Indra

Akasha—space; etheric atmosphere Amba—mother

Ananda—bliss

Anandamaya kosha—pure ego sheath

Ananta—five-headed king of snakes; symbol of the elements of nature

Ananya bhakti—one-pointed devotion

Apana—nerve current which governs the abdominal region; the down-going breath

Arjuna—son of Pandu; sincere seeker in the *Bhagavad Gita*

Aryaman—one of the Adityas; revered ancestor

Asa—to desire to obtain

Asana—Hatha Yoga poses; pose or seat

Asat—untruth

Ashram—a spiritual community where seekers practice and study under the guidance of a spiritual master

Asura—demon

Asvattha—sacred fig tree

Atma jayam—Self-victory

Atman—the Self; The Supreme God; the inner Consciousness

Avvayaar—South Indian saint and poetess

Baba(ji)—brother

Bhagavan—the Lord; he who is endowed with power, virtue, fame, detachment and freedom

Bhakti—devotion; love (of God)

Bharatavarsha—India; the kingdom of Bharata

Bhaya—fear

Bhrigu—*rishi* who dwells constantly on the superconscious plane

Bhutas—ghost

Brahma—great Hindu deity; the Creator Brahman—the Absolute One

Brahma Sutras—teachings about the Absolute

Brahmacharya—continence; sense control; celibacy; the stage in life of the celibate student

Brahmana—spiritual aspect of the *Vedas*

Brahman jnana—knowledge of God

Brahmin—priestly caste

Brihaspati—priest of the *devas*

Brihat—sublime music

Buddhi—discriminating intellect

Buddhi Yoga—Yoga of discernment

Caste—mental tendency

Chakra(s)—subtle nerve center(s) along the spine which when concentrated upon yield experiences of various levels of consciousness

Charvakas—school of Hindu thought

Danam—charity

Deva(s)—gods

Dhammapada—Buddhist teachings

Dharana—concentration

Dharma—virtuous teachings; destiny; duty; righteousness; morality

Dharmaputra—a name of Yudhishthira

Dhritarashtra—brother of Pandu; blind patriarch of the Kauravas

Dhyana—meditation

Drishti—vision

Dvandva—lit. "and"; that which combines two parts without lessening either one

Gandharva—heavenly being; celestial musician

Gandiva—bow of Arjuna

Ganesh—son of Shiva and Parvati; god of wisdom

Ganga—sacred river Ganges

Garuda—vehicle of Vishnu, half-man, half-bird

Gayatri—most sacred verse of the *Rig Veda*

Grihastha—householder

Guna(s)—qualities of nature: *sattva* (balance), *rajas* (restlessness) and *tamas* (inertia)

Guru—spiritual guide; teacher

Hanuman—monkey king in the *Ramayana*; the perfect servant

Hatha Yoga—physical aspect of Yoga practice

Himsa—injury

Ida—one of the major *nadis* (subtle nerves)

Indra—king of the Gods

Indriyas—senses

Ishvara—the Supreme God

Janaka, King—enlightened king; father of Sita

Japa—mantra repetition

Jnana—wisdom

Jnani—person of wisdom

Jiva—individual self; individual soul

Jivanmukta—one who is liberated while still in a body

Jivatma—egoistic self; individual soul

Kalpa—cycle of eons

Kama—desire; sense pleasures

Kamadhenu—wish-fulfilling cow

Kamadhuk—same as Kamadhenu

Kandarpa—god of romantic love

Kannappar, Saint—one of the Shaiva saints; lit. "eye-fixer"

Kapila—founder of Samkhya philosophy; a great sage

Karma—action and reaction

Karma Yoga—performing actions as selfless service without attachment to the results

Karna—half-brother of the Pandavas by Kunti; Kaurava warrior

Kauravas—opponents of the Pandavas; representative of all selfish desires

Kevalam—independent

Koran—sacred scripture of Islam

Krishna—incarnation of Vishnu; the Lord; teacher in *Bhagavad Gita*

Kshatriya—warrior or ruler caste

Kshetra—field; the body

Kshetrajna—knower of the field

Kubera—lord of wealth

Kurukshetra—lit. "field of the Kurus"; location where *Bhagavad Gita* was imparted

Kutastha—essence of every creature

Lakshmi—Goddess of good fortune; wife of Vishnu

Lingam—symbol of Lord Shiva

Lokas—joyful realms

Mahabharata—Hindu epic in which the *Bhagavad Gita* is found

Mahatma—great soul

Mahatman—Supreme Self

Maheshvara—a name of Shiva

Mala(s)—beads used for counting the number of mantra repetitions

Manas—mind

Manomaya kosha—mind sheath

Mantra—lit. "that which makes the mind steady"; sound formula for meditation

Manu—law-giver; ancient founder of humanity

Margashirsha—month in the beginning of the Hindu calendar, auspicious for worship

Marichi—lord of the wind and storm powers

Maya—illusion

Meru—lit. spine; axis of all the heavenly bodies

Moksha—liberation

Nadi(s)—subtle nerves

Nakula—a warrior

Nandinar—an ancient sage

Narada—a great *rishi*

Neti—"*Neti, neti*"—"not this, not that"

Nirvana—lit. nakedness; the state of liberation

Ojas—subtle energy resulting from the preservation of sexual energy

Om—the cosmic sound vibration which includes all other sounds and vibrations; the basic mantra

Om Tat Sat—"*Om* that is the truth"

Pandavas—righteous family; represents virtuous people

Paramatman—Supreme Self

Parameshvara—Supreme Lord

Parvati—wife of Shiva

Patanjali—codifier of Yoga philosophy

Patanjali's Yoga Sutras—aphorisms which form the basis of Yoga philosophy

Pavaka—the purifying fire

Pingala—one of the major *nadis* (subtle nerves)

Prahladan—ardent devotee of Vishnu

Prajapati—the Creator

Prakriti—nature; creation

Prana—the vital energy

Pranava—the basic hum of the universe; *Om*

Pranayama—the practice of controlling the vital force, usually through control of the breath

Prarabdha karma—karma which causes one's present birth

Prasad—consecrated offering

Pratyahara—sense control; withdrawal of the senses from their objects

Preta—a spirit or ghost

Purusha—the essence behind the changing forms in nature

Purushottama—Supreme Consciousness

Puja—worship service

Raja Yoga—the "Royal Yoga"; path of concentration and meditation, based on ethical perfection and control of the mind

Rajas—activity; restlessness; one of the three *gunas*

Rakshasas—minor demons

Rama—an incarnation of Vishnu; protagonist of *Ramayana*

Ramakrishna, Sri—Indian saint of the 19th century

Ramalingam, Saint—Indian saint of the 19th century

Ramana Maharshi—great spiritual teacher of 20th century India

Ramayana—oldest Sanskrit epic poem, written by Valmiki

Rasam—peppery Indian soup

Ravana—king of demons in the *Ramayana*

Rig Veda—one of the major *Vedas*

Rishi—a sage

Roshi—Buddhist teacher

Rotis—an Indian bread

Rudra—a name of Shiva

Rudras—dispellers of ignorance

Sadhana—spiritual practice

Sadhu—a spiritual person; often a wandering mendicant

Sama Veda—one of the major *Vedas*

Samadhi—superconscious state; contemplation, absorption

Samkhya—direct information about the Self

Samsara—round of births and deaths

Samskara(s)—mental impression(s)

Sanatana Dharma—eternal Truth

Sanjaya—Dhritarashtra's charioteer with gift of clairvoyance; narrator
of the *Bhagavad Gita*

Sankalpa—thought; desire; imagination

Sannyasa—renunciation

Sannyasi—member of the Holy Order of *Sannyas*; a Hindu monk

Sarasvati—Goddess of Wisdom

Sat-Chid-Ananda—existence-knowledge-bliss

Sattva—purity; balanced state; one of the three *gunas*

Satya—truth

Shaivites—worshippers of Shiva

Shakti—energy; the Divine Mother

Shakti Purana—ancient legends of Shakti

Shalom—peace (Hebrew)

Shankara—a name of Shiva

Shanti—peace (Sanskrit)

Shastra—recognized scripture or authority

Shiva—major Hindu deity; the destroyer of ego; king of yogis

Shiva Purana—ancient legends of Shiva

Shivagocharya—*brahmin* priest in the story of Saint Kannappar

Shivalingam—symbol of Lord Shiva

Shraddha—whole-hearted sincerity; sincere belief

Shruti—lit. "that which is heard"

Siddha—an accomplished one, often with supernatural psychic powers

Siddhis—psychic powers; attainments

Skanda—a name of Muruga; god of War

Sloka—sentences; verses

Soham—lit. "I am That"

Soma—a creeper whose juice was used in *vedic* sacrifices; the "essence" of the moon

Sthitapragnya lakshana—description of the enlightened person

Subrahmanya—son of Shiva

Subda rishi—great sage

Sudra—laborer

Sukha—pleasure; happiness

Sushumna—one of the major *nadis*, or subtle nerves

Sutras—lit. "thread"; aphorism

Svadhyaya—reading scripture; spiritual study

Svadharma—predestined duty

Swami—title of a *sannyasi*; renunciate

Tamas—inertia; dullness; one of the three *gunas*

Tapasya—lit. to burn; spiritual austerity; accepting but not causing pain

Thirukkural—a major South Indian scripture

Thirumulai—South Indian saint

Thiruvalluvar—South Indian saint, author of *Thirukkural*

Tinnappar—lit. "hefty boy"; young boy who became Saint Kannappar

Torah—Hebrew scripture

Triguna Rahitam—"Beyond the three *gunas*" (God)

Triputityagan—three-fold renunciation

Tyagan—renunciation

Ucchaisravas—white horse of Indra, produced at the churning of the ocean of milk

Upanishads—end portion and culmination of the *Vedas*

Ushana—poet with great intuitive and psychic power

Vairagya—non-attachment; dispassion

Vaisya—tradesperson

Index

ANGER: Origin and danger of: 2:56; 2:62-63; 3:37; 4:10; 5:23, 5:26-28; 12:15; 13:29; 16:2, 16:4, 16:12, 16:18; frustrated lust: 16:21; 18:53.

ATMAN: nature of: 2:10-30; 3:42-43; 4:41-42; the peace within: 4:11; 9:22; inaction of: 4:18; mind is controlled by: 6:6; identification with: 2:55; 3:17, 3:30; 5:8-9, 5:17; 6:7, 6:14, 6:18, 6:20-22, 6:25-26; 7:29; 15:5; not the doer: 5:13-14; 13:29, 13:31; true knowledge: 5:7, 5:16-18, 5:26; 6:20-22; 13:11; its own friend or enemy: 6:5-6; as Brahmacharya: 10:11; the true Self is: 2:45; 4:18; 6:29; 10:20; 18:16, 18:18; Adhyatman: 8:3; results of knowledge of: 10:32; 11:1; ways of realizing: 13:31; 14:4; within every creature: 13:32; Atma jayam (self victory): 15:6.

ATTACHMENT: confusion resulting from: 1:27-31, 1:45-47; 2: introduction; to the fruits of actions as possessions: 2:48-50; 3:25; 4:20-23; 5:10-5:13, 5:26; 18:23, 18:26; freedom from: 2:57; 3:9; 15:3,

15:5; 18:12, 18:71; origin of: 2:62-63; 3:7, 3:9, 3:19; 18:53; to externals: 5:21; 6:4; story of the two boatmen: 6:35-36; devotees renunciation of: 12:16, 12:\18; 18:10; to family, children, home: 13:9; Jivanmukta is free of: 14:24-25; cause of possessiveness and fear is: 16:3; bound by: 16:12; extremes in tapas motivated by: 17:5-6; need to renounce: 8:11.

BEING: see Purusha and also Atman.

BIRTH: 2:20-22, 2:25-27, 2:36, 2:50-51; 4:4, 4:6-7, 4:9; Yogabrastha: 6:41-43; deluded at: 7:27; due to desire: 9:21, 9:24; 13:23; race, sex, caste are unimportant: 9:32; 10:4; coming together of the gunas: 13:23, 13:26; prakriti, Purusha and: 14:2, 14:4, 14:20; 15:4, 15:10, 15:18; 16:19-20; value of human birth: 16:21; God's examination room: 16:21; temperament, dharma and: 18:47; mother nature prepares for: 18:66.

BODY: 1:28-29; 2:introduction,

2:13, 2:18, 2:20, 2:30, 2:41; 9:34; identification with: 9:10; "I'm not the": 2:59; actions of the: 3:7, 3:22; 5:8-9; actions required to maintain: 3:8; part of prakriti: 4:18, 4:21; 6:32; to purify one works with the: 5:11; cleanse the: 6:12; preparation for meditation: 6:13; satisfaction of the: 6:17; death of the: 8:12-13, 8:23-27; birth of body due to desire: 13:23; Atman present in: 13:32; birth and death of: 14:4, 14:15; tree of life and the: 15:1, 15:3; the prisoners of: 15:4; obeys the mind: 15:5; God enters: 15:8, 15:10; purity of: 16:3; needed for spiritual development: 17:6; disciplines of the: 17:14; can not renounce all actions while in the: 18:11, 18:14; inherent nature to protect: 18:59, 18:66.

BONDAGE: 2:51; 3:9; 4:41; 5:12; 9:28; cause of: 14:5-9; seeking anything is: 14:19; demonic traits that lead to: 15:5.

BRAHMACHARYA: 6:14; 10:11; 17:14.

BRAHMAN: 4:24, 4:25; 5:19-21; 6:31; 8:11, 8:13, 8:24; 10:12; 13:4, 13:12-18, 13:30-32; 14:26-27; 17:23.

BRAHMA NIRVANA: 2:72; 5:24-26; 6:15, 6:27-28; 7:29; 18:51-56.

BUDDHA, THE: 6:15; 5:22; 17:6.

BUDDHI (Intellect): 2:65; 3:37, 3:40, 3:42-43; 5:11, 5:22, 5:27-28; 7:10; 10:4; 12:8; 13:5-6; 18:48-49; those of small: 16:9; result of confused: 18:16; no longer tainted: 18:17; three types of: 18:29-32; pure understanding explained: 18:51.

BUDDHI YOGA: meaning of and need for: 10:10; result of: 10:11; recommended: 18:57; fix the mind on God: 18:57.

CITY OF NINE GATES: explained: 5:13; gates of the body: 8:12; 14:11.

CONCENTRATION: 5:27-28; 6:10, 6:13, 6:19; 8:13; 10:10, 10:25; 12:6-8, 12:12; 18:72, 18:78.

COSMIC FORM: described: 11:5-32, 11:39-40; 13:13.

CREATION: creator of all: 3:10; evolution and involution: 7:6-7; 8:17-19; 9:5-10; Purusha pervades all: 8:22; the cycle of: 9:7-8; seed of: 9:18; 10:5-

6, 10:34; 13:21, 13:30, 13:33; 14:3; 15:16-18; described as Asvattha Tree: 15:1-4.

DANAM (Giving or Charity): giving person described: 2:49; five types of giving and taking: 3:12; 9:27; 10:5; 11:48, 11:53; 16:1; 17:20-22, 17:24-27; 18:3; should not be renounced: 18:5; should be performed without attachment to the fruits: 18:6.

DEATH: 1:38; transmigration of the soul: 2:11-13, 2:19-2:22, 2:25, 2:27, 2:36, 2:72; dishonor worse than: 2:34; cause of: 2:50; Yogabrastha: 4:9; 6:41; 7:30; control of mind at time of death: 8:2-6, 8:10-13, 8:16; story of parrot chanting Ram: 8:13; story of Lord Shiva and Parvati discussing blind man: 8:13; death: 9:3, 9:19; 10:4, 10:34; 13:21, 13:23, 13:31; birth and death explained: 14:2-4; effect of gunas at time of: 14:14-15; transcending the gunas: 14:20; 15:4, 15:8, 15:10, 15:18; 16:11; two-fold paths at time of death: 8:23-27.

DELUSION: 2:10, 2:52; 3:6, 3:29; cause of: 3:40-41; 5:15, 5:20; 7:14-15, 7:25-28; 9:12; 11:1; 14:8, 15, 22; freedom from: 10:4; 15:5, 15:10-11, 15:19; 18:53, 18:60; the ego sees things its own way: 6:5-6; 18:16, 18:18, 18:73; renunciation and: 18:7.

DEMONIC TRAITS: listed: 16:4, 16:6-19; lead to bondage: 16:5, 16:20; in performance of austerities: 18:5-6.

DESIRE: 2:43, 2:55, 2:62-63, 2:70-71; 3:4, 3:10, 3:19, 3:36-41, 3:43; 4:19, 4:21; 5:12, 5:22-23, 5:27-28; 6:2, 6:4, 6:10, 6:24, 6:45; 7:11, 7:20, 7:22; 9:21, 9:28; 12:16-17; 13:6, 13:23; 15:5; 16:10, 16:21, 16:23; 17:11-12, 17:18, 17:21, 17:25; 18:24, 18:27, 18:34, 18:49, 18:53-54.

DEVOTEES: 4:3; 7:16-18, 7:21-22; test of the: 8:13; protection of: 9:22-23, 9:31; divine traits of. 12:13-20; 16:1-3; required understanding of: 13:18; teaching of: 18:68; beloved of God: 18:69.

DEVOTION (Bhakti): many paths of: 4:11; highest forms of worship: 6:47; Ananaya Bhakti explained: 9:22; the way of: 8:10, 8:22; 9:13-14; 11:54; (story) Saint Kannappar: 9:23; offering of love: 9:26-

27; results of: 9:29, 9: 33-34; 10:10-11; transforming power of: 9:30-31, 9:33-34; is fostered by knowledge: 10:7-9; 11:53; Yoga of devotion: 12:1-20; 13:7, 13:10; to the teacher: 13:11; Bhakti Yoga discussed: 13:25; a means to transcend the gunas: 14:26-27; ritualistic compared to sincere sacrifice: 17:1; devotional offerings: 17:23-27; 18:54, 18:65-66; leads to knowledge: 18:54-55; cherished for: 18:64, 18:67-70.

DHARMA: 1:38; potency of practice of: 2:40; 3:13; virtue or righteousness: 4:7-8; 7:11; 9:31; lack of faith in: 9:3; guardian of: 11:18; faith in: 12:20; 14:27; 18:31, 18:32; Dharma, Artha, Kama: 18:34; temperament and the: 18:46-47; "relinquish all dharma": 18:66; also see Duty and Svadharma.

DISCIPLESHIP: see Service and Surrender.

DISCIPLE SUCCESSION: 4:1-2.

DISCIPLINES: of the body: 17:14; of speech: 17:15; of the mind: 17:16.

DIVINE EYE (Eye of Wisdom):

11:7-8; 13:34; explained: 15:10-11.

DIVINE TRAITS: listed: 12:13-20; 16:1-3, 16:6.

DOUBT: 2:52; 4:40-42; 5:20, 5:25; 6:39; 8:7; 18:73.

DUALITY: tossed about by: 2:53; free from: 2:64; 4:22; 5:25; 6:7, 6:29; 7:2; 9:19; source of. 2:14; 7:27-28; remain the same in the midst of. 12:17-19; 13:6; the mind creates: 13:29; talking is in the realm of: 15:17; likes and dislikes: 14:22; 18:51, 18:57; pairs of opposites: 2:45; 5:20; 15:5; nonsense of: 10:10.

DULLNESS (Negligence, Heedlessness, Laziness): 4:13; drive away: 6:12; tamasic energy: 14:8, 14:12-13, 14:15-17; 17:2, 17:10; 18:39; also see Tamas.

DUTY: need to perform: 1:38, 1:45; 2: introduction, 2:4, 2:7, 2:10-11, 2:31-33, 2:36-38, 2:47, 2:49; how to perform: 2:38, 2:47, 2:50; 3:8, 3:17, 3:19; 5:22; 9:28; no duty for man of knowledge: 2:50; 3:17-18; 4:15; to perform yajna, danam and tapas is one's: 18:5; should not be renounced: 18:7-10; attain perfection through performance of: 18:45-47; imperfection is no reason to abandon: 18:48; relinquish all duties: 18:66; also see Dharma and Svadharma.

EGO: 2:10, 2:71; 3:27; 4:21, 4:34; 5:22; 6:6, 6:17; 7:4; 8:14; 9:12, 9:34; surrender of the: 12:11; 13:5, 13:8, 13:11; need to be free from: 15:5, 15:19; chop away little by little: 16:3, 16:18; motivation of extremes in tapas: 17:5-6; 18:14, 18:17; functioning of: 18:18, 18:24-26; can not achieve liberation through: 18:49; egoistic choice versus natural change: 18:47-49; sense of my and mine: 18:53; danger of projecting: 18:58-59.

ENLIGHTENMENT: see Moksha.

EVOLUTION: involution: 8:17-19; the cycle of: 9:7-8; Darwin's theory of: 10:6; all levels of: 11:15; from Purusha: 13:30; 14:3-4; human birth (a time to be tested): 16:21.

FAITH: see Shraddha.

FEAR (Bhaya): 2:35; protection from: 2:40, 2:50, 2:56; 3:35; 4:10; 5:22, 5:27-28; 6:14; 10:4; a lack of faith: 8:7; 16:1; attachment causes: 16:3; renunciation due to: 18:8, 18:30; tamasic nature of: 18:35.

FEARLESSNESS (Abhaya): 6:14; 10:4; 16:1; 18:30.

FOOD: offering of: 3:13-14; 9:26; all is Brahman: 4:24; 6:15; three types of: 17:7-10.

GARDEN OF EDEN: 3:10; 16:21.

GOD or LORD: see Purusha and also Brahman.

GRACE OF GOD: 18:53, 18:58, 18:62, 18:73.

GREED: 1:38; rajasic behavior: 14:12, 14:17; insatiable nature of. 16:12, 16:16; gateway to hell: 16:21-22; 18:27.

GUNAS: need to transcend: 2:45; 3:37; 4:13, 4:18; 7:12-15; origin of: 7:12; all qualities "good and evil" are of God: 9:17; everything is a combination of: 9:17; Triguna Rahitam explained: 9:17; 13:14, 13:19; arise from prakriti: 14:5; mind tossed about by: 14:8; use of will to overcome: 14:16; all actions performed by: 14:19; characteristics of one who has transcended: 14:20-25; sattva and tamas sometimes look alike: 14:24-25; tree of life nourished by: 15:2; God experienced through the: 15:10; 17:1-2; renunciation and the: 18:introduction; kinds of knowledge and the: 18:19-18:20, 18:29; must pass through rajas: 18:21; all on earth and in heaven are subject to the: 3:5; 18:40; see also Rajas, Sattva, Tamas.

HAPPINESS: to do one's duty brings: 2:32, 2:56, 2:66, 70; 4:11; the absolute ttuth is permanent: 7:27; 9:22; temporary nature of: 5:22-23; finding: 5:24; who is: 15:5, 15:10; 16:23; types of: 18:37-18:40, 18:49, 18:57, 18:78.

HEAVEN: gates to: 2:32, 2:37; the goal of: 1:19; 2:2, 2:32, 2:37, 2:43; 6:6, 6:41; 9:20-21; 18:40.

HELL: three gates of: 1:42, 1:44; 6:6; 16:21.

HUMILITY: required in order to learn: 3:14; 4:34; 13:11.

IMMORTALITY OF THE

SOUL: 2:11-30, 2:36; 9:19; also see Atman, Brahman, Jiva, Purusha.

INCARNATIONS: Reasons for: 4:7-8; explanation of: 3:22; 4:11.

INTEGRAL YOGA: 2:39; 7:30; complementary nature of Yogas: 13:25; need for: 14:27; 18:44, 18:65.

JANAKA, KING: 3:6, 3:20.

JAPA YOGA: 10:25.

JESUS, LORD: the Bible: 2:41; 7:2; 9:22.

JIVA, JIVATMAN (The individual souls): 6:20; explained: 10: introduction; 14:4; 15:7-11; difference between Paramatman and jivatman: 15:8.

JIVANMUKTA (One who is liberated while living): 5:16; is beyond the gunas: 14:20, 14:22-25; characteristics of. 14:24-25; 15:5; also see Sthitapragnya.

JNANA: see Knowledge.

JNANA YOGA: 2:39; 3:3; compared with Karma Yoga: 5:4-5; method of worship: 9:15; a means to realize Atman: 13:24; equal in importance to Raja and Karma Yoga: 13:25; 14:27; study of Gita as Jnana Yoga Yajna: 18:70.

KAMADHENU (Kamadhuk): 3:10; 10:28.

KANNAPPAR, SAINT: 9:23.

KARMA—(As actions in the present): harmony in thoughts, words and: 2:11; the cause of birth and death: 2:50; quality of: 2:49; 3:9; renunciation of: 3:4-6; the gunas force: 3:5, 3:10, 3:27; 4:19; source of: 3:15; inaction in action: 3:7; 4:16, 4:18-22; 15:5; need for action: 3:8, 3:20-24; 4:15; not every action should be renounced: 18:3, 18:5-19,48; standard for selfless action: 3:25-26; 4:14-15; 18:23-28; nature of: 3:27-29; 4:17-18; 7:29; 17:27; scriptural guidance: 16:24; dedication of: 3:30; 4:41; 5:10; how to transcend: 4:23; 18:12; constituents of every action: 18:13-15; not bound by all actions: 4:22; 18:17, 18:49, 18:56-57; incitements to action: 18:18.

KARMA—(As resulting from past actions): ridding oneself of: 4:23, 4:37; 9:28; purging of: 18:40; past actions: 4:32; next birth selected by: 18:47; bound by: 18:60.

KARMA YOGA (Selfless Service): standard for selfless action: 3:25-26; basic principles of: 2:47, 2:48-50; 3:25-30; 6:1, 6:3; advantage of: 2:40, 2:50-51; greatness of: 3:13-15; twofold path, Jnana and: 3:3; King Janaka: 3:20; does not mind: 4:20-23; 5:3; 9:28; need to perform: 4:41; liberation through: 5:1-2, 5:6; 3:19; compared to Jnana Yoga: 5:4-5; renunciation is hard to reach without: 5:6; purification of the mind through: 5:6, 5:7, 5:11, 5:13; knowledge of: 7:29; explained: 9:27; prescribed for certain devotees: 12:10; 15:19; some realize Atman through: 13:24-25; conversion of rajasic actions: 14:27; analyze the mind during: 15:5; appropriate action during: 18:10.

"KNOW THAT BY WHICH EVERYTHING ELSE IS KNOWN": meaning: 14:19; 13:2; "Seek ye first the Kingdom of Heaven", meaning of: 2:41; 14:19.

KNOWLEDGE: practice should be based on: 2:11;

sacrifice of: 4:28, 4:33; 9:15; no duty for the person of: 3:17-18; the glory of: 4:9-10, 4:19, 4:33, 4:35-39; 5:29; 10:3, 10:7; 13:28-29, 13:34; 14:1-2; 15:19; sever all doubts through: 4:41-42; the seeker of: 7:16; how to acquire: 4:34; 5:16; 7:29; 8:7-10, 8:14, 8:22; 9:1; 10:10-11; when it can be acquired: 4:38; 13:30; fosters devotion: 10:7-9; true discriminition (*viveka*): 2:18, 2:63, 2:66-67; 3:32, 3:37; 5:16; 7:15; 10:10, 32; 13:2; 15:1; 16:21; 18:40; story of children buying chocolate: 13:2; secular: 13:2; description of person with: 13:7-11, 13:27, (also see Sthitapragnya); the goal described: 13:17; Self-realization: 13:6, 13:25; the gunas and: 18:20-22.

KOSHAS (Sheaths or dresses of the soul): Manomaya, Vijnanamaya and Anandamaya Koshas: 13:6.

LAKSHMI DEVI: 14:19; 18:38.
"LOVE YOUR NEIGHBOR AS YOURSELF": explained: 5:18.
LUST: 5:26; thirsting after things: 14:12; craving for types of sense gratification: 16:8,

16:11-12, 16:16, 16:18, 16:21; extremes in tapas motivated by: 17:5-6.

"MADE IN THE IMAGE OF GOD": meaning of: 13:2.

MAHAT BRAHMA (Prakriti): the great creator: 14:3-4; also see Prakriti.

MANUS (lawgivers): 10:6.

MAYA (Illusion): 7:14-15, 7: 25, 7:27; defined: 13:6; 18:61; also see Delusion and Prakriti.

MEDITATION: 2:61, 2:66; 3:6; 5:7; on Brahman: 5:21; place for: 6:11; method: 5:27-28; 6:12-15, 6:24-29; characteristics and benefits of: 6:18-22; for selfpurification: 6:12; 18:33; moderation needed: 6:16-17; one pointed: 6:23; 8:8-10, 8:12-13; meaning of "constantly thinking of me": 8:14; 10:11; relationship to knowledge and renunciation: 12:12; steadiness through meditation: 12:14; best time for: 13:21; realization of Atman through: 13:24; 15:5; in action: 12:12; 18:52; on the truth: 18:63.

MERU: the spine (symbolically): 15:1.

MIND: openness of the: 2:7; agitation of the: 1:30-31; 2:7, 2:60, 2:63, 2:67; 3:6, 3:40; 11:45; strength of: 3:42; the fleeting and unsteady: 3:41; fixing the mind on God: 3:30; 7:1; 12:2, 12:8; 17:11; 18:58, 65; a clouded mind: 3:27; actions happen through the: 5:8-9; control of mind at time of death: 8:2; equilibrium, peace or Vyavasayam: 2:13, 2:41, 2:44-45, 2:48-53, 2:64-2:66, 2:68-71; 4:11, 4:22; 6:15-29; 8:7; 9:22; 12:12; 15:11; senses and the: 2:59, 2:60; seat of desire is the: 3:40; part of prakriti: 4:18; purification and purity of: 5:6-7, 5:11-13; 8:7; 15:11; 16:1-3; 17:16; 18:5, 18:18, 18:51; control of the: 3:7, 3:41; 4:21; 5:26-28; 6:12, 6:33-36; 18:33; friend or enemy: 6:5-6; story of man lying on the side of the road: 6:6; self-disciplined: 6:7, 6:18-19; equal vision: 6:8-9; 5:18-20; concentration of. 6:10; nature: 7:4; 9:10; surrender of: 9:34; steadiness through practice: 8:7-10; 10:22; 12:6-9; 12:14, 12:16-19; 13:5; need to refine and keep clean: 13:6-11; 15:11; Supreme is beyond the grasp: 13:12; Presence of God in: 13:22-23; disturbing thoughts are of the: 13:32; tossed about by the gunas: 14:8; need to analyze activity of the: 14:8; need to keep clean: 14:22; of the Jivanmukta: 14:22, 14:24-25; how to analyze "who is doing what": 15:5; the sixth sense: 15:7-9; the Supreme is beyond the: 15:19; functioning of: 18:18; qualities of: 18:28, 18:30-31.

MODERATION: needed in practice of Yoga: 6:16-17; The Buddha and path of: 17:6.

MOKSHA (Liberation, Perfection): 2:46; 6:15, 6:21-22; realization: 4:36-39; difficulty of attaining: 6:36; 7:3; 8:15; 11:47-48; how to attain: 4:23, 4:34, 4:39; 5:28; 8:5, 8:7-10, 8:14, 8:22; 9:1, 9:27-28; 13:18, 13:23; 14:26; 15:3; 16:22; 18:66, 18:71; freedom from gunas: 14:19-20; qualifications for: 15:5, 15:11, 15:19-20; 18:30; divine qualities lead to: 16:5; seekers of: 17:25.

NADIS: 6:13; 15:1.

NAMES AND FORMS: 2:18; 4:7; 6:29; 7:21; 8:7, 8:20;

formless nature of God discussed: 7:22, 7:24; 9:16-19; 10:10; 13:2, 13: 6, 13:16, 13:21, 13:26; modification of the gunas are: 14:5; 15:17; 16: introduction.

NIRVANA: see Brahma.

NITYANANDA, SWAMI: story of his life: 14:24-25.

NON-ATTACHMENT: see Vairagya and Attachment.

OM: 6:15; 7:8; 8:13; 9:17; 10:25; 17:23-24.

OM TAT SAT: meaning of: 17:23-26.

OMNISCIENT: 6:15.

PAIN AND SUFFERING: of no consequence to firm mind: 2:41; 10:4; sense contact and: 2:14-15; 5:22; 4:18; 5:20; 6:17, 6:23, 6:32; 7:2, 7:16; 8:15; solution to: 9:33; 12:17-18; 13:6; fruit of rajasic guna: 14:16; 15:4; it is the mind that feels: 15:5; foods which cause: 17:9; renunciation of duty due to: 18:8; see also Rajas.

PASSION (Restlessness, Desirefulness): 4:10; 6:27; 7:11; rajasic energy: 14:7, 14:12, 16-17; faith and the passionate: 17:2; control of: 18:51.

PATANJALI'S YOGA SUTRAS: 2:58; 5:22; 6:15; 7:2; 15:11.

PATHS OF LIGHT AND DARKNESS: 8:23-27.

PEACE: see Tranquility.

PERFECTION IN ACTION: 2:50; is meditation: 12:12; meaning: 14:11; is Yoga: 15:11.

POTENCY OF YOGA PRACTICE: 2:40; 4:38.

PRAKRITI (Nature, God's Manifestation, the Known, Kshetra, Vibhuti): 3:5, 3:27, 3:29; 4:6, 4:13, 4:18-19; 6:9; the manifested: 2:28; 7:2, 7:24; 8:18, 8:20; 9:4; the doer: 5:14-15; 13:20, 13:29; bodies and minds are made of: 13:19, 13:21, 13:26-28, 13:30; the eight aspects of: 7:4-5; lower and higher explained: 7:2-7; adhibhuta: 8:4; function of: 9:7-10; divine manifestations: 10:16-42; kshetra explained: 13:1-3, 13:21; constituents described: 13:8; benefits of understanding: 13:18, 13:23, 13:34; the gunas and: 13:19; 14:4-5; afflictions of the body and mind resulting

Paramatman and jivatman compared: 15:8; transcends perishing and nonperishing: 10:15; 15:19; recognized by undeluded: 15:19; imperishable aspect: 15:16-17; realization of: 18:50-56; Ishvara in the heart of all: 18:61.

RAJA YOGA: 2:39; 13:24-25; 14:27.

RAJAS: qualities of: 14:5; type of action: 14:7, 14:9; predominates: 14:10; characteristics of: 14:12, 14:22; predominence at time of death: 14:15; the fruits of: 14:16; traits arising from: 14:17; conditions upon rebirth: 14:18; compared to Sattva: 14:12; quality of faith: 17:2-4; method of worship: 17:4; food preference: 17:9; types of sacrifice: 17:12; practice of discipline: 17:18; charitable acts: 17:21-22; renunciation of duty: 18:8; kind of understanding: 18:20-22; actions: 18:24; individual: 18:27; intelligence: 18:31; willpower: 18:34; pleasures: 18:38, 18:40.

RAMAKRISHNA: quote: 13:29; story of the parrot chanting Ram: 14:14; on learning: 15:19.

RAMALINGAM, SWAMI: quote: 6:15; 8:14.

RAMANA MAHARSHI: 18:57.

REFUGE: 2:7; 4:10; 7:14, 7:19, 7:29; 9:13, 9:18, 9:32; think on me constantly, meaning of: 8:14; of the universe: 11:38; by surrendering ego: 12:11; in the Absolute: 15:4; 18:62, 18:66.

REINCARNATION: 4:5; 6:41-6:42; 7:27; 8:26; 9:24; 17:3.

RENUNCIATION: comes automatically: 3:5; the state of true: 3:6; 5:6-9, 5:11-13, 5:26; leads to freedom: 3:4-6; 5:1-3; the "true renunciate": 6:1; as the essence of Yoga: 6:2; how to achieve: 9:28; of the fruits of actions: 2:51; 12:6, 12:11-12, 12:16; is selflessness: 16:3; is being neutral: 16:3; enlightenment through: 18: introduction; letting go of personally motivated actions and fruit thereof (tyaga): 18:2-4, 18:11-12; not every action should be renounced: 18:5; likes and dislikes to be: 18:51; renunciation of one's duty: 18:7-18:10, 18:66.

"RISE TO MY STATE": the meaning of: 13:18.

SAMADHI: transcends desires: 2:59; description of the state of: 6:19-22; references to: 2:44,

2:54; 6:6; also see Jivanmukta and Sthitapragnya.

SAMSARA: deliverence from: 12:7; also see analogy of Asvattha tree: 15:2-4.

SAMSKARAS (Mental Impressions): 3:10; 7:27; determines next birth: 18:47.

SARASVATI DEVl: 14:19; 18:38.

SAT AND ASAT: 13:12; 17:28.

SAT-CHlD-ANANDA: explained: 17:23.

SATTVA: qualities of: 14:5; types of happiness and knowledge: 14:6, 14:9; predominates: 14:10; characteristics of: 14: 12, 14:22; predominence at time of death: 14:15; the fruits of: 14:16; traits arising from: 14:17; conditions upon rebirth: 14:18; confused with tamas: 14:8, 14:24-25; compared to rajas: 14:12; quality of faith: 17:2-4; method of worship: 17:4; food preference: 17:8; types of sacrifice: 17:11; practice of discipline: 17:17; charitable acts: 17:20, 17:22; renunciation of duty: 18:9-10; kind of understanding: 18:20-21; actions: 18:23; individual: 18:26; intelligence: 18:30-31; willpower: 18:33; pleasures: 18:37.

SELFLESSNESS: the main trait to acquire: 18:53; also see Karma Yoga (Selfless Service).

SENSES: contacts with the objects of the: 2:14-15, 2:64, 2:68; 5:8-9; lack of control of: 2:60, 2:67; 3:6, 3:16; source of attachment to objects of: 2:62; need to control: 2:7; 3:34; nature as the object and the: 3:28; seat of desire is the: 3:40; sacrifice of the: 4:26-27; control of, by concentration: 6:12; satisfaction of the: 6:17; 12:3-4; are of prakriti: 13:5; in relation to Brahman: 13:14; under influence of sattva guna: 14:11; objects of the: 13:5; 15:2, 9; 18:38; taken on by the jivatman: 15:7-10; organs of the: 18:14, 18:38; inner and active: 18:18, 18:33; control of senses leads to Brahman: 18:51; also see Sense Gratification and Pratyahara (control of the senses).

SENSE GRATIFICATION: seekers of: 9:20; rajasic in nature: 14:7; temporary nature of: 18:38.

SERVICE: of the Guru as teacher: 4:34; 13:7; 17:14.

SEXUAL ACTIVITY: need to constrain: 10:11; 16:8, 16:18.

SHRADDHA (Belief, Sincerity): 4:39-40; 6:47; practice of: 7:21-22; (story) worship of the dunghill: 7:22; (story) worship of Shivalingam: 7:22, 7:24; faith: 8:7; 9:1, 9:3, 9:23, 12:2, 12:20; application of will: 17: introduction; depends on temperament: 17:2-4; lack of: 17:28; 18:71.

SILENCE: the sound in: 7:8; the secret of: 10:38; devotees take refuge in: 12:19; mental discipline: 17:16; so golden: 18:18.

SIN: 1:39, 1:45; 2:33, 2:36; 3:13, 3:36-41; 5:10, 5:25; is of the mind: 6:27-28, 6:36; burnt away by worship: 9:30; 17:14; relieved from: 18:66.

SHIVA, LORD: 7:22, 7:24; 8:13; 18:38.

SHIVAGOCHARYA: story: 9:23.

SHIVALINGAM: worship of explained: 7:22.

SIVANANDA, SWAMI: quote: 13:2; 18:44.

SOLITUDE: of the seeker: 18:52.

SPEECH: harmony with thoughts, deeds and: 2:11; limitations of: 15:17-19; false: 16:2; austerity or discipline of: 17:15; truthfulness in: 17:15; importance of proper: 17:23; is an action: 18:18.

STHITAPRAGNYA LAKSHANA (the One of Steady Wisdom, Enlightened): 2:7, 2:50, 2:52-53, 2:69; characteristics: 2:54-72; 3:25; 4:19-20; 5:16, 5:18-21, 5:24-26; 6:8-9, 6:29-32; 12:13-20; 14:21-26.

SURRENDER: to the master: 2:7; 4:34; 6:47; 9:34; 13:11; also see Service.

SVADHARMA: Bhishma's: 1:12; explained: 2:31-33, 2:36-38; 3:33, 3:35; 18:41-46; incur no sin in performance: 18:47; you are directed by: 18:48; nature will force you to perform: 18:59-61; when you have peace of mind you know your: 18:51; relinquish all duties: 18:66; also see Duty and Dharma.

TAMAS: qualities of: 14:5; type of confused thinking: 14:8-9; predominates: 14:10; characteristics of: 14:13, 14:22; predominence at time of death: 14:15; the fruits of: 14:16; traits arising from: 14:17; conditions upon rebirth: 14:18; confused with sattva: 14:8, 14:24-25; quality of faith: 17:2-4; method of worship: 17:4; food preference: 17:10; types of sacrifice: 17:13; practice of disciplines: 17:19; charitable acts: 17:22; renunciation of duty: 18:7; kind of understanding: 18:20, 18:22; actions: 18:25; individual: 18:28; intelligence: 18:31-32; willpower: 18:35; pleasures: 18:39.

TAPAS (Austerity): 4:10, 4:28; 7:9; 8:28; 9:27; 10:5; 11:48, 11:53; 13:2; 15:8; 16:1; extremes are to be avoided: 17:5-6; of the body, speech and mind: 17:14-16; influence of the gunas: 17:17-19; Om Tat Sat used with: 17:24-27; 18:3; should not be renounced: 18:5; should be performed without attachment to fruits thereof: 18:6.

THAYUMANAVAR, SAINT: 6:15.

THIRUMULAR: need for body in spiritual development (quotes): 17:6.

THIRUVALLUVAR: 3:11; 5:27-28; 11:32; 13:11; 15:4.

TRANQUILITY (Equaminity) IS YOGA: 2:48, 2:50-51, 2:64-65, 2:70-71; 4:22; 6:17, 6:33; 8:7; 10:4-5; 12:18-19; 14:16; 15:11; 17:16; 18:20.

TREE OF LIFE: 15: introduction; how to cut down: 15:1-20.

TRIPUTI (Seer, Seen, Seeing): explained: 14:19; incitements to action: 18:18.

TWO-FOLD PATH (Jnana and Karma Yoga): 3:3.

UNWISE: 2:42; not to be disturbed: 3:26, 3:29; ignore God: 9:11-12; the way of the pleasure seekers: 9:20-21; fate of: 7:20-24; 16:23.

UPANISHADS: 11:52; 15:8; Mandukya: 15:19; 17:23.

VAIRAGYA (Dispassion): conditions of: 2:52; need for: 6:35; 13:8; 18:10, 18:52.

VARNA (Caste): 1:41-43; 4:13; unimportant: 9:32; intent explained: 18:41-44; the four Yogas and: 18:44.

VEDAS: 2:42-45, 2:54; 7:2; 9:17; 10:22, 10:35; 11:48, 11:53; 15:1, 15:15, 15:18; 17:23.

VEDANTA: 9:17; 15:15, 15:19.

VIVEKANANDA, SWAMI: quote: 7:2; 18:20.

WILL and WILLPOWER:
3:36; arises from prakriti: 13:6;
use to overcome the gunas:
14:16; development of: 16:21;
application of the: 17:4; free
will explained: 3:10; 18:49,
18:63; the higher will: 18:53;
three types of: 18:29, 18:33-35.

WITNESS: of actions: 4:18;
5:8-9; 9:9-10, 9:18; is all you
really do: 15:5; 18:66; Purusha
witnesses all: 13:22; true Self
is actionless witness: 13:29;
14:20.

WORK: see Karma Yoga (selfless
service).

WORSHIP: of the Gods: 4:12;
6:47; 7:2, 7:20-21, 7:23;
reasons for: 7:16; 9:13, 9:15,
9:19, 9:22-23; the Lord of:
9:24; result of: 7:22-23, 7:28,
7:30; 9:25, 9:29; different
forms of: 9:25, 9:30; offering
love as a part of: 9:27; 10:8;
the real meaning: 10:10-11; of
the unmanifest and manifest:
12:1-5; saguna method of:
12:6-12; by those free of
delusion: 15:19; the gunas and
methods of: 17:4; purpose of:
17:4.

YAJNA (Sacrifice): 3:8-16;
different kinds of: 4:23-33;
9:20; 11:53; 16:1; the Lord of:
5:29; 7:30; 8:4; the enjoyer of:
9:24, 9:27; influence of gunas:

17:11-13; as early rituals:
17:23-24; 18:3; should not be
renounced: 18:5; performed
without attachment: 18:6.

YOGABRASTHA (One Who
Practiced Yoga in a Former
Life): fate of the: 6:37-45;
14:15; 17:3.

YOGI: see Sthitapragnya and
Jivanmukta.

Index of Stories

About the Author

Swami Satchidananda (Sri Gurudev) was born on December 22nd in 1914 during the month known as *Margali*, the Dawn of the *Devas*. He was the second son of Sri Kalyanasundaram Gounder and his wife, Srimati Velammai. Their home had always been a meeting place for poets, musicians, philosophers and astrologers. *Sannyasis* (monks) and holy men passing through the area were directed to the home of Sri Kalyanasundaram and Srimati Velammai for food and lodging. Srimati Velammai was inspired by the holy men and decided that her next child should be this type of person. She and her husband traveled sixty miles to Palani, the holy hill, to the Ashram of Sri Sadhu Swamigal, where she was given a mantra to invoke the Divine Light as manifested in the Sun. She repeated it constantly, developing a vibration conducive to receiving the type of soul she desired.

From the time he was a little boy, Sri Gurudev (then known as "Ramaswamy") was deeply spiritual. Even as a young child, he spoke truths and displayed insights far beyond his years. His devotion to God was strong, and he looked at people of all castes and faiths with an equal eye, always recognizing the same light within every being. That recognition of the universal light, equally present in all people, remained as he grew to adulthood and became a businessman and a husband.

When he lost his young wife, he turned his attention to spiritual practice and studying with many great spiritual masters, including Sri Ramana Maharshi. Finally, in 1949, Ramaswamy met his Guru—His Holiness Sri Swami Sivanandaji of the Divine Life Society, Rishikesh. He received *Sannyas Diksha* (initiation into monkhood) from his spiritual master and was given the name Swami Satchidananda.

So began a new level of dynamic service for Sri Gurudev. Sri Swami Sivanandaji recognized the gift that his newly-initiated *Sannyasin* had for touching the lives of others and did not let this disciple stay in the Rishikesh Ashram for long. Soon, he sent Swami Satchidananda to serve in various parts of India and Sri Lanka.

In 1966, Sri Gurudev made his first global tour, sponsored by an American devotee. The intended two-day visit to New York extended to five months as he was surrounded by hundreds of students, eager for his teachings and guidance. In 1969, he opened the Woodstock Festival. The peaceful atmosphere that prevailed throughout the event has often been attributed to his message and blessings.

Sri Gurudev is the founder and guiding light for the Integral Yoga® International, with centers located throughout the world. Integral Yoga, as taught by Sri Gurudev, combines various methods of Yoga, including Hatha Yoga, Karma Yoga (selfless service), Raja Yoga (meditation), Bhakti Yoga (prayer), Japa Yoga (mantra recitation), and Jnana Yoga (the path of wisdom contained in the ancient Indian sacred texts and philosophy that helps one find the peace and joy within).

The teachings of Swami Satchidananda have spread into the mainstream and many thousands of people now practice Yoga. Integral Yoga has trained over 20,000 Yoga teachers and pioneered advances in Yoga therapy and specialized applications of Yoga for specific populations. Integral Yoga now certifies Yoga therapists and is the foundation for Dr. Dean Ornish's landmark work in reversing heart disease, Dr. Michael Lerner's Commonweal Cancer Help program, Sonia Sumar's Yoga for the Special Child, Jivana Heyman's Accessible Yoga, among many others.

In 1979, Sri Gurudev was inspired to establish Satchidananda Ashram–Yogaville® in Virginia, USA. Based on his teachings, it is a place where people of different faiths and backgrounds can come to realize their essential oneness. Yogaville is the home of the Light Of Truth Universal Shrine (LOTUS). This unique interfaith shrine honors the Spirit that unites all the world religions, while celebrating their diversity. People from all over the world come there to meditate and pray. In 2014, LOTUS India was completed and dedicated in honor of the 100th Birth Anniversary of Sri Gurudev.

Not limited to any one organization, religion or country, Sri Gurudev received invitations for over fifty years from around the world to speak about the way to peace. In addition, he served on the advisory boards of many world peace and interfaith organizations. He was invited to share his message of peace with many world leaders and dignitaries, and received many honors for his public service. Among them were the Juliet Hollister Interfaith Award presented at the United Nations in 1994 and the prestigious U Thant Peace Award in 2002. The James P. Morton Interfaith Award was posthumously given to Sri Gurudev in 2014 to honor his contributions as an "interfaith visionary."

Sri Gurudev is the author of many books, including *Integral Yoga Hatha, To Know Your Self, The Yoga Sutras of Patanjali, Beyond Words, The Yoga Way, Enlightening Tales* and *The Golden Present*. He is the subject of four biographies, *Swami Satchidananda: Apostle of Peace, Portrait of a Modern Sage, Boundless Giving: The Life and Service of Sri Swami Satchidananda* and *Swami Satchidananda: A Yoga Master's Early Days in India and Sri Lanka*. He is also featured in the documentary, "Living Yoga."

In August 2002, Sri Gurudev entered *Mahasamadhi* (a God-realized soul's conscious final exit from the body). His *Mahasamadhi* Shrine, known as Chidambaram, is located at Yogaville.

For more information, visit: swamisatchidananda.org and integralyoga.org

Notes

Notes

Notes